A HISTORY
OF WOOD-ENGRAVING

Dürer   *The Nativity* (11¾″ × 8¼″)

A HISTORY OF WOOD-ENGRAVING

by Douglas Percy Bliss

WITH ONE HUNDRED AND
TWENTY ILLUSTRATIONS

SPRING BOOKS · LONDON

ORIGINALLY PUBLISHED 1928
THIS EDITION PUBLISHED 1964 BY
SPRING BOOKS · WESTBOOK HOUSE · FULHAM BROADWAY · LONDON

PRINTED IN ENGLAND BY RICHARD CLAY AND COMPANY LTD, BUNGAY, SUFFOLK

TO
PHYLLIS DODD

PREFACE

In the copious literature on Wood-Engraving there are instances to be found of treatises, both technical and historical, written by men who were themselves skilled in the practice of the art. It is enough to mention J. M. Papillon and W. J. Linton. But among the moderns, apart from Mr. Gordon Craig's diverting volume, Wood Cuts and Some Words, which on the historical side does not go back beyond the Beggarstaff Brothers, engraver-authors of this craft are rarer than those who have contributed to the literature of Etching.

There has been, however, a remarkable revival of interest in woodcuts, dating from about the close of the Great War. The phenomenon is noticeable in almost every country of Europe; recent exhibitions have proved to us in London that the woodcut flourishes in Russia, Poland and Czecho-Slovakia as it does in more western countries, and the art has its votaries also in the United States. In London two societies of wood-engravers compete vigorously for our custom every year in the weeks preceding Christmas.

I have spoken of an interest in woodcuts. This interest has been felt primarily by the wood-engravers themselves, whose new and not always well-informed enthusiasm for their ancient art has communicated itself only by degrees to dealers and collectors, while their productions have still to stand the test of revaluation in the auction-room. It is not yet clear how far the wave will spread, but it may lose its force in time and die down in gentle ripples at a distance from the wellspring of enthusiasm that bubbles up at the centre, at the many centres, of the movement.

It is a natural outcome of this interest that some of those who engrave should also write, and that a modern literature of the craft of Wood-Engraving, written by engravers on wood, should come into existence, parallel to the many books on the craft of Etching which have been written in recent years by etchers.

Mr. Bliss, who was already the author of a good little pamphlet on Wood-Engraving illustrated by himself and by reproductions of woodcuts by Joseph Crawhall (a publication of the Dryad Handicrafts, Leicester), and had won *his spurs still earlier, at the Royal College of Art, South Kensington, by editing a clever students' magazine,* Gallimaufry, *here enters the lists with a much more serious challenge to the elder knights of scholarship. Let not this metaphor be taken to imply any kind of flippancy. Mr. Bliss writes, as he engraves, with humour, but he has made a conscientious study, remarkably wide in its range, of the old woodcuts themselves and of what has been written about them, and his book, though every assertion in it may not be accepted by experts acquainted with the latest German research, gives evidence of a genuine effort to acquire and impart sound information. Nor is it a mere compilation ; it is constantly kept alive by frank and outspoken expression of personal preferences, and a reader who knows the facts about woodcuts already may always learn something fresh, which the facts alone will not give him, by noticing how the critical taste of a gifted young engraver of to-day reacts to time-honoured masterpieces and settles the claims of secondary engravers whose respectability is generally taken for granted.*

Mr. Bliss, moreover, explores by-paths, among chapbooks, for instance, and Images d'Épinal, *which have been too often neglected by professional historians. He would approve, I feel sure, of a certain large Milanese calendar, with a painted woodcut caricature, published in 1816 at* trenta centesimi *(coloured), which the British Museum acquired, at much greater cost in shillings, at the famous Leipzig sale of woodcuts last May.*

He has his message also, not wholly couched in complimentary terms, to the wood-engravers of to-day, who cannot fail to profit, whether or no they accept certain strictures on their own art, if they follow his example and make a serious study of the achievements of five centuries.

CAMPBELL DODGSON.

PUBLISHER'S NOTE: Mr. Dodgson's preface to the original 1928 edition has been retained unaltered for its valuable comments on the author and his book. Nor has any attempt been made, despite recent developments in the field, to revise the book, in the belief that Mr. Bliss's lively and discerning survey of the history of wood-engraving remains an important and essentially undated contribution to the literature on the subject.

CONTENTS

NOTE

OUR thanks are due to all the generous people who facilitated the making of our set of illustrations by granting us the necessary permissions. Specific acknowledgment of each is made in our list opposite. In particular, we are indebted to the artists who lent us original wood-blocks, from which casts were made to illustrate the closing chapters. These were Madame Raverat, Miss Hermes, Mr. John and Mr. Paul Nash, Mr. Daglish, Mr. Ravilious and Mr. Hughes-Stanton. Mr. Gibbings not only lent us one of his own blocks, but those by Mr. Eric Gill and Mr. David Jones. We are also much indebted to Les Éditions, C. Van Oest, for two illustrations from *Origines de la Gravure en France*, Messrs. Bernard Quaritch Ltd., Messrs. R. Piper & Co. for two illustrations from *Die Altdeutsche Buchillustration*, M. Bruno Cassirer of Berlin, M. Karl W. Hiersemann for five illustrations from *Der Bilderschmuck der Frühdrucke*, the Imprimerie Nationale of France, Messrs. Kegan Paul, Trench, Trübner & Co. Ltd., the Oxford University and Harvard University Presses, Mr. J. Schretlen and Messrs. Ernest Benn Ltd., the Keeper of Fine Arts, Ashmolean Museum, the Librairie de France, Messrs. Robert Scott, Messrs. Chatto & Windus, Messrs. Chapman & Hall Ltd., Messrs. Etchells and Macdonald and Messrs. Brown & Phillips. Finally our thanks are due to Mr. Campbell Dodgson, who lent us the modern French prints from his private collection, and to Mr. R. A. Walker for valuable advice and encouragement when it was sorely needed.

LIST OF ILLUSTRATIONS

AN ELEMENTARY ACCOUNT OF THE TECHNIQUE OF WOODCUTTING AND OF WOOD-ENGRAVING WHICH MUST BE READ

THERE are three kinds of Prints, namely Relief Prints (corresponding to Woodcuts and Wood-Engravings), Intaglio Prints (corresponding to Line-Engravings or Etchings upon metal) and Surface Prints (corresponding to Lithography). With the third we will have no concern in this work; but it is necessary to distinguish carefully the first and second processes. In Wood-Engraving and Woodcutting, between which I will shortly distinguish, the design is drawn upon the block and the parts which are to read as white are cut away with the knife or ploughed out

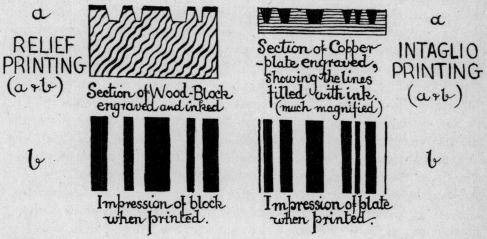

RELIEF PRINTING (a & b)

Section of Wood-Block engraved and inked

Impression of block when printed.

Section of Copper-plate engraved, showing the lines filled with ink. (much magnified)

Impression of plate when printed.

INTAGLIO PRINTING (a & b)

with the graver, leaving so much of the surface in relief. This surface is then covered with ink applied by a dabber or roller (care being taken lest any ink get into the incised portions) and prints are taken by burnishing the back of the paper which is placed upon the block, or by the vertical pressure of the printing-press. Woodcuts and Wood-Engravings,

I

then, have this in common that they are Relief Prints, and this distinguishes them from Intaglio Prints (that is to say from Engravings and Etchings upon copper and other metals) where a more liquid ink is forced into the intagliate or cut-away portions, and, the surface of the plate being wiped clean, prints are taken by the pressure of the paper *into* the incised lines. The diagram on the previous page will make this clear.

But here ends the similarity of woodcuts to wood-engravings, though the words are applied loosely even in textbooks.

Woodcutting is the ancient method and the one in use until about 1800, when Wood-Engraving was developed and largely superseded it. Woodcuts are made upon soft wood cut plankwise with a knife pulled or drawn towards the user. On the other hand, wood-engravings are made upon the end-grain of box, a very hard wood, by the action of the graver or burin, which is pushed by the hand away from the worker. The wood is always fairly close-grained and the surface of the blocks is smoothed very carefully. Since woodcuts and wood-engravings have to a very great extent been used in book-decoration and have had therefore to be printed with types, the blocks are made of the regulation height of type; that is about seven-eighths of an inch.

To consider Woodcutting or Knife-Work by itself. Woodcuts were used before the development of paper-manufacture and typography for the multiplication of patterns upon textiles. When paper became plentiful, wood-blocks were employed for the printing of images of saints upon devotional broadsheets and also for playing-cards. After the development of printing with movable types (i.e. about 1450) they were used in book-illustration. In Germany the engravers were called "Formschneider"[1] or cutters of "forms" or wood-blocks from which the patterns on the textiles were printed. The "Formschneider" were classed with the carpenters in the old civic guilds, and it was they who cut the images of saints and the book-decorations. In some cases they may also have been designers as well as engravers; but it is almost certain that they confined themselves to the task of engraving the designs of more skilled workers. There is no evidence that any of the older artists whose names we know were actually woodcutters, although many of them were famous line-

---

[1] "Formschneider" was the most common term; but "briefmaler," or card-colourer, was often used. In France the woodcutters were called "tailleurs d'images," "faiseurs d'images," "imagiers" or "tailleurs de molles." In Italy the term for a woodcutter was "intagliador de figure de ligno"; in Flanders it was "printer." The Latin words were "incisor lignorum" and "sculptor."

engravers on copper; and there is ample evidence by the year 1500 to show that they contented themselves with making drawings with quill or brush upon the surface of the block for the "Formschneider" to engrave. This he did by cutting away with knife and chisel all those portions of the surface which did not bear the lines of the artist, so as to leave those lines alone in relief. By the close of the fifteenth century this subdivision of labour is very marked. The designers are very skilful and the engravers are wonderfully accurate and painstaking craftsmen. The earliest cuts may have been done by humble draughtsmen and hacked by themselves upon the block; but Dürer and his contemporaries work in connection with the workshops of well-known "Formschneider."

In a series of woodcuts dealing with artisans of his day (1568) the artist Jost Amman shows us a "Formschneider" at work upon a block. In the verses which accompany the picture he is made to say, "I am a good woodcutter and I cut so well with my knife every line on my blocks, that when they are printed on a sheet of white paper you see clearly the very lines that the artist has traced, his drawing whether it be coarse or fine reproduced exactly line for line."

Anonymity is well-nigh the rule not only for the "Formschneider" of the fifteenth century but for the artists who made the designs. But when artists like Dürer and Cranach begin to design the cuts, a few names of woodcutters begin to appear. Sometimes the engraver put his monogram on the block along with that of the designer and often added a little figure of a knife below it. In 1542 we get the first portrait of an engraver. This occurs in a beautiful Herbal by the German botanist Fuchsius, which contains five hundred large and noble cuts of which the good man is very proud; so that he not only trumpets their praises in his Introduction but he devotes the last page of the Herbal to the portraits of the artists, the "Pictores Operis," who adorned this the most lovely book of its kind. The subdivision of labour is very clearly seen. Two of the artists are shown at work together. Albrecht Meyer is seen drawing a plant placed before him in a vase. Beside him Heinrich Füllmaurer is engaged in copying such a drawing on to the wood-block. Below them is the "Sculptor," Veit Rudolf Speckle—"by far the best engraver in Strassburg," as Fuchsius boasts. He is not at work, unfortunately, but it is good to see so worthy a man. He wears a scone-shaped hat with ear-flaps, is heavily cloaked and sadly needs a shave. He looks complacent enough, as well he might, for was not his the hand that with but knife and gouge cut all these great plant-forms with all their flowers and roots and tendrils and wreathing tenderness and curl of life!

The wood which the knife-workers used was fairly soft and close-grained, as pear, apple, or sycamore, and the blocks were cut in longitudinal section. Sometimes box was used, and one block of boxwood is preserved at Basle upon which Holbein drew a portrait of Erasmus which Lützelburger engraved. The same artists may have used box in the famous cuts of the *Dance of Death* which are among the most wonderful pieces of knife-work known. Some critics have suggested that the *Dance* cuts were done upon metal with the graver and printed in relief. This is possible and may have been done often. We know that the cuts in the French *Book of Hours* of the late fifteenth century were done in metallic relief, and later on we shall notice a wonderful kind of dotted metal-cut which was printed as woodcuts or types are printed.

Mistakes could be remedied and alterations made at later times by boring a hole in the block and driving in a plug of fresh wood shaped like a wedge, so that it grips the sides of the hole very tightly. The block is then levelled down and smoothed at that place and the cutting can be done again. This practice has left amusing traces. In the edition of *Josephus* published by Vérard (Paris, 1490) we see a knight wearing a bishop's mitre. In the *Froissart* from the same press three years later the block has been plugged, and the knight now wears a royal crown; but the tell-tale pendants from his old headgear still hang over his shoulders. In the edition of *Launcelot du Lac* of the year following (1494) there is yet another change of headgear, and the knight has now been fitted with a helmet. Another instance of plugging is seen in an Elizabethan edition of Turberville's *Book of Faulconrie* (London, 1575), which contains a charming cut of the Virgin Queen out hawking on horseback. In a later edition of the same book published during the reign of her successor the block was plugged, and King James now rides out amid the company which before surrounded Queen Elizabeth.

In 1766 the French woodcutter Papillon published a valuable treatise on the technique and history of his art. Although he was aware of a practice known as "lowering" (of which more anon) and had added other little refinements to the technique, it is clear that the practice of Wood-cutting was substantially the same in Papillon's time as it had been in that of Dürer. But a great change was at hand. At that time, says Papillon, there came a foreigner to Paris who claimed to use the graver upon the end-grain of box. "But this man" (he continues) "reasoned without principle and without art. He was ignorant of the impossibility of engraving properly upon the end of the wood with such a tool, for the graver could only lift the wood and could not cut the lines sharply and cleanly as it ought. What is more it renders them all ragged (*barbellées*), from which it follows that they blot in the printing." Poor Papillon! Here was the secret of modern Wood-Engraving. He had but to take the graver and try it on the end of a piece of boxwood to see what could be done; but he condemned it without experiment. One wonders who the "étranger" was. Perhaps he was an Englishman, for in London certain engravers were exploiting this method with success—for example, the artist of Croxall's *Fables*, 1722. But it was not until Thomas Bewick (1753–1828) took it up (learning something from them and perfecting their teachings for himself) that the new method won fame, and replaced as a polite art the ancient and long-discredited craft of Woodcutting.

This new method which was perfected by Thomas Bewick was the antithesis of Woodcutting proper. In the latter you cut away the surface of the block so as to leave islanded in relief the *black lines* which form the design. But in "white-line engraving," as the new method is called, you use the plain surface of the block (considered as though already covered with ink) as a black ground upon which you make your design with the graver in the form of white lines. It is like drawing upon a blackboard with white chalk as compared to drawing with a pen upon paper. Or it can be thought of as a photographic negative as opposed to a print therefrom.

Wood-Engraving is a freer, more spontaneous and more truly creative method. Moreover, it is vastly quicker and less mechanical. To cut a line with a graver may be done with one push, to cut the same line with a knife requires four incisions. As Linton says, you can draw the four lines of this diagram with four strokes of the pen or four thrusts of the graver. To cut them in facsimile with the knife (as the "Formschneider" had to do) would take thirty-two or thirty-six incisions and in the end have less life in the lines.

You cannot use the graver upon the plank or longitudinal section of wood because it tears up the fibre. Engraving is therefore done upon the cross-section (cross-grain), and the cross-section of boxwood is very hard, so that there are remarkable opportunities for delicate lace-like engraving. Indeed, you can get effects of fineness comparable to any obtainable upon the copperplate and vastly superior to anything that can be cut with the knife upon the plank. It was by demonstrating the possibilities of Wood-Engraving as a "polite art" capable of elegant effects that Bewick saved it from the depths of humiliation to which it had been reduced by its more refined sister.

To talk about "white-line engraving" is not to imply that black lines can be dispensed with altogether. Only an engraving with very little range of colour can be without a certain percentage of black lines; for example, if you were to engrave the forehead of an old man, it is pretty obvious that to get the effect of the wrinkles on his brow it would be convenient, if not absolutely necessary, to leave black lines. So most engravings of any range combine both white- and black-line passages, or rather the new method contains within it all the possibilities of the old. By the method of Bewick any intelligent apprentice-engraver of fifty years since could have executed a perfect facsimile of the most closely shaded of Dürer's woodcuts, while it is obvious that no "Form-schneider" could possibly have copied a Bewick. In fact white-line engraving has suffered through its almost unlimited capacity for representation, for in displaying their skill in the engraving of tone and colour the engravers of the nineteenth century neglected the fundamentals of their art—Form and Pattern.

We mentioned before in passing that Papillon was aware of a practice known as "lowering." He claimed to have discovered it for himself, as did Bewick at a later time. "Lowering" means that those parts of a cut or engraving where a greyer effect is desired are lowered slightly below the surface of the block, and thus escape with less inking, and less pressure from the platen of the printing-press. To take the most common example, the edges of a vignette which were required to fade off gradually into the white of the page were always lowered slightly with flat chisels so that an unpleasant hard edge was avoided. By lowering portions of the block before engraving on them, distance and tonal effects were made very clear and detached, and the subject is not confined to one "dead level" as is almost unavoidable if all lines get the same evenness of inking. This practice being peculiar to Wood-Engraving should not be valued too slightly as it is to-day. Let us suppose that we have engraved and are about to print the disk of the sun going down in a blaze of light represented by a few thin lines at a distance from the darker portions of the block. If these thin black lines were to receive the same inking and the same pressure as the rest of the block, they would blot and "come up" in the impression too prominently. There are only two possible precautions against this: (1) that the lines should be "lowered" below the surface of the block; (2) that the pressman should so "overlay" the darker portions of the block that the lighter portions would receive less pressure. An "overlay" is a piece or pieces of paper carefully shaped and stuck on the platen of the press over against the places requiring greater pressure. We shall have more to say about "lowering" and "overlaying" in our essay on Bewick. In the meantime, it must be said that such delicate precautions are no longer demanded by the engravers nor yielded by the printers of our own time.

The box is a slender tree, its cross-section seldom more than about six inches; so that it was almost impossible to get a block for an octavo page. The block-makers used to try cutting the trunk in oblique sections to get a larger size. Or they would veneer a number of pieces of box together upon a plank of cheaper wood or clamp small blocks together in an iron chase. We read of these makeshift composite blocks warping and splitting, with reports fearful to the ear of the poor engraver who beheld the destruction of weeks of patient toil. In 1860 Charles Wells devised a method of riveting together smaller pieces of box to form blocks of great dimensions, which is now universally employed. The amalgamation of the smaller pieces is done by drilling holes at the back and sides and fixing bolts in the grooves. The comparative ease with which assembling and dispersing of portions could be done was of great value to the reproductive engravers of last century.

A question that is often asked by polite people who do not like one's wood-engravings and yet desire to show a general interest is, "How many prints can you take from a wood-block?" Well, Papillon's grandfather cut upon pear-wood a large "Virgin in Glory" and this cut lasted for ninety years at the rate of five or six hundred pulls a year. After that, says the grandson, "le bois semble un peu usé." One of Papillon's own cuts resisted wear to the extent of 120,000 proofs. Now this was soft wood. Boxwood has even longer life and Bewick calculated that one of his cuts was sound after 900,000 impressions. However, printing was much less heavy and mechanical in those days, and it is doubtful if a wood-block would be used for so long in the modern machine-presses. In fact most woodcuts used in books to-day are printed from metal casts of the original blocks.

It is necessary to say something about Colour-Printing from Wood-blocks, although we are little concerned with it in this book. In making a colour-print the first block to be cut, the "key-block," gives the main black parts of the design, and with the aid of this, other blocks are cut, one for each colour or tone. By means of careful registering these blocks can be printed one by one upon the same sheet and a colour-print obtained. "Chiaroscuro" is the name given to these early prints which imitated broad effects of light and shade. The chiaroscuros generally required three or four printings. The practice of using a tint-block with high-lights cut out upon it was introduced about 1508 by Cranach, Burgkmair and other German artists, and developed in Italy by Ugo da Carpi, who made prints after designs by Raphael.

Colour-printing from boxwood blocks was common throughout the nineteenth century and is still used on the Continent. By cross-hatching the block with a mesh of delicate lines the colour was sobered down to suit Victorian tastes. In this way the engraving firm of Edmund Evans Ltd. reproduced the charming children's books of Randolph Caldecott, Kate Greenaway, and other designers.

A word about Japanese colour-prints. The designers of these popular prints (called "Ukioye") were content with making drawings upon paper. These were transferred to planks of soft wood and cut by artisans, with one block for each colour. Printing was done by powder-colours mixed with rice paste, and not from inks, as in Europe, and the whole standard of design and execution is immeasurably higher than in the West. As many as twenty blocks were often used for one picture, and were printed by burnishing the back of the paper by hand.

Colour-printing from wood-blocks in the Japanese style has been practised in this country since the War, but chiefly by art-masters. Until the designer can send out his drawing to a workshop of engravers who will perform all the labour of cutting a dozen or so blocks, one for each colour that is required; until, in fact, the executive side, the cutting and printing, is done by skilled artisans as it is in Japan and was long ago in Europe, then the colour-print is not likely to be firmly established in the West. Two or three colour-blocks are often used with good effect by French engravers, but a larger number, as used by the English pioneers of the movement, ends in the production of confused and smudgy things like water-colours. The only good colour-prints of recent times that I have seen were by René Ben Sussan, now working in Paris, who did two delightful two-colour illustrations for an edition of Marston's *Pigmalion* published at the Golden Cockerel Press. Brangwyn has designed several colour-prints, and these were brilliantly executed by Urushibara, a Japanese engraver. This is the only sane usage. It is ridiculous to expect the artist to cut a dozen blocks for one little print; but since Urushibaras are few in the West, the artist has to do so. Even then, of course, one would not complain, if the finished thing seemed worth the trouble; but English Utamaros or French Hiroshiges do not seem likely to arise.

The best book on the technique of Wood-Engraving for those desirous to learn is by R. J. Beedham (with a foreword on God and Commercialism by Eric Gill), published by the St. Dominic's Press, Ditchling, 1921. But for the fullest and clearest account of the practice, ancient and modern, one must still go to Chatto and Jackson's mighty treatise published in 1839. Chatto as critic and bibliographer has, of course, dated sadly, but Jackson, the pupil of Bewick, must still be read on the craft. He omits nothing. He even tells engravers not to chew pieces of boxwood, warning us that it is equally indigestible for worms and rabbits and men. You will find no worm-holes in boxwood as you do in the old wood-blocks of the knife-workers. A fellow-apprentice of Jackson was poisoned by chewing the chips that he cut from his block, and Jackson's rabbit, left unprovided with nourishment in his little garden, ate up everything and at last, reduced by hunger, nibbled a few leaves of the tree sacred to engravers and therewithal he died

THE BEGINNINGS

PAPER—DEVOTIONAL PRINTS—CARDS

WHO was the first wood-engraver and how and what did he engrave? Papillon the eighteenth-century writer had his answer ready for that: The Children of Seth. For the Bible says that they engraved upon hard materials, such as stone and brick, so what could be more likely than that they began upon wood? But what they engraved will only be known when we can tell what song the sirens sang, or what name Achilles assumed when he hid himself among women. However, Papillon has furnished us with one inscription which, if not the oldest, is certainly of great antiquity. It was cut (says he) upon a piece of wood preserved to this day in a museum at Pekin, and expresses the heart-longing of a Chinese princess, unhappily wedded to a Tartar king. The lines have a familiar and eighteenth-century ring, but they are none the worse for that:

> Ah chère patrie, je pense continuellement à vous.
> Mon cœur est mortellement blessé.
> Que ne suis-je oiseau
> Pour aller vous rejoindre.

We are told that the good Papillon late in his life lost command of his wits; but he had a sweet imagination, and his account of the "beginnings" of engraving is the only one that we have been able to read.

It is, however, a matter of fact that a Chinese manuscript in the British Museum bears a woodcut, very skilfully executed, which is dated A.D. 868. This represents Buddha discoursing to Subhiti amid a great number of figures all drawn in flowing black lines. Mr. Laurence Binyon further states that the art of Wood-Engraving in China was in "no rudimentary stage even in the ninth century."

In Western Europe Wood-Engraving as we know it had to wait until the manufacture of paper, which was centuries later than in the East. It had even to wait until paper was cheaper than parchment.

Long before this came to pass wood-blocks had been utilised for the repetition of designs upon fabrics. The most ancient blocks for this purpose known are Coptic and of the sixth century after Christ, though the printed cloths of India were carried by Phœnicians to the Near East before the age of Alexander the Great. The invading Arabs and the Venetians and Genoese carried the stuffs, and the practice of printing them, into Western Europe, so that we have European specimens dating from the twelfth to the fifteenth century, and in Spain, by a sumptuary law of James I. in 1234, the wearing of "estampados" or printed fabrics was forbidden. Roger of Sicily established the manufacture of printed stuffs at Palermo in 1146, and it was practised in the thirteenth century at Genoa, Venice and Lucca. In his delightful and invaluable "Trattato" (chapter 173) the fourteenth-century artist Cennino Cennini describes the method, "Il modo di lavorare colla forma dipinti in panno," the *forma* being the matrix or block of wood.

The most ancient European example extant is assigned by the learned Henri Bouchot to about the year 1350. This cloth is printed with woodcut designs (about 2.50m square) illustrative of the History of Œdipus, and purely decorative passages of ladies and gallants dancing to the sound of lute and tambourine, busts of women, battle-pieces, etc. Bouchot,

Le Bois Protat. Anonymous Woodcut, about 1370 (24" × 7¼")

arguing from internal evidence, inclines to think it is of the neighbourhood of Avignon and of the time of the "bel exil de la Papauté" in that city.

Not many years ago an actual block, which was almost certainly cut for the same purpose, was discovered near the Abbey of La Ferté-sur-Grosne in Burgundy. This piece of worm-eaten walnut-wood, known as the *Bois Protat*, was probably one of three pieces intended to be printed together representing a Crucifixion in the traditional arrangement of central cross with groups on either side. The *Bois Protat* shows the right-hand group, of the Centurion and Three Soldiers, designed in outline without any shading or any intricacies in the costume. From the mouth of the centurion issues a banderole bearing the words, "Vere Filius Dei erat iste." His tunic, the high basnets of the soldiers and the whole spirit of the figures, simple and frail with "leur pose miniaturale," point to a date no later than 1370, while the use of the block for printing stuffs can be safely deduced from its size (60 cm. × 23 cm.), which is larger than that of any sheets of paper prepared at this time.

Everything, then, was ready for the production of "Prints" except paper. Mediaeval goldsmiths were engravers, so were enamellists and the designers of the monumental brasses. Nor was the widespread use of paper much longer delayed. By the end of the fourteenth century it was to be had in abundance. Peter the venerable Abbot of Cluny in one of his "Tractates" (1130) had mentioned paper "ex rasuris veterum pannorum contracti." Pace da Fabriano brought the recipe of paper-making from linen and rag to his native town and by 1276 there were paper-works at Fabriano. From Fabriano it spread to Padua, and from Padua to Treviso. In 1373 the Venetian Senate forbade the exportation of rags, thereby assuring Venice of a full supply of paper in the fourteenth century, and it was to the excellence and cheapness of its paper that the fame of Venice as a printing centre was to some extent due. In 1377 one Collo da Colle rented a fall of water in the Val d'Elsa near Florence to drive his paper-mill. As for France, generations of Frenchmen had worn linen chemises, and the vast quantities of rags thus forthcoming were utilised in the manufacture of paper. Bouchot quotes Simeon Luce, the historian of the age of Bertrand du Guesclin, to show that by 1360 every Frenchman, no matter how poor, had a few "chemises de toile," and there is documentary evidence that one particular valet had thirteen. "The fourteenth century" (says Luce), "by the fact alone that it is the century of body-linen and rag paper, is the indispensable preparer of Printing." In Germany, paper-making was known at Nuremberg by 1390, the instructors being Genoese. Parchment was unsuitable for printing blocks, apart from its great expense. Proper presses could not have been known at this time and the brittle nature of parchment would make hand-burnishing difficult.

But now that paper was cheap and plentiful there was nothing to retard someone from taking a block for printing stuffs—the *Bois Protat*, for example—and utilising it for the multiplication of facsimiles upon paper. The much-discussed "St. Christopher" of 1423, now in the John

St. Erasmus. Anonymous Woodcut (about 1400)

Rylands Library at Manchester, was long considered to be the oldest dated print extant. This and an "Annunciation" are both preserved, pasted upon the covers of a MS. book dated 1417. The date has given rise to much controversy into which we will not enter, and, at any rate, a print bearing an even earlier date has since been discovered— namely, the "Virgin and Child with Four Virgin Saints" of 1418, now in the Royal Library at Brussels. There may have been multitudes of lost prints of an earlier date.

Two social factors made for the development of prints: pilgrimages and card-playing. Always popular in the Middle Age, the habit of making pilgrimages was encouraged by the act of Pope Boniface IX. at the end of the fourteenth century. Indulgences could now be gained by visiting other holy places than the Roman basilicas. At these holy places single-sheet prints were sold to the pilgrims just as they are distributed to this day to those who visit the monasteries of Mount Athos. These prints were simple representations in outline, coloured rudely and brightly, of the great incidents of the Life of Christ, and figures of Sebastian, Christopher, Dorothea and others of the favourite saints. The great popularity of these prints in Germany is evidenced by the large number which have survived, a remarkable number when one thinks of their popular nature and the dangers to which they would be exposed, pasted upon the walls of houses, exposed to smoke and damp and innumerable other risks. Those that have survived owe their existence to having been pasted into manuscript or early printed books as illustrations, or inside coffers or upon the insides of book-covers. These "Helgen" or "Heiligenbilder," as the pictures of saints were called, would be purchased at the shrines through much the same instinct as that whereby modern tourists purchase pictorial post cards. Pilgrimages were a form of mediaeval holidaying, combining spiritual benefits with enjoyment. With the sweet showers of April, says the most famous of all pilgrims, Wives of Bath, Prioresses and Millers all get restive—"Thanne longen folk to goon on pilgrimages." And just as Chaucer's Pardoner, who had been at Rome, bore a pewter vernicle upon his hat and when he had got to Canterbury would pin an ampulla beside it, so if you went to a shrine or convent in Germany at a later date, you would buy a print or even, at some places, a block-book. At Maestricht, for example, they sold a little xylographic "Vita Sancti Servati" illustrating the life of the patron saint of that place, or at Einsiedeln you might buy a life of the martyr St. Meinrad. Luther, in one of his writings (says Mr. Dodgson), grumbles at the Pope "who lets convents remain empty and only puts in a monk to say mass and sell pictures." [1]

Indeed it is more than likely that these prints were not only sold but executed by monks. Only inside the monastic houses was the designer

[1] *British Museum Catalogue of early German and Flemish Woodcuts*, p. 8.

free to make them. Outside, he was pursued by the enmity of the Guild of Scribes and Illuminators, who forbade multiplication of images by other means than by the hand.[1] The woodcutter, like the forger of money, was outside the law. He worked by stealth and sent out his prints disguised as drawings, tinted with water-colours to make the deception easier. In France the maker of prints was not safe from the jealousy of the guild until the installation of the printing-press at the Sorbonne in 1470. Monastic artists, however, were safe, and the great houses passed on the prints to filial houses. This was doubtless the case in Burgundy, where many of the existing prints were produced, and Bouchot has created a hypothetical artist to whom he assigns a large number of these and whom he calls "Le Maître aux Boucles" from his way of representing draperies with round loops. As in all primitive forms of art, the figures are short and large-headed. The technique is very simple, the lines thick and open and the forms rounded. No hatching is employed except in the later prints, and lettering gave such trouble that it was often added by hand. Later prints, however, show Netherlandish influence in the stiff angular treatment of forms and the hooked draperies such as we see in paintings of the school of the Van Eycks. Such simple designs called for the added richness of colour, especially since the print-makers had to contend with the draughtsmen who lived by the sale of coloured drawings. The colour is boldly and vigorously washed on, sometimes with charming results. The washes are loose and transparent, not opaque and laboured as in the illuminations of MSS. and early printed books, though sometimes gold-leaf was applied. The colouring is an essential part of the design and is often very boldly patterned as when the Man of Sorrows appears, His face and body evenly covered with drops of His blood.[2]

The popularity of card-playing was another opportunity for the development of Woodcutting. The cards, which differ considerably from those in use to-day, were cut upon wood and coloured with the aid of stencils. The game is said to have been devised as an expedient to soothe the mind of the mad king Charles VI. of France. In the royal account-

---

[1] Lettering could not be done by mechanical means without infringing the laws. In 1260 a French statute said, "Nus moleres ne puet moler ne fondre chose là où il i ait lettres et si il le faisoit, il seroit en la merci le Roy de cors et d'avoir, hormis lettres chascune par li."

[2] Schreiber reproduces a very beautiful cut of a Pietà, dating from about 1440. It was printed upon rose-coloured vellum with the nimbi painted yellow. Vellum prints are rare, and this is particularly lovely.—*Manuel de l'amateur, etc.*, vol. vi., pl. ii.

books of the year 1392 there is an entry of a payment to a certain
Jacquemin Gringonneur, painter, for three sets of cards in gold and
divers colours.[1] But the game was known before that, for it is included
in a by-law issued by the magistrates of Lille ten years before which
forbade card-playing along with dicing and another game of hazard.[2]
In Germany in the fourteenth century the love of cards had developed
into a vice, to an extent which alarmed the pious, so that play had to be
forbidden by law in many cities, and San Bernardino fulminated against
it in his city of Siena. Germany produced packs in great quantities and
cards are known to have been used there as early as 1377. In 1441 the
Venetian woodcutters appealed to the Signoria to forbid the importa-
tion of "Carte e figure stampide" (playing-cards and printed figures,
doubtless of saints), for these, it seems, were sent out from Ulm and other
German towns in bales. They were probably printed "au frotton" (by
burnishing) and hand-coloured. In any case, no existing cards can be
dated before 1460.[3] Lyons was a famous centre for the card industry,
and we know that King Charles VII. was presented with a pack of Lyons
cards in 1454, and in 1476 Good King René of Anjou bought another pack.

[1] "A Jacquemin Gringonneur peintre, pour trois jeux de cartes à or et à divers couleurs de
plusieurs devises pour porter devers ledit seigneur roi pour son esbattment . . . LXI sols parisis."

[2] "De non juer as dez, as taules (au jeu de dames), as quartes, ne a nul aultre gieu. Que nuls
ne soit si hardis uns ne aultres quelz que il soit qui depuis maintenant en avant en ceste ville,
jueches, de jour ne de nuict, as dez, as taules, as quartes, ne a nul autre geu quelconques."—
Ordonnances de police de Lille, 1382. Cited by Blum, *Origines de la Gravure en France,* 1927.

[3] In the following year the poet Villon in his *Grand Testament* bequeaths to his friend Périnet
de la Barre "ung beau joly jeu de cartes."

BLOCK-BOOKS

ABOUT the middle of the fifteenth century in Germany and the Netherlands books were produced in which not only the picture but the explanatory text which accompanied them were drawn (in reverse) and boldly cut upon the plank. These so-called Block-Books have given rise to much discussion. On the face of it the text cut out upon wood seems a foreshadowing of the text printed in movable characters. It seems reasonable that the one step should precede and suggest the other, and according to the old story, Coster, to whom some ascribe the invention of printing, first used letters cut upon pieces of wood and juxtaposable so as to form words and sentences. So that it comes as a shock to our logic-loving minds to find that scholars no longer believe that the block-books are anterior to the invention of movable types. It is extremely unlikely that any block-book was published before 1450, the date provisionally assigned to the Mainz *Donatus*, which is in all probability the work of Gutenberg and the earliest example of type-printing known. At any rate, no copy bears a date earlier than 1470, and the great group of Netherlandish block-books have been ascribed to the period 1460 to 1465 which is subsequent to the achievements of the proto-typographers. Moreover, there are block-books of the sixteenth century and one was printed at Rome as late as 1548.

What, then, occasioned the production of books so laboriously made, which could so much more easily have been printed in the press with movable types? In the first place, it may be answered, these productions were small, no larger than pamphlets. To this it may be added that the amount of types possessed by the earliest printers must have been very limited, and, after a few pages had been printed off, the types had to be distributed to be used again in setting up other pages. It therefore would pay the publisher to engrave the text as well as the picture of his block-book and thus be able to meet the demand for new editions without re-setting his types. Moreover, early metal types were soft and easily worn out, but wood-blocks were durable.

In any case, wood-engravers working independently for their own gain, not printers like Schoeffer or the Zainers, probably devised the block-books and multiplied those which won popularity. These venerable works, surviving for the most part as meagre *fasciculi* of sad yellow hue, were printed as the Japanese print their colour-prints. The surface of the block was inked with a watery brown ink; sheets of damped paper were superimposed upon it and impressions taken by rubbing the back of the paper with a dabber or frotton. Only one side of each sheet could be printed thus. In some cases the text was added by hand (the so-called xylo-chirographic books). The popularity of these productions is attested by the numerous editions which have survived, and later printers some-times got possession of the blocks and used them, often mutilated, to serve as book-illustrations. Strange as it seems to us, these books were the favourites of the time, the books in constant demand.[1] Donatus, for example, the fourth-century Latin grammarian, whose *De Octo Partibus Orationis* was the most important school-book of the Middle Age, was constantly printed, and of course appears as a block-book. So great was the demand for "Donati," indeed, that Ulrich Zell, the first printer at Cologne, and a pupil of Gutenberg, says that the first idea of the invention of printing was taken in 1440 from the Donati which were printed before this time in Holland.

Other famous block-books were the *Biblia Pauperum*, the *Ars Moriendi*, *Speculum Humanae Salvationis* and the *Canticum Canticorum*. These are of Netherlandish origin shown in the prevalence of straight lines and stiff angular draperies with hooked terminations.

The *Biblia Pauperum* is a short picture-book of the Old and New Testaments in forty or fifty leaves, each leaf showing a New Testament subject flanked by two Testament subjects accompanied by four verses from the Prophets and three rhymes, each of two lines. Mediaeval MSS. had worked out the scheme thoroughly of "figurae typicae veteris atque antitypicae novi testamenti"; for example, Jonah and Samson are the Old Testament types of the Resurrection of Christ. According to Schreiber, the poor, or "pauperes," for whom this Bible was intended, were needy priests who could not afford a Bible, and this with its pictures

---

[1] "The Donatus always being in demand was generally one of the first books printed at a new Press. It was the first book issued by Pannartz and Sweynheym when they started at Subiaco."— O. Jennings, *Early Woodcut Initials*.

"The word Donatus was a synonym for Grammar—thus in a mediaeval schoolroom when a boy complained to the Pedagogue, 'Please, Sir, Jones has torn my Grammar,' he would say, 'Joannes Donatum meum dilaniavit.'"—Pollard, *Old Picture Books*, p. 102.

and Old Testament types and references would be very valuable in getting together a sermon.

Temptation to Impatience. From the "Ars Moriendi," about 1465 (7½" × 5½")

The block-book was essentially a picture-book with explanatory text; but in one case the text far outvalues the pictures. This is the *Mirabilia Urbis Romae*, which has 184 pages and is a sort of mediaeval

Baedeker giving a short history of Rome, its churches and the wonder-working relics contained in them. It was probably produced for the benefit of pilgrims to Rome in 1475 and bears the pontifical arms of Sixtus IV.

The *Ars Moriendi* is the most interesting, as it was in its own time, the most popular and widely circulated of all xylographic booklets. The cuts were engraved thirteen times and as many as twenty editions are known. For a century the Black Death had swept and re-swept Europe—that appalling "Peste noire" which the debonair Froissart so calmly describes, "Car en ce temps par tout le monde généralement une maladie que l'on clame épidemie couroit, dont bien la tierce partie du monde mourut." And so long as the pest endured the clergy were overworked. Such a book as the *Ars Moriendi* could teach a man how to meet Death without priestly assistance, and the preaching friars had long driven home the necessity of being ready to meet Death, for which, after all, Life is but the preparation. "Souvent aves preschié de Mort," jeers the skeleton as he leads away the Franciscan in the Danse Macabre of Les Innocents in Paris.

The very powerful woodcuts, which may have been derived from copper-engravings by the Master ES but are stronger in design, illustrate the Temptations to Unbelief, Despair, Vainglory and Avarice which attack the dying man, and the angelic inspirations which serve to frustrate them. The edition in the British Museum, which is German and of about the year 1465, consists of twenty-four pages, two pages of text, then eleven pictures each accompanied by a page of text. The original text was Latin and is ascribed to the great Chancellor Gerson, but it was translated into several languages and no book was more popular. The struggle of good and bad angels for the soul of Man, represented as a little babe, which the body exhales with its last breath, is as old as Christianity and older. The duel between St. Michael and Satan is only one of the many forms of this psychomachia—a divine type of the everlasting earthly struggle of Virtue and Vice for the soul of Man. The little shivering soul awaits the issue or is pulled between them in their celestial tug-of-war. It is thus that Dante describes the dispute between St. Francis and the Black Cherub for the soul of Count Guido da Montefeltro, when the latter cries in diabolic glee, "You did not know that I was a logician." In the *Ars Moriendi* we see the demons awaiting the momentary weakness that will suffice to betray the dying man. One careless word, one errant thought, and the day is theirs. They hang over his bed like an

Temptation to Avarice. From the "Ars Moriendi" (about 1465)

incubus. They induce despair by producing the man he had slain, the woman with whom he had been adulterous. They condole with his sufferings and praise his fortitude. They are dreadfully potent, creations of the fear which beset the minds of the age; but the good inspiration in each case frustrates the temptation, and in the final design the emaciated man gives up the ghost amid the throng of spirits, good and bad, which have made his bedside their battleground. A monk places a taper in his hand, a band of angels is in readiness to receive his soul, Our Saviour appears upon the bitter Tree, and the obscene band of demons rage impotently, crying, "Confusi sumus," and beat away on their bat-wings to besiege another bedside.

The delusion that the block-books preceded the type-printed book lent them in the past a glamour which we do not feel to-day. It is difficult to rouse any interest in these crude and stammering achievements except in the case of the first edition of the *Ars Moriendi* to which we have alluded. Here a real poignancy of expression and power of design is apparent which gets less and less in the many subsequent versions in xylographic or printed books. The technique is somewhat surprisingly mature in these cuts, and a certain amount of tick-like shading is employed, as we shall notice again when we come to write of Netherlandish *incunabula*. The forms are not rounded, like those in the earliest single-sheet prints, but straight and angular; the draperies are not looped, but are represented by straight lines with hooked terminations.

METAL-CUTS OF THE MANIÈRE CRIBLÉE

THE metal-cuts of the fifteenth century, since they were designed for relief-printing, must be considered along with wood-engravings rather than with line-engravings or etchings. A considerable number of so-called woodcuts may have been prints from metallic relief. The French Books of Hours, for example, were decorated with metal-cuts, the plates of metal being nailed upon wood-blocks to be rendered of a height with types. The printers of Basle in the sixteenth century used metal-cuts after the drawings of Holbein and others, and some of these (copper-plates) have survived.

But the metal-cuts which we must now consider are of a distinct species easily distinguishable from other prints. The main feature of this manner, namely the use of dots disposed more or less regularly over the plate as a means of covering the black ground, has gained for it the name of the Dotted manner, or more commonly the Manière Criblée, from the French word "crible" meaning a sieve (because Laborde was reminded by these dots of a sieve which at one time was a sheet of metal punctured with round holes). The enormous difficulty of lowering large spaces of metal to form a white passage may have suggested the employment of dots as a rapid means of covering the ground. The task of scooping a ditch on the shallow plate has often been too much for the patience of the old cutter, and the print by its smudged or rain-like appearance shows that the printing-ink had been pressed into these passages, and thus picked up on the impression. The mediaeval metal-workers used to decorate their plates with dots made with a punch, and their practice is described by Theophilus, the monkish writer on technique, in his *Schedula Diversarum Artium*.

Indeed, it is very likely that the metal-cuts of the manière criblée are derived from the practice of the mediaeval metal-smiths, particularly of the niellists. A niello (Latin "nigellus," black) is a plate or other metal object upon which a design has been engraved or stamped, and these incised portions which form the design have then been filled with a black enamel powder which, on the application of heat, is melted and hardens in these portions so that the plate when polished reveals them as black lines.

The nielli were a decorative end in themselves; but it is only natural that the metallurgist having elaborated a large plate would like to take an impression before completing it for his client. This could easily be done either by printing the plate in relief or in intaglio, or even by rubbing a sheet of paper stretched over it as one might take a rubbing of a monumental brass in an old English church. According to Vasari, Maso Finiguerra the Florentine goldsmith used to take impressions of his plates by intaglio printing before he applied the niello, and this led to the invention of line-engraving. Two things point to the origin of the criblé

St. Francis receiving the Stigmata. Anonymous Metal-cut, about 1450 (6¼″ × 8¼″)

prints in the workshop of the niellist. First, that although about 700 have been described, almost all of these prints are unique, and, secondly, that the lettering upon the scrolls sometimes appears in reverse, as would not have been the case had the plates been intended for reproduction. But these two reasons will not stand close scrutiny, and there is little doubt that most of the criblé cuts were executed for printing as devotional single-sheets like the woodcuts of saints or "Heiligenbilder."

The drawing on the plate was made with the graver, thus yielding white line, so that the criblé artists anticipate the white line of nineteenth-century Wood-Engraving. Quite delicate effects could be obtained by the graver, and close cross-hatching of certain parts is a common feature of these splendid prints. The engravers used punches for the dots or pecked them out with the graver. Punches were of various shapes such as lozenge, star, quatrefoil and fleur-de-lys. Rich textures were got by the use of these punches and sometimes of additional hatchings and cross-hatchings over the portions punched. Many of the prints have frills of cloud-forms, so severely conventionalised as to resemble a lady's neck-band, which enclose the whole design as a passe-partout, and are studded at the corners with little medallions containing the symbols of the four Evangelists such as are found in monumental brasses of the period. The floors behind the saints are chequered, and the walls often covered with rosettes or mail-like patterns. The rocks amid which St. Christopher strides or St. Francis kneels to receive the stigmata are diapered with great white plants and mushrooms of sternest conventionality.

The earliest dated print is 1454 and the extension of the style seems to belong to the latter half of the fifteenth century. The earliest cuts are the most thickly and irregularly dotted. The background is cut right out from the plate around the figures which are covered with a plague of spots of various sizes gradated so as to suggest the relief of the forms. Great scrolls are arranged above the figures. In these earlier prints the very faces and other exposed parts of the figures are spotted, but this practice was abandoned later and the faces are white without any shading. Dots become larger and more irregular and the design less hieratic in character. The figures are no longer against a background of white, and looser cloud conventions are introduced. The pounced devices, hatched for greater variety, give these cuts an incomparable richness, splendidly exemplified in the "St. Jerome" and the "St. Christopher" of the British Museum (Nos. 2673 and 2591 in Professor Schreiber's Catalogue). The latter (perhaps made in Cologne about 1475) is one of the noblest prints ever produced, and is reproduced here as the finest example of the manière criblée which the writer has encountered. There are other dotted St. Christophers of similar design, for the arrangement is traditional; but none is so inevitable in placing or pattern, so rich in textures and so beautiful in drawing. The ogival cloud-shape of the earlier style has

St. Christopher on Horseback.   Anonymous Metal-cut

not been entirely displaced, but a new flecked cloud-system occupies the main part of the sky. There is a great deal of pure white line, the spots are marshalled in orderly groups and the inner side of the cloak is further lightened by cross-hatching across the dots. Unfortunately for the purpose of our reproduction the original has been slightly tinted.

Most of the criblé prints are of German and Flemish provenance. The metal employed may have been copper, but is much more likely to have been pewter or zinc or an alloy of such softer metals. Though it will be noticed again in due course in our study of the French printed Books of Hours in which the cuts were made in metallic relief, it may be added here that one printer, Du Pré, informs us that his pictures were "imprimées en cuyvre," that is to say engraved upon copper. The backgrounds of these Books of Hours were criblé, but in no other places were dots employed. This use of dots for a background reminds us that dots have ever been the heraldic convention for gold. Where dots are used in heraldic stonework, for example, gold-colour is implied; but it is certain that in the Books of Hours as in the single-sheet criblés the dots were *not* meant as a guide to the illuminator as to where to apply his gold.

Printing from metallic relief was also practised much later by William Blake, who was obliged to devise some means of publishing his own little books of poetry and prophecy. His brother Robert, who was dead, appeared to him in a vision and revealed a method of relief-etching whereby the words and designs could be drawn upon plates with a varnish and the rest of the surface bitten away with an acid. In this manner, Blake with the aid of his Kate, whom Swinburne has called "about the most perfect wife on record," printed the *Songs of Innocence* and other little books which he coloured by hand. The same artist also made several white-line engravings upon pewter which were printed like woodcuts. One of these decorated a broadsheet with a pathetic ballad by Hayley on the death of a certain "Little Tom the Sailor." Another existing in a unique proof in the possession of the son of Samuel Palmer is the tremendous design of "Death's Door," which was used again and re-engraved for intaglio printing in Blair's *Grave*.

EARLY GERMAN BOOK-ILLUSTRATION

THE first German printer to use woodcuts in books printed with movable type is Albrecht Pfister of Bamberg, working about 1460. These books are thin folios, nine in number, the first of them being the *Complaint of the Widower against Death* (*Ackermann aus Böhmen*), with five large cuts, while an edition of Boner's *Edelstein* contains a hundred cuts, the most immature things conceivable. They are obviously intended for hand-colouring, being in simple outline with no hatching. Pfister also used metal-cuts in his *Sieben Freuden Mariae* and *Leiden Christi*. They are slightly dotted, and the marks of the nails by which the plates were attached to the wood-blocks, to be rendered type-high, are very noticeable.

Not until ten years later was the practice of employing woodcut decorations resumed in Germany with a delight-ful little garner of Ulm

Bathers. From the Augsburg Calendar (about 1480)

and Augsburg books. As these cities had been noted for their output of playing-cards, there was no lack of woodcutters to provide the blocks for the printers. But before the first of these printers at Augsburg could begin, he had to overcome the resistance of the professional "Formschneider" of the city, jealous of innovation, as guilds or trade unions have ever been. However, the Abbot of SS. Ulrich and Afra, who was interested in printing and was soon to install presses at his monastery, arbitrated, and through his good-will it was finally agreed that Gunther Zainer should be permitted to use woodcuts in his books, provided that he employed the "Form-schneider" of the Civic Guild. Zainer was a prolific printer and, of his hundred books, twenty were fully illustrated with simple cuts, for the most part small and of varying merits. The designs are traditional and therefore good, the type of line firm and thick, which harmonises with the massive black letter in which these books are printed. William Morris in his essay on the earliest Ulm and Augsburg books, says the most that can be said for these cuts: "Their two main merits are first their decorative and next their story-telling quality; and it seems to me that these two qualities include what is necessary and essential in book pictures."

Melancholy. From the Augsburg Calendar (about 1480)

Johann Bamler and Anton Sorg are other Augsburg printers who work in the same tradition, and achieve results not very different in quality from those of Gunther Zainer, though Bamler is more niggard of cuts, and Sorg, if prodigal, is an imitator of the works of Zainer, Pfister and others. Sorg's most notable work is his edition of Ulrich von Reichenthal's account of the Council of Constance, which he decorates with hundreds of shields bearing the arms of the grandees who attended that mighty conference.

Johann Zainer, who was some relative of Gunther, worked at Ulm, in which city he published, in 1473, a well-known Boccaccio, *De Claris Mulieribus*; one of those long-winded biographical dictionaries which the Middle Age loved, and best known to English readers in the much sprightlier Chaucerian exercise in the kind—*The Legend of Good Women*. All the great women of the Bible or of classical antiquity and the Middle Age are mustered, and have their histories related, while, to every life, Zainer attached a woodcut illustration. These cuts, which

sometimes contain more than one incident in the same life-story, are
remarkably to the point in their way—blunt and embarrassingly outspoken, like the remarks of children. One in particular, a vigorous scene
of the accouchement of Pope Joan, is sometimes found defaced in remain-
ing copies. This most remarkable of all successors of St. Peter gives birth
to a child amid the throng of cardinals. The names of the characters are
engraved above them and the designer, to speak proleptically, did not
know his Lemprière. Nessus, for example, is not a centaur, but an old

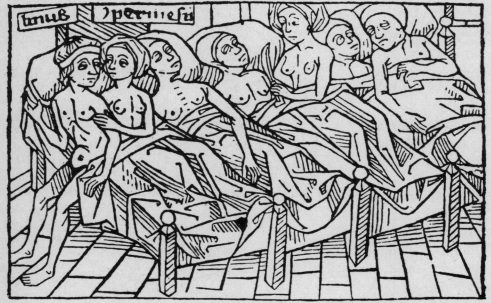

Lynceus and Hypermnestra. From Sorg's edition of Boccaccio,
"De Claris Mulieribus" (Ulm, 1479)

man on a horse; but Morris was surely right when he saw in this book
"the mediaeval reverence for the Classical period without any loss of
romanticism on the one hand, and epical sincerity and directness on
the other, which the flood-tide of Renaissance rhetoric presently inflicted
on the world."

In the cut of the Roman Virgin in prison there is an elementary
attempt at the rendering of cross-hatching, which was evidently too much
of a task for Sorg's engraver, who abandoned it in his version. Sorg's
translation into German appeared in 1479 with seventy-nine cuts, imitated
without reversing from Zainer's, so that swords are now wielded in the
left hands of soldiers or hunters.

At the risk of giving the *De Claris Mulieribus* disproportionate attention here, we must notice that it contains the first large woodcut border. It is true that before this the Augsburg printers had begun to use side vignettes of a sort, the need for something being keenly felt by those who knew the very ornate borders of contemporary MSS. But none before this had been historiated or of any pretensions, and even this did not enclose the whole page of text, being only for top and side margin. It

Nero and Popea. From Boccaccio, " Von den berühmten Frauen" (Anton Sorg. Ulm, 1479)

shows Adam and Eve receiving the fruit from the human-headed serpent whose tail ascends, twists round so as to form a large initial S and dwindles away to the right into little figures, emblematic of the Seven Deadly Sins.

Johann Zainer's other influential book was his *Æsop*, with a large cut of the fabulist as a humpbacked dwarf, surrounded by tiny figures with some reference to the fables. There are many smaller cuts of considerable charm and great clarity of statement, which were extraordinarily widely known and were copied in France, the Netherlands, Spain and even in England.

Conrad Dinckmut, another Ulm printer, is responsible for forty books, many of which are illustrated with cuts, while they get a look of profusion through the conscienceless practice of reprinting the same block many times over, one cut being used as many as thirty-seven times in one volume. Conrad's German translation of the *Eunuchus* of Terence (1486) is his chief claim to our gratitude. The play is illustrated by eighteen full-page cuts where the scenes are represented as being enacted in streets made to recede in some sort of perspective. The dramatis personæ, who have their names cut beside them, are lank and angular

Woman and Peacock. From the "Æsop" of Johann Zainer (Ulm, 1475)

and wear long black shoes. The black is left for windows and doors; the cutting is strong and careful.

The *Cosmographia* of Ptolemy was printed in a large and splendid folio by Leonhard Holl in 1482. This book is interesting to us for its fine series of woodcut capitals, called Maiblümchen or Lily of the Valley capitals (a kind common in MSS. and adopted by the early printers), and for two large initials, one containing the figure of Ptolemy and the other showing the editor, Nicholas Germanus, offering his book to the Pope. But the main interest of Holl's *Cosmographia* is its twenty-seven large maps, the first of their kind, each of them occupying two folio pages, printed on the verso of the one and the recto of the other. The names of the places are cut upon the blocks. It is not unnecessary to mention this, for it became the practice in the next century to print place-names by drilling holes in the blocks and inserting movable types. One of these, a large Mappa Mundi bordered by winds which puff out their cheeks, bears the engraver's name as "Insculptum est per Johannē Schnitzer de Armszheim," *Schnitzer* being the term for engraver used at Ulm.

Another book by the same printer that merits our attention is the remarkable edition of Bidpai's *Buch der Alten Weisen*, a collection of fables, illustrated with 126 full-page cuts of great boldness and freedom of design, characterised by a convention of shading which consists of short lines

From the "Eunuchus" of Terence (Conrad Dinckmut, Ulm, 1486. 6⅞″ × 4½″)

arranged with regularity like bricks in a wall. Schreiber declares that they are the finest to be found in any fifteenth-century book, and though this is an over-statement, they certainly have an arresting quality like the best cuts in Spanish *incunabula*.

At Basle, Martin Flach and Bernhard Richel are the earliest printers to employ woodcuts, but the fame of Basle as a centre for illustrated books dates from the *Ritter von Turn* of 1493 and the *Narrenschiff* of 1494–5, both ascribed to a certain "Master of the Bergmann Printing House" of whom nothing is known. Guided by the internal evidence of style, however, many of the best critics have not hesitated to class these among the unsigned works of Dürer's first period and to identify this unknown "Master" with the great designer of Nuremberg. The great printers of the city were Froben and Amerbach. The position of Basle in the history of European culture was assured by the character of these men distinguished for their industry and intellectual attainments, as well as for personal charm. The greatest scholars of the day were their friends and correspondents. Reuchlin was at one time corrector for the press of Amerbach; Erasmus bestowed upon Froben the glory of publishing his books. But, although we shall have occasion to speak of the

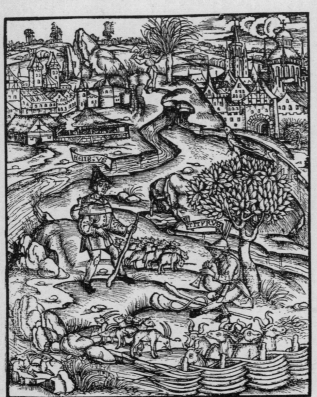

Arcadians. From the " Eclogues of Virgil" of Grüninger (Strassburg, 1502. 7½″ × 5¼″)

latter again in a later place in this book, we must pass for the moment to another scholar of Basle more immediately concerned with our subject.

Sebastian Brant, humanist and author of the world-famous *Ship of Fools*, though a professor at the University of Basle did not disdain to interest himself profoundly in book-illustration. Brant's maxim was "Imperitis pro lectione pictura est"; and, since the cuts in the great *Virgil* printed by Grüninger are expressly ascribed to him ("expolitissimis figuris atque imaginibus nuper per Sebastianum Brant superadditis"), we cannot be over-bold in assuming that he at least roughed out suggestions for the designer of that series of cuts; and probably with more graphic ability than was displayed by that other lover of illustrated books—his patron the Emperor Maximilian—in whose fingers the charcoal of Albrecht Dürer kept breaking when he tried to sketch out for the artist some alterations he desired in a design. In any case, Brant's *Nar-*

renschiff or *Ship of Fools* was launched in 1494 from the printing house of Bergmann von Olpe and sailed into the world with great effect. Appearing originally in German, the poem reached the cultured of all lands in the Latin version (*Stultifera Navis*) of Brant's friend, Jakob Locher. Men had conceived of Life in many images; as a pilgrimage in Deguileville's weary poem it had delighted the later Middle Age in which Romance and the

The Duel of Sir Æneas and Sir Turnus, Venus among the Onlookers. From the "Virgil" of Grüninger (Strassburg, 1502. 6¾″ × 5¼″)

three great "Matters" of Romance had given place to Allegory. But here was an image never worked out before, a metaphor capable of endless embellishment and variation—Life a ship at sea manned by a crew of fools. The success was instantaneous. The original edition was a quarto with 115 illustrations, strong, capably designed and full of character, but the vigour is not qualified by good taste, a circumstance often to be deplored in German book-decorations. Beginning with the well-known cut of the Bookful Blockhead in his library, each type of fool is dealt with in turn and the moral is, in the words of Ecclesiastes (words often

quoted at this time when Erasmus was engaged upon his *Praise of Folly*):
"Stultorum infinitus est numerus."

Brant's return to his birthplace, Strassburg, proved a great incentive
to book-illustration in that town. The influence of men like Brant can
hardly be understood to-day in an age which has ceased to worship
scholarship. The humanists of the Renaissance progressed from university town to Court and from Court to university town and were received
everywhere with pride and enthusiasm. At no time has learning been
so reverenced and rewarded, and the great scholars of the Renaissance,
though in their academic combats often extraordinarily passionate and
acrimonious, were always glad to learn and teach and always sure of an
audience. Three German humanists have left a beneficent influence upon
book-illustration—Brant at Basle and Strassburg, and at Nuremberg
Hartman Schedel and Conrad Celtes. The last-mentioned, a peripatetic,
whose motto was "Errando discitur," wrote many important books,
founded a club of scholars, the Sodalitas Celtica, was honoured by
Kaiser Max with the laureateship and is portrayed by his friends the
artists Dürer and Hans Burgkmair in laurels and singing-robe.

It was from the press of Johann Grüninger of Strassburg that the
remarkable *Virgil* of 1502 was published. This is the most important
outcome of Brant's belief in the educative power of the picture. We have
seen that the author of the *Ship of Fools* is even credited with the
execution of the designs, and in a preface in Latin verse he claims that
by the study of these book-pictures the ignorant will be able to read
Virgil as well as the learned.

> Hic legere historias commentaque plurima doctus
> Nec minus indoctus perlegere illa potest.

The famous book has hundreds of large cuts illustrating the Eclogues and
Georgics as well as the Æneid, the figures being carefully labelled and two
or three stages in their progress being sometimes included in one picture.
The Troy of Grüninger's artist, for all that a humanist be at his elbow,
remains a mediaeval city, from whose battlements a mediaeval Helen
looks down upon Alsatian soldiery solemnly carving each other as Greeks
against Trojans, or manœuvring the gawky horse inside the gates. Virgil
is shown to us laureated and at his desk, while the Muse with music-
book and quill sings to him of Arms and the Man. In the right-hand
corner Paris proffers the apple to the most fair, while Juno and Minerva

converse unheeding. The immortal goddesses, like other ladies of the period, seem to think it indecorous to remove their head-tires; otherwise they reveal their charms, characterised as always in Gothic representations of the nude by a notable protuberance of the belly. Hebe meanwhile ministers unto Jupiter upon his throne, while across a stream in the background Ganymede is ravished by an eagle and the Fates spin the fatal thread around Carthage. All the figures have their names on scrolls beside them. The whole is admirably lucid.

Grüninger's cuts may be said to belong to the Transitional period of German Woodcutting. They have not the maturity of the Nuremberg cuts which Wohlgemuth and his pupil Dürer were soon to achieve, and they have a "body," which such cuts as Zainer's and Holl's patently lack. The influence of Martin Schongauer is noticeable in the types which are full of vigour and character and have a certain amount of grim hatching to suggest form. Here is God's plenty of notable cuts, yet we find ourselves regretting that so much honest German effort should remain so unqualified by more sensuous qualities. Still, take it for all and all there are few picture-books more desirable than the Strassburg *Virgil*.

One other book from the press of Grüninger requires to be noticed here. This is the *Terentius cum directorio* (1496), in which the influence of Brant first makes itself felt, and is remarkable for its use of "factotum" cuts, a practice popular with Strassburg printers. The cuts of dramatis personæ and décor, which number eighty-seven, are arranged side by side in groups of five, making in all one hundred and fifty different combinations, an ingenious, economical and charming way of illustrating a play. Thus there may be one cut for the senex and one for the hetæra and every time he or she appears in a scene that cut is set up along with others of the different characters that figure in that scene, or even with a piece of décor such as a tree or a group of houses. The scrolls which accompany each character are left blank to allow of the names being inserted in types. In addition to the factotum cuts, there is a large full-page cut of the theatre.

As Grüninger's edition was influenced by the *Terence* of Trechsel, published at Lyons three years previously, it will be convenient to treat of that book at this point as well as of Vérard's *Therence en Francoys* (*c.* 1500) which derives from Grüninger. Trechsel's cut of the theatre is amusing but difficult to understand. Two men sit in a box marked

"Ædiles," a boy provides music with his whistle; there are tiers of seats
and underneath the ground-floor are shown the stews ("fornices") where
daughters of joy accost spectators. In the versions of Grüninger and
Vérard there is even less clarity—they are quite fantastic and inexplic-
able. Trechsel's cuts for each scene are massive and full of interest and no
block is employed more than once. The dramatist himself is shown at
work in a mediaeval scriptorium with pen and scraper in hand. A double

Moses praying for the Victory of Israel. From the Cologne Bible, 1480
(7⅓″ × 4¾″)

eagle upon a shield over the doorway signifies that the scene is laid in
ancient Rome.

Vérard takes over Grüninger's labour-saving device and perfects it.
He illustrates 297 scenes with groups of juxtaposable blocks set up
in fives. The characters are pleasantly drawn without the coarse
hatching that disfigures Grüninger's figures and are less scraggy and
lean in type. A muster of the "Personnages et Décors" from
Vérard's *Therence* makes a most decorative ensemble. One of the
earliest of our English printers used these figures to illustrate a book
of the "interludes" which preceded Elizabethan drama. Pynson inserted
new names in the scrolls so that "Everyman," "Hyckescorner" or
"Jacke Jugeler" now assume the shapes of the Terentian *senex* or

"miles gloriosus." The idea of factotum blocks is charming and deserves to be revived to-day.

Of the book-illustrations of Cologne in the fifteenth century, we have encountered nothing comparable to the Bibles in High and Low German printed by Heinrich Quentell. These long oblong cuts, full of surprising strength of design, are marked by a certain squareness of treatment and great simplicity of statement. Nothing could be franker or more in-

Egyptians Plagued. From the Cologne Bible, 1480 (7⅓″ × 4¾″)

genuous than the illustrator's methods, seen at their clearest in the cuts dealing with the Ten Plagues of the Egyptians, where the locusts are few but notably wicked and come whizzing down like aeroplanes; or Moses scattering boils and blains from his hand with excruciating effect upon a representative group of Egyptians, God the Father meanwhile looking over a ribbon of cloud, to direct operations. The Wars of Israel offer opportunities for admirable battle-scenes, while the Apocalyptic scenes were used by Dürer as the starting-point of his famous series. Quentell's Bible was a very influential book and was imitated and adapted in many countries, notably by the great Venetian printer Foresti in his *Supplementum Chronicarum* of 1486.

Lübeck, a German town, otherwise undistinguished for its illustrated books, is the birthplace of a Low German Bible, printed by Stephan Arndes in 1494, which rivals and is generally held to excel the Cologne Bible. It is certainly a work very much more mature in technique and with far greater variety in the use of line. Quentell's straight thick lines and comb-like shading seem very primitive beside these more nervous linear statements, and use of dots and ticks, which postulated some skill from the Formschneider; but the older cuts have a massive dignity which is lacking in the Lübeck series.

In the first Italian book to contain woodcuts, the *Meditationes* of Cardinal Turrecremata, it is stated that the designs are based upon the frescoes which once adorned the walls of Santa Maria sopra Minerva in Rome. These Italian cuts were of the crudest nature, but upon them were based a remarkable set of metal-cuts, tiny in scale, but large in feeling, which came from the press of Johann Neumeister at Mainz, and were used again by the printer at Albi. This set of thirty-four metal-cuts surprises by its force and directness, which is in no small measure due to the superior opportunity offered by the use of white line, though there is dotting as might be expected upon a metal plate. One cut in particular, the largest of the series, gives an admirable version of a genealogical tree of Dominican saints issuing from the side of St. Dominic, the Stamm-Herr.

To Mainz, the cradle of typography, must also be assigned the credit of bringing forth the first piece of conscious artistry in the decoration of printed books. For with Bernard von Breidenbach's *Peregrinationes in Montem Syon* (1486) we are entering into a new era of illustration. Breidenbach, the author of this extremely interesting narrative, took with him two gentle companions and, what is of extreme interest to us, "an ingenious and learned painter," by name Erhard Reuwich, to illustrate the itinerary with plans and sketches of inhabitants of the Holy Land. Starting from Venice the voyagers passed Modon, Parenzo, Corfu, Candia and Rhodes, each of which is represented in a large woodcut panorama. The largest of these, a careful and valuable map of Venice, is 64½ inches by 10½ inches, in four sections, equivalent to eight leaves and folding to allow of inclusion in the volume. In addition to these are half a dozen sketches of types of folk encountered by the artist, which are full of observation, and one full-page cut for which we would certainly hesitate to say as much. This is of animals "truly depicted as we saw them in the Holy Land," as the author claims, and includes a unicorn,

a salamander, a giraffe ("sereffa"), a crocodile ("cocodrillus") and a
great ape-man of unknown name ("non constat de nomine").[1] The
large and pretentious frontispiece shows a lady, quaintly tricked out
with ornaments, who perhaps personifies the city of Mainz and stands

Erhard Reuwich   *Janissaries. From Breidenbach's "Peregrinationes in Montem Syon,"* 1486

between the shields of the voyagers under an arch of interlacing branches,
in which scraggy children clamber.[2] Reuwich personally supervised the
printing which was done with some of Schoeffer's types. The book was an
enormous success, as such an enterprising production deserved to be.

[1] Mr. Pollard calls this a "jest." If so, there were few jests more successful. All the editions
of Breidenbach follow it carefully and in the following century you will find most of the animals
in the Natural History of the learned Conrad Gesner. Of the missing link Gesner says that he
had got the likeness from a German book on the Holy Land—"ex Germanico quodam libro
descriptionis Terrae sanctae mutuati sumus" (*Icones Animalium*, p. 95), and he quotes the
authority of Cardan, an actual eyewitness to its existence! But Gesner boggles at the salamander.
He includes it but reduced in scale and with a warning note: "Salamandrae figura falsa; quam
addidimus reprehendi tantum causa illos qui eam publicarunt."

[2] "Der Maler Erhart Rewich geheissen, von Uttricht geboren, der all disz gemelt yn diesem
Buch hatt gemalet und die Truckery yn synem Husz volführet."

It was translated into several languages and the cuts re-cut in Spain and Italy. The French version of Nicolas de Huen, 1488, contains the panoramas copied upon copperplates and is interesting as being the first case of a French book including "plates."

It is significant that Reuwich is the first designer for the printed book whose name is given. Erhard Reuwich is the first of the artists to take a hand in book-decoration. Those who preceded him, like the designers of the popular prints and pamphlets of a later date, were of a different social caste. They were not "Herren," not artists, but craftsmen ignorant of the new science of anatomy and perspective, and have to be content with the splendid anonymity of the mediaeval illuminators whose tradition they brought to a close. The subsequent course of Wood-Engraving in Germany lies along these lines. "Ingenious and learned" painters are called in to design for the publishers and employ cross-hatching to obtain more naturalistic effects. Reuwich's title-page, already noticed, is richly cross-hatched with fine lines which the Formschneider has succeeded in rendering very faithfully. The draughtsmen who followed him set the Formschneider even more formidable tasks, and that he succeeded so admirably in his task that the thought of the engraver's knife never comes into the minds of the many who admire the woodcuts of Dürer and Cranach, is a tribute to human intelligence and assiduity. This is not the place to stop and consider how much or little this power of creating facsimiles of pen-drawings was æsthetic gain, but the name of Erhard Reuwich heads the list of painters who designed upon blocks for reproduction. At any rate, it is very significant that the advent of the "great artists" upon this field coincides with the decline in printing in Germany. The printers have slain the scribes. The demand for books causes over-production, a consequent lowering of the standard of press-work and the use of inferior paper. To make matters worse, the wood-blocks are so fine and closely lined that, in the inferior state of craftsmanship, good impressions are now not the rule but the exception.

We are brought very near to the most famous of all wood-block designers with the *Schatzbehalter* of Nuremberg (1491), another ambitious book with ninety-one woodcuts by Michael Wohlgemuth, the master, as the printer Anton Koberger was the godfather, of Albrecht Dürer. Wohlgemuth's designs are not in themselves of much intrinsic value and are chiefly interesting as showing in what conventions his apprentice

Michael Wohlgemuth   *From the " Schatzbehalter " (Nuremberg, 1491. 9¾″ × 6¾″)*

had to learn. Some of the designs show an acquaintance with the copper-engravings of Martin Schongauer.[1]

Two years later Koberger published the *Liber Chronicarum* of Hartman Schedel which is well known as the Nuremberg Chronicle, illustrated with an enormous profusion of woodcuts, large and small, to be exact 654 cuts, repeated so as to form a total of 1809 pictures. The time allowed to the artists was nineteen months, so that there is some excuse for their ill-success, seen both in the coarseness of the cutting (there must have been a great gang of Formschneider employed—a perfect lumber-camp, one would imagine) and in the dullness of the designs. Wohlgemuth had the assistance of his stepson Pleydenwurff in the undertaking, much of which bears all the stigmata of "donkey work." How far we have got from the noble and fastidious industry of the proto-typographers! Paper and press-work are indifferent and quantity is shovelled up for quality. The Nuremberg Chronicle is the first great picture-book for the bourgeoisie —your money's worth of pictures—sold unbound and uncoloured at two Rhenish florins, bound and coloured at six. It has many large maps borrowed where possible from Breidenbach's or others' panoramas, or purely imaginary and conventional. The type of line is scraggy, curly and unpleasant; there is neither shrewdness of characterisation nor vigour of movement to compensate for the total absence of severity or sweetness in the drawing, and the cross-hatching serves neither to express the form of objects nor to enrich the general "colour" of the design. Animals and birds are still unobserved from nature and are of the common mediaeval unnatural type, prodigious and fantastic. Forty-four cuts of kings are used two hundred and twenty-six times and one and the same bearded head does service as Thales, Anastasius, Paris, Odofredus and Dante.

---

[1] Mr. Campbell Dodgson (in the *Catalogue of German and Flemish Woodcuts in the British Museum*, p. 25) notices that "the author in explanatory text to the tenth woodcut requests that if the cut be coloured the Cow may be painted red, since the animal he has in his mind is the red heifer of Numbers xix."—"und wenn man die egenanten tyer mit verbe ausstreichen so sol die kurot geferbt werden."

EARLY FRENCH BOOK-ILLUSTRATION

We have devoted a special chapter to the Livres d'Heures, but French books of the fifteenth and early sixteenth centuries are in general remarkable for the quantity and excellence of their woodcut illustrations. The most common format of French *incunabula* is the two-column folio in Gothic types with many full-page cuts and smaller ones in the columns and calligraphic initials. Let us begin by considering one folio of this kind which is chosen at random, but is quite typical—the *Æneid* of 1509 in the French version of Octavien de St. Gelais. The title-page contains a large calligraphic initial L from which a grotesque head flowers. Then follows on the verso page a full-page cut of King Charles VIII. holding a bed of justice and seated aloft on a dais diapered with great fleurs-de-lys within a rich columnar setting in the ogival style. After the prologue addressed to Louis XII. comes the translation, which Brunet says is not a translation but a romance in prose, of which the Æneid has furnished the subject and part of the details. The text is interspersed with full-page cuts showing Judith and Holofernes, a lady embarking on a boat from a castle, a tournament, and Orpheus and Eurydice (where Orpheus harps so sweetly that Cerberus lays down three sleepy heads at his feet and a devil with a face on his belly delivers Eurydice from out of a whirl of flame). Other pictures show Pallas and Arachne, a battle within a town (used also in a *Josephus* and a *Froissart*), the siege of a town, three judges, and a man slaying a dragon while the same or another man behind lifts out a naked lady from what may be a well (perhaps Perseus and Andromache?). Finally the device of the publisher, Anthoine Vérard.

Now what, it may be asked, have these pictures got to do with the Æneid? And this question, recurrent whenever we open a book by that most popular and indefatigable of early French publishers, requires no answer. It was Vérard's praiseworthy habit to adorn his books with cuts as richly as he could; but another habit was to be careless of how he obtained them, to what purpose he applied them or with what "damned iteration" he repeated them.

48

As his business increased—and it grew enormous by the end of the first decade of the sixteenth century, when the worthy man ceases to publish and is referred to by another publisher as "feu"—the store of wood-blocks must have accumulated enormously, so that ceasing to order new series Vérard continued to cram his books with the old stock. Not himself a printer but a publisher or bookseller ("marchant libraire"), Vérard is not entitled to the praise justly bestowed upon his smaller rivals, Du Pré

Initial Q. From the "Recueil des Hystoires troyennes"
(Heremberck et Topie, 1490)

or Pigouchet, but in enterprise and output he outdistances all competitors. Although primarily a popular publisher producing the favourites of the late Middle Age without a thought for the cultivated readers with neo-classic tastes so soon to have their day, Vérard produced sumptuous editions upon vellum and glowing with gold and colour for princely patrons like King Charles VIII., Louis XII. and Anne de Bretagne, Henry Tudor, the Seventh, and Le Comte d'Angoulême. His output has been divided into five main parts: (1) Horæ, Books of Devotion, (2) Books of Chivalry, (3) Poems and Light Literature, (4) Quasi-scientific Books, and (5) Translations of the Classics. All these kinds allow of ample illustration and all are in the vernacular, for Vérard is not concerned with scholarly texts of Latin and Greek classics or even with the tomes of mediaeval theology. How far away the Renaissance seems, as we look at a list of his books, the *Roman de la Rose,* "ou lart damours est toute enclose," *Fais Alain Chartier,* Deguileville's *Pèlerinage de Vie Humaine, Boccace des nobles Dames, Boece de Consolacion,* Chronicles of *Froissart* and *Enguerrand de Monstrelet,* Romances of *Ogier le Danoys, Tristan, Merlin,* and *Les Quatre Fils d'Aymon, La Légende Dorée, La Danse Macabre, Gestes Romaines* and *L'Art de Bien Mourir,* and a hundred others.

From "*Le Proprietaire des Choses*" (Paris, Duvost, 1500)

There is no class of French incunabular illustration of which Vérard does not offer examples, so that a survey of his main classes of cuts covers the whole field of early book-decoration in France. Perhaps the most interesting, as they are the largest in scale, are the full-page cuts for folios like *Froissart* or *Josephus*—truly grand works, nobly printed in double columns in handsome Gothic letters. The column of printed text alone, not counting margin, in the *Josephus* is twelve inches long. No other country has anything to show like these folio cuts, which are generally set within juxtaposable borders decorated with floral or grotesque patterns. These cuts are designed with great freshness and freedom and packed with charming details in the manner of the Gothic tapestries of the century. Very little hatching is employed and there is little attempt at characterisation, the great gift of the northern schools; nor are these sweet and simple designs vigorous like those in

Adam and Eve. From Vérard's "Bible en Francoys," 1505

German *incunabula*; but the figures in them have something of that dreamy frailty of pose that you find in mediaeval tapestries as though they were dazed by the perfume of the great flowers among which they stand.

Under the battlements of cities stand knots of placid warriors around one who bears the lilies on his surcoat and might be a king of France if he were not intended for Joshua or Judas Maccabæus. Perhaps a siege is going on and single combats are waging, while, in the borders around, rabbits browse and birds are intent on insects; or Priam's noblest son lies fully armed on his bier and they read the service over his corpse. "Hic Iacet Hector" is engraved around the bier which lies under the high altar of a Gothic church.

Vérard's greatest publication is the *Speculum* of Vincent of Beauvais, in five massive folio volumes, faultlessly struck off upon vellum and decorated with innumerable cuts. Towards the end of his career his energies abate and the great folios give way to octavos, often undecorated; but while he dominated the publishing world of Paris no successful work could remain any time on the market without being plagiarised or imitated by Vérard. We shall speak of his debts to Du Pré and Pierre le Rouge later, but all successful book-ventures provoked his emulation. Thus in 1484 Jean Bonhomme published Milet's *Destruction de Troye la Grant*, a small folio with many charming and distinctive woodcuts which were promptly snapped up by Vérard for his *Végèce* and his *Commentaires Iules César* of a few years later. The cutter (whether from laziness or happy instinct, no one can say) has left much black space between figures or around the fallen forms of the battle-pieces and this enriches the design considerably. Indeed, this is one of the best sets of cuts of the period. The death of Penthesilea is very vigorous, while splashes of red are richly employed upon the wounds of Ajax and Hector who are falling slain in the charge of knights.

When Guyot Marchant had a success with his *Danse Macabre*, Vérard followed him up with another version, and Du Pré's noble *Livre d'Heures* prompted Vérard to new activities upon this class of book. And he has an eye for what is adaptable in the foreign market. From Grüninger's *Terence*, as we have seen, he derives one of his happiest ideas, the employment of factotum blocks. For his *Bible des Poètes* he copies the designs of Colard Mansion of Bruges probably, by pasting prints upon the blocks, and thus engraving them so that they print upon the reverse. In his *Exposicions des Epistres* of 1511 he borrows from an unpleasant design of the Swiss artist Urs Graf, while in his *Triomphes de Petrarque* of 1514 he follows uncongenial Italian models and in his *Art de Bien Mourir* revives the cuts from the old German block-books.

Theatre. From the "Terence" of Trechsel (Lyons, 1493)

Thus all sizes and types of cuts are to be found in Vérard's books, so that in spite of his very questionable business methods, revealed by Macfarlane in his valuable monograph, we cannot be too grateful to a publisher who has so liberally decorated with unpretentious designs the old favourites of the dying Middle Age.

One very characteristic feature of French *incunabula* and therefore largely used by Vérard—calligraphic initials—requires special note, so that we will speak of it now in connection with the name of Pierre le Rouge, in whose *La Mer des Hystoires* of 1488 it made its first and most wonderful appearance. Pierre le Rouge, who is believed by the very learned Claudin to have given the greatest impetus to book-decoration in France, belonged to a family of calligraphers who, like so many of their calling, turned printers. He began to print at Chablis in Burgundy in 1478 and ten years later printed "pour Vincent Commin, marchand libraire," the two great folio volumes of *La Mer des Hystoires*, which contain four famous initials. At the beginning is the great letter L, almost a foot high, called the "Man-at-Arms 'L'" because of its large figure of a man-at-arms, and to differentiate it from other famous L's, as the "St. George" or the "Eve," L being the favourite letter of designers of calligraphic initials. This is the culmination of the miniaturist's love of great initials which are kinds of enclosures from which wild elements emerge, flowers intertwine and struggle forth to climb up or down the borders, hounds issue forth in pursuit of the hare, or pygmies spear griffins across the base. Pen-flourishes, madly incessant, are the foundations of these initials which look as though the calligrapher, weary of his task, had suddenly gone hysterical, and out of the flourishes emerge grotesque profiles, dragons or fierce-beaked birds and insects, while monkeys, lovers, zanies, St. George and Mother Eve mingle freely and have equal rights of citizenship in this queer world. So much for calligraphic initials, of which it may be said in passing, that their subsequent popularity was great and scores of excellent examples large and small are to be found in the books of the period.

The other three full-page initials of *La Mer des Hystoires* are of a different kind. The second is an S formed of two dragons coiled mouth to mouth and the whole page surrounded with historiated borders. The third, an I, is surrounded with flowers and foliage, and in the stem of the letter God the Father stands blessing the world. The fourth contains the author at work upon his book. In addition to these there are other great cuts in pure line with very little shading, and small column cuts of less interest.

Jean du Pré is another French proto-typographer to whom we owe many handsomely illustrated books. His great edition of St. Augustine's *Cité de Dieu* was produced in collaboration with Pierre Gérard at Abbeville in 1486. The two folios contain twenty-three large cuts (subsequently used by Vérard) which are among the most delightful works of the age.

In the history of early French printing the name of Lyons is hardly second to that of Paris. Woodcuts were as freely employed in the books of Lyons as in those of Paris, but they have a different character, for the Lyonnese publishers did not address themselves (at least until 1540) to so refined an audience as that of the capital. Their appeal was to tastes more popular, to the need of "tous citoyens et habitans en ville et chasteaux" who could read, but were indifferent as to whether or not the new art of the book equalled or surpassed the works of scribe and miniaturist. Thus we find no sumptuous editions from the earlier presses of Lyons to compare with those of Paris or of Abbeville. The simple designs which a more popular taste preferred have bold lines and little shading—the backgrounds are baldly summarised and the *mise-en-page* is not so tasteful as in Parisian *incunabula*. Cut by the "cartiers" or card-manufacturers established for some generations at Lyons, these cuts make up for their deficiency in grace by their vigour and fun; and the printers were keenly alive as to what was coming out in other book-centres. Aldus complained of their bold piracy of his italic; they acquired blocks designed by Holbein for the great Basle printers—for example, the famous portrait of Erasmus with the god Terminus, and they utilised cuts from Grüninger's *Virgil* to decorate a *Quatre Fils d'Aymon*. Du Pré's *Vies des Pères Eremites* and Guyot Marchant's *Danse Macabre* are taken over by these sharp publishers, and Breidenbach appears in a French version with his great maps engraved upon copper, being the first appearance of this deadly foe of the woodcut in a French book. But interesting as all this bustle and excitement is, there remains the evidence that these earlier printers were not great craftsmen. Too many mediocre blocks, grossly cut like those of the most pathetic chapbooks, are printed carelessly in this vast typographic output, where indeed they linger throughout the century some time after the advent of the new "antique" style which the Renaissance carried over into France. Few changes in the history of taste have come so swiftly as this new amazing orientation given to the art of the book by the influx of Italian ideas; so swift it was that for a time the two fashions run alongside as though invisible to each other—graceful Apollo, abroad again after the sleep of the Middle Age, pursues the shrinking Daphne even alongside the ungainly sons of Aymon mounted

From Boethius, "De Consolatione Philosophiæ" (Paris, Jean de Vingle, 1498)

all four together upon their wonderful steed and still going about the old chivalric business.

But not for long can the sons of Aymon (personifying the old popular taste as against the worship of Antiquity) keep the pace upon their ancient charger. Before long they disappear into subterranean haunts to appear only in the cheapest form of chapbooks for the amusement of the poorer classes in town and country.

Michelet in his splendid way has described the effect upon France of the invasion of Italy by Charles VIII.: "La découverte de l'Italie eut infiniment plus d'effet sur le XVI siècle que celle de l'Amérique. Toutes les nations viennent derrière la France; ils s'initient à leur tour, elles voient clair à ce soleil nouveau. . . .

"Cette barbarie [the army of Charles VIII.] étourdiment heurte un matin cette haute civilisation; c'est le choc de deux mondes, mais bien plus de deux âges qui semblaient si loin l'un de l'autre; le choc et l'étincelle; et de cette étincelle, la colonne de feu qu'on appela la Renaissance."

France now looks to Italy as her spiritual home. Army after army descends upon the plains of Lombardy and great battles are fought between Papacy and Monarchy, and Monarchy and Empire, for it is a strangely rough courtship that France makes of this country of amazing beauty, which it ruins while it adores. Italian artists are tempted to the Court of François Premier. The divine Leonardo breathes his last in his arms; Andrea del Sarto, Primaticcio, Rosso, the ruffian Benvenuto Cellini, all come to France, and some stay long and found a new style or school of art, introducing the "antique" with all the enthusiasm it arouses. Soon the spirit of the country, that spirit which Brantôme defines as "prompt, gaillard, actif et toujours en cervelle," begins to work upon the imported styles and there is a French School with Goujon and Pillon among its sculptors, Bullant and Philibert de l'Orme among its architects and Cousin and Clouet among its painters. And in the domain of book-decoration there are Geoffroy Tory and Bernard Salomon.

The older book-decorations had followed the tradition of the manuscripts which preceded them; but with Tory and the Renaissance which he personifies, decoration got a new form. Geoffroy Tory, at once humanist, artist, author, typographer and reformer of orthography, seems to be an example of that human synthesis for which the Renaissance yearned, the "uomo universale." Of humble parentage, Tory studied at Bourges and at Rome, was Professor of Philosophy at Paris in 1512, then, fired with passion for antiquity, vacated his chair, journeyed to Italy whence he returned in two years with a style and a conviction which were to revolutionise the art of the book in France. He was working for Simon de Colines in 1520 and designed borders, initials, and new types, roman and italic, which soon superseded the favourite black letter of French *incunabula*. Tory created a new formula for the book, his ornaments are clear and supple and admirably suited to the elegant roman and italic types with which they are arranged. He made use of fine outline cuts in which the new affected grace of the "antique" manner is evident.

His arabesque borders are designed with exquisite taste, and his famous grotesque borders full of Italian motives, swags, shields, amorini, flowers and garlands and the like, all drawn in the thinnest outlines, have a certain charm, thin and insipid as they seem beside the livelier, more vital borders of the early French Horæ. But Tory remains a very significant figure, because, as we have said, it was through him more than through any other man that the Renaissance style in book-decora-

Death of Penthesilea. From Milet's " L'istoire de la Destruction de Troye la Grant" (Paris, 1484)

tion reached France. The undecorated 8vos and 16mos printed in small italics with which Aldus had done so much for the study of Latin and Greek classics were influencing the trend of book-production in every country and especially in France, which drank most deeply of the intoxicating draught of the Italian Renaissance. No longer is the most common format a folio with gothic type in two columns and cuts correspondingly heavy to match, but 8vos, 16mos and even 32mos are in more general demand. The elegant small italics demanded elegant small cuts to harmonise—for the Gallic taste could not be content for long without decoration. It was in such a style that Lyons printers produced Holbein's very influential *Danse* and his *Old Testament* and it was in such a style that Bernard Salomon did his most notable work.

Le Petit Bernard, as he was called from the modest scale of his designs, was influenced by the artistic conventions of the School of Fontainebleau. He is inspired by the rhetoric and theatricality of Primaticcio and his work is elegant, facile and effeminate. A native of Lyons, Bernard lived in that city at a time when it was agog with the intellectual excitement of the age, in touch with Italian culture by reason of its position on the Trade Route and full of savants, artists and printers. His two most celebrated works are the *Quadrins historiques de la Bible* and *La Métamorphose d'Ovide figuré*, both from the press of Jean de Tournes. The latter is considered by Mr. Francis Meynell, the distinguished typographer of the Nonesuch Press, to be the most beautiful arabesque book in the world; for it is in the arabesque that Bernard Salomon finds his most exquisite expression. The thirty borders of the Ovid which are used 168 times, each time enclosing a vignette and a quatrain in italics, are of three types: (1) Arabesques or moresques in white upon black or black upon white, derived through the patternbooks of Pellegrino and other Italians domiciled in France, from the traditional ornament of the East and varied with wonderful taste and invention. (2) Rabelaisian motives, grotesque figures, pygmies, nymphs, etc. (3) Architectural motives, pilasters, urns, swags and the like. The vignettes which these wonderfully rich and delicate borders enclose are cleverly composed but quite frigid and affected. The heads of the figures are now made tiny and the limbs elongated, for the fashion is all for the elegant and the picturesque. The four sons of Aymon, to whom we waved farewell a few pages back, had large heads and earnest bulging eyes, as had their charger. Their bodies, it must be confessed, were stumpy and their limbs deplorably short. But how we long for their homely beauties among the refinements and prettinesses of these nymphs and baroque heroes!

Bernard has little or no individuality, but of course is highly eclectic. He borrows from Holbein for the Apocalyptic designs of his *Novum Testamentum* of 1541 and he knows the work of Dürer and of Hans Sebald Beham, Dürer's pupil and a prolific designer of small cuts not unlike those of Salomon in character.

Much of what has been said in criticism of Salomon is applicable to Jean Cousin, another famous artist of the period of the Italianisation of

France. Born at Soucy in 1530 he saw the change from the style of the Gothic "imagiers" to that of the refinements of Italy. The phrase "histoires à la mode d'Ytalie" occurs in the colophon of a Book of Hours published in 1507 by Gillet Hardouyn, and Cousin was a prime mover in the nationalisation of this style. Another synthetic artist, being painter, sculptor, designer, as well as author and poet, and illustrator of books on Perspective, Anatomy and Drawing, Cousin has left very little which is demonstrably his except the books with their diagrams. The designs of the French *Songe de Poliphile* have been ascribed to him as well as two series of triumphal entries of French kings, and it is certain that he was a highly skilled but cold and uninspired designer.

The great enthusiasm of the fifteenth century died slowly out throughout the ensuing century. France takes over from Italy the pre-eminence in fine printing, holds it until the terrible religious troubles cripple the book trade. By the mid-sixteenth century there was little room for freethought in France. The printer Etienne Dolet was burned for his atheistic tenets, Robert Estienne and Jean de Tournes the younger had to flee from the land, and the depression in the book trade meant depression in the art of Wood-Engraving. When the decorated books of France again became interesting it was due to the skill of Moreau, Cochin and other line-engravers.

LES LIVRES D'HEURES

By the fifteenth century, Illumination, which a century before had been identified by Dante with the art as practised in Paris, reached its last great height of excellence in the French Books of Hours. In Italy as in England the art had sunk very low. When a great noble like Talbot Earl of Shrewsbury wanted a Book of Hours he went to French illuminators to get it done. The famous "Bedford Hours," that superb manuscript which the Regent presented to his bride Anne of Burgundy, was decorated in France, while the culminating achievement of the school is seen in the "Very Rich Hours" of the art-loving Duc de Berry. No words of ours can describe the strange beauty of this manuscript painted by Pol de Limbourg and others under the influence of the great school of Netherlandish painting, then at its prime, and known by the title, appropriately fragrant, of "Les Très Riches Heures du Duc de Berry," wherein all that is most sweet and bright and uncontaminate of Middle Age and Proto-Renaissance is mingled.

As the Books of Hours enormously outnumber all other manuscripts of the time, so the printed Horæ form so important a class of books as to require separate treatment. The printed Horæ as usual follow, with few deviations, the traditions of their manuscript predecessors. Instead of the illuminated borders we now have juxtaposable blocks animated with figures or rich with flowers, leaves or birds which enclose every page. And for the larger pictures, which are so conspicuous a feature of the manuscript Hours, we have engravings of the same subjects. Before we go any farther let us look at these subjects in the order which tradition prescribed and from which deviations are exceptional:

(1) To begin with there is usually a Calendar with advice moral and medical, generally in Latin, but sometimes in French verse. The picture shows an anatomical man, the different members of whose body show the influence of the planets—Cancer upon his heart, for example, and Aries upon his knee. Beneath his

62

me domine quoniam conturbata sunt ossa mea.
Et anima mea turbata est balde: sed tu domine bsquequo. Conuertere domine et eripe ani-

Bathsheba. From Pigouchet's "Heures à l'usage de Rome," 1498

The story of the chaste Susannah is narrated in the little side-blocks.

legs crouches a jester and in the little interchangeable blocks which compose the border are the inevitable signs of the Zodiac or the pastimes and occupations of the months.

(2) Four Lessons, one from each Evangelist, called "Sequentiæ" or "Cursus Evangelii"; from John, the opening of his Gospel, "In Principio erat Verbum"; from Luke, the Annunciation; from Matthew, the Adoration of the Magi; from Mark, the conclusion of his Gospel. This section is illustrated with from one to three pictures. Thus you may have St. John meekly boiling in a cauldron while ruffians stoke and blow the fire, or seated on his island of Patmos; or, as likely as not, both stages in his career are shown on the one block. Sometimes you may have an Annunciation or an Adoration of the Magi, or a Fall of Lucifer and his Host, God the Father sitting with a papal hat on His head and the rebel angels already transformed into absurd devils with evil additional faces *circa genitalia*. Sometimes you may find a Betrayal with Judas kissing the Christ and angry Peter with great deliberation slicing off the soldier's ear.

(3) Private Prayers. Here in the manuscripts it is not infrequent to find a picture of the owner of the book kneeling to the Virgin with the prayer "O Intemerata, Obsecro te" issuing from his mouth upon a banderole. Upon a tree his shield is hung and in the printed Horæ these shields are generally blank so that the owner may fill them with his bearings, if he is so minded, as did the possessors of manuscript Horæ.

(4, 5 and 6) Hours beginning with "Deus in adjutorium meum intende," except Matins which begins, "Domine labia mea aperies"; Hours of the Virgin, of the Passion and of the Holy Ghost. The Hours are seven and are accompanied:

(*a*) Ad Laudes by the Visitation.
(*b*) Ad Primam by the Nativity.
(*c*) Ad Tertiam by the Annunciation to the Shepherds.
(*d*) Ad Sextam by the Adoration of the Magi.
(*e*) Ad Nonam by the Circumcision.
(*f*) Ad Vesperas by the Flight into Egypt.
(*g*) Ad Completorium by the Assumption of the Virgin.

(7) The Seven Penitential Psalms. Here the subject is either the

angel appearing to David with a choice of three weapons wherewith to do penance for his sin in numbering the people, or more commonly the affair of Bathsheba. David looks out of the palace window. He wears a crown, or, in one case at least, the "Chapeau fleurdelisé" or "Chapel de Montauban" which only kings of France can wear. Bathsheba sits bathing in the fountain of her garden with her ladies all around. She has all the beauties that mediaeval folk desired and that Villon's "Belle Heaulmière" had in her youth:

> Ces gentes espaulles menues,
> Ces bras long et ces mains traictisses,
> Petiz tetins, hanches charnues.

She poses so chastely with a flower in her hand and her long hair floating down behind, while the king seems calm enough for all her charms, and, in the mêlée that is going on in the background, the unfortunate Hittite is falling slain—"le noble chevalier Urye" as they call him in their old sweet way.

(8) Litanies of the Saints. Here you may have a picture of the Trinity or of a saint, as the mysterious Vision of St. Gregory at the Altar, and in the borders you will always find little cuts of saints with their emblems.

(9) Vigils of the Dead, Vespers called "Placebo" and Matins "Dirige." This gives an opportunity for a picture of the Three Dead and the Three Living or of a Burial Service in the Choir. The Story of Dives and Lazarus is found in this section. To Dives feasting with his friends enters Lazarus the leper. He bears the "cliquette" or leper's clapper in his hand and the bowl for the food he hopes to beg. He is covered with sores which a dog licks, but his clapping has aroused a flunkey who advances to eject him and outside the window you see Lazarus lying dead. Sometimes their fate is contrasted in higher regions where Lazarus lies in Abraham's bosom, while Dives in torment implores the one drop of water that Divine Justice denies him.

(10) Commendation of Souls beginning "Beati Immaculati." This section seems to be variable and to have received no traditional treatment. Other subjects that are common in the Livres d'Heures are the Jesse Tree, the Church in Heaven and on Earth, the

Descent from the Cross, and a "mesure de la playe du coste de nostre seigneur Jesu Crist" or chalice upheld by angels that was the shape of the wound in Our Lord's side—the Saint-Graal.

In any case you will not get all these pictures in any one edition. Actually few editions have more than twenty cuts, though borders enclose each page throughout. These borders are made up of woodcuts or cuts upon soft metal for printing in relief, with some use of dots or the manière criblée in the backgrounds where they wanted to kill a black. The number of motives that accumulated during the vogue of the printed Horæ, i.e. between 1486 and about 1525, is considerable, and the tiny cuts are juxtaposed in a schemeless, happy-go-lucky mediaeval way—dances of death, saints and sibyls, shepherds dancing, boys bird-nesting, pigs playing the bagpipes, cats performing their toilets, insects, plants, zodiacal animals, fools and loves and huntsmen.

Anthoine Vérard, chief of the Parisian publishers, was the first to bring out a printed *Livre d'Heures*. But this little book with ten rude cuts, published in 1487, is no fit representative of the kind. It was intended for complete illumination, the cuts being the guide to the miniaturist; whereas colour has no place in a really characteristic printed Book of Hours, although it was the practice to add the initials by hand in gold and colours, and two-colour printing from blocks was known. The real inaugurator of the kind is Jean du Pré who brought out his *Heures à l'usage de Rome* in 1489, which was the model, within limitations, to most subsequent editions for thirty years. Here the use of borders to every page is established. Du Pré informs us that his pictures were "imprimées en cuyvre"—engraved upon copper. These plates of metal, engraved in relief and very delicately shaded and hatched, show a use of dots in the backgrounds. One of these plates, which belonged to a set used by Pierre Pigouchet, is still in existence, and is nailed upon a block of wood to make it type-high for printing in the press. Vérard, as was his wont, followed up the success of Du Pré's venture with his *Grandes Heures*, but it was not until 1491 that the most delightful of all printers of Hours produced his first edition. This printer is the afore-mentioned Pigouchet who worked chiefly for Simon Vostre. He continued to produce Hours for thirty-five years and comprises in his *œuvre* the most perfect examples of every motive. His first set of pictures served for many editions but was replaced in 1496 (with additions two years later) by another and

Eus in adiutorium meũ intende.
Domine ad adiuuãdũ me feſtina.
Gloria Patri & Filio & ſpiri.
Sicut erat in princi.   Hymnus.

Geoffroy Tory. From a Livre d'Heures (Paris, 1531)

much more graceful set. Any book bearing the famous device of the Wild Man and the Wild Woman, so carefully and tastefully shaded and dotted, is a book to treasure. While Pigouchet continued to work, the Gothic fragrance still clung to the Horæ, the designs were light, sensitive and unassuming, but with the next century' the German virus begins to permeate the designs of Vostre and the other printers of Horæ. The figures in Vostre's larger cuts, when his collaboration with Pigouchet had ceased, are too large in scale for the borders, and the borders themselves reveal new motives in the heavy naturalistic manner of the north. In some editions half the blocks are old and French and half show the new influences in the lack of restraint or sweetness of line. Everything whirls, branches interlace wildly to form an arch above, flames, weeds, draperies, all are in movement. It is the influence of Nuremberg books and prints by Martin Schongauer. The dotted backgrounds are replaced by white spaces, the quietness of drawing by rant and vigour, the old placid faces by grimacing German ones, the architectural details of the original style by the porticoes of the Renaissance. Paris was the centre for the production of these little books which spread everywhere and were enormously popular. In the Parisian libraries alone M. Paul Lacombe has described 630 Books of Hours belonging to 500 editions and believes that this number is very far below the number of editions extant. Other printers who require mention, even in these narrow limits, are Gillet Hardouyn and Thielman Kerver. Kerver was the first to replace blackletter types with a roman letter. His books are in the best tradition of the kind, and after his decease his widow, Yolande Bonhomme, who aptly quotes the old adage, "Pictura est laicorum scriptura," continues to produce delightfully decorated editions.

But in 1525 appeared Geoffroy Tory personifying the New Outlook. The old haphazard mixing of styles, the sleepy aimless ways of mustering border-blocks is replaced by a new clarity of thought, a new precise insistence on form. Tory produces a new formula for the book. He is first and foremost a typographer, anxious to produce fine type-faces and then to design ornaments to harmonise with them. His clear roman letters demanded and received a new treatment, arabesques and grotesque ornaments, motives from the antique, Italian amorini with shields and swags and what-nots, all designed and cut in simple outlines. But by the time that Tory and the Italian Renaissance began to touch it with their cold hands, the Livre d'Heures had not long to live. The great industry languished, new interests followed the discovery of Italy by France, and in 1568 the Pope in his revision of the Breviary, by forbidding its translation into the vernacular and decreeing that the clergy need no longer use the office, extinguished the demand for Books of Hours.

EARLY ITALIAN BOOK-ILLUSTRATION

IT is popularly believed that on the sack of Mainz in 1462 by the army of Bishop Adolf of Nassau the disciples of Gutenberg and Schoeffer scattered themselves far and wide, came buzzing out like bees from a burning hive and carried their honey with them. At any rate peripatetic Germans with printing-presses passed from city to city of Western Europe. Thus Sweynheim and Pannartz came to Subiaco in Italy, and thence to Rome, whither, too, came Ulrich Hahn and Arnold Buckinck. To Venice came John and Wendelin of Spires, and the partners Bernhard Maler, Peter Loselein and Erhard Ratdolt, while Lambert Palmart set up the first printed pages in Valencia, and other Germans are found at work at Ferrara, Foligno, and other cities.

Ulrich Hahn was the first of these who printed in Italy to employ woodcuts in his books. There had been a block-book of an earlier date, which perhaps originated at Venice, where the blocks were later utilised in an edition of the *Devote Meditatione* of St. Bonaventura (1487). But Hahn's edition of the *Meditationes* of Cardinal Turrecremata is the first book to demand our notice here. The cuts, thirty-four in number (one to each of that number of folio pages), are very dull and clumsy, quite without salt or savour of any kind, though said to be based upon the frescoes which at that time covered the walls of S. Maria sopra Minerva in Rome. Notwithstanding the quality of these cuts, Hahn was flattered by the call for three editions of the *Meditationes*, and by their imitation by other printers in subsequent editions of the work. A remarkable case of adaptation has been described before in our comment upon the edition published, presumably by Neumeister, at Albi with a great set of metal-cuts based on Hahn's designs.

Despite this success, fifteen years were to elapse before woodcuts were employed again in printed books. After this date the practice of illustrating books of a popular or devotional nature became fairly well established. Isolated volumes with cuts appear at Rome, Verona and Naples, while at Florence the pace begins to quicken notably and at

Venice an enormous harvest of picture-books was reaped between 1490 and 1500.

In the year 1472 John of Verona printed at his press in that city an isolated book with many woodcuts of interest. This was the edition of *De re militari* of Valturius appropriately dedicated to Sigismondo Malatesta, Lord of Rimini, that extraordinary product of the Renaissance, at once humanist and condottiere, who

> Mit à sang la Romagne et la Marche et le Golfe
> Bâtit un temple, fit l'amour et le chanta.

The woodcuts are based upon drawings in manuscript copies of the Valturius and it is certainly not unlikely that the author of these drawings was Matteo de Pasti, best remembered for his amazing medals, among them one which moulds forever the unforgettable profile of the Lord of Rimini. Still such an attribution, even were it irrefutably established, could add nothing to the fame of Matteo de Pasti, for these designs are interesting merely for their simple and lively renderings of most fantastic instruments of warfare at a period when the cannon and the battering-ram were used alternatively for one purpose. Mangonels, paddle-boats, chariots, bombs, ballistæ, the clepsydra or water-clock (registering seventeen hours on its dial), all worthy of the ingenuity of a Heath Robinson, are soberly drawn in simple outline and capably cut and printed in this book, which lies, however, off the main current of Italian book-decoration and has no influence upon its trend.

Another exceptional book with a style rather of its own was printed in 1485 at Naples for Francesco Tuppo, a jurist, by certain "very faithful Germans." This is an edition of *Æsop* with thirty-seven strong and certain cuts all unmistakably Spanish in character and enclosed in each case in one of three stock borders with architectural features, and entablatures in which are shown the struggles of Hercules and Antæus, Samson and the lion, and a combat of pygmies. The borders are enlivened by various repeating units boldly cut in white upon the black ground. The pictures are more remarkable for their strength than for their grace. The figures are squat and large-headed, the animals full of spirit, particularly the microbes which are as large as pigeons and mean mischief. The conventions for water or earth or trees could hardly be simpler yet are quite expressive, and there is a massive feeling about the whole. In the accompanying cut, which shows the wife of Xanthus asleep, the drawing of the limbs and the arrangement of the draperies are admirable. But Tuppo's *Æsop* is another book which lies off the beaten track of book-production.

In Quattrocento Italy Venice is of paramount importance both for the number and quality of its books, and 268 Venetian presses are known

The Wife of Xanthus asleep. From Tuppo's " Æsop"
(Naples, 1485)

as against 41 in Rome, 63 in Naples and 37 in Florence. Though some have given the priority to Jenson, there is little doubt that Joannes de Spira or John of Spires was the first Venetian printer, and in 1469 the signoria granted a monopoly of printing in their state for a period of five years to this German by whom "inducta est in nostram inclytam civitatem ars imprimendi libros." John, however, died before the expiration of that period and the privilege was not extended to his brother and successor Wendelin. Two years later appeared the first book from the press of the illustrious Nicholas Jenson, the Frenchman who for his noble books was made Count Palatine by the Pope. But it is not until Erhard Ratdolt of Augsburg commences work at Venice with his two brother

Thais and the Youth. From "Æsopus Fabulæ"
(Venice, 1487)

Germans that woodcuts are employed as book-decorations. The firm of Ratdolt produced some very beautiful initials and borders cut in white upon black with elegant leaf or interlacing patterns, shields and wreaths which are the first and among the finest of the century. Though these borders only surround three sides of a page they are the first to be free from illumination. For although Jenson had used woodcut patterns for the borders of his books it seems probable that the blocks were not printed with the type but were stamped on, possibly in the shop of the illuminator, as a labour-saving device and as a guide to his later procedure

Title-page (reduced from 11¼″ × 7¼″*). From the*
"*Vita di Sancti Padri*" (*Venice, about* 1500)
The medallion bearing the printer's device and the xylographic title
were originally printed red.

with gold and colour. To Ratdolt's borders, sometimes printed in red, the addition by hand of second or third colours would be ruinous. They are sufficient decoration by themselves. It seems, however, that the essay was premature, that the taste for illuminated borders was still too prevalent at this time, or it may have been that the dissolution of the partnership lost to Ratdolt the designer of the firm, as Bernhard Maler (or Pictor) doubtless was, for, on the former's return to Augsburg where he worked for many years, he discontinued the employment of the famous borders. Ratdolt's later books are sometimes illustrated with cuts, but they are third-rate German productions and add nothing to his prestige.

Niccolo Mallermi's translation of the Bible into Italian is another book famous by reason of its woodcuts which did much to set a standard for Venetian book-decorations. The Mallermi Bible is a two-column folio with four hundred small cuts, each of them the width of a column of text, which was printed by Giovanni Raggazo for Lucantonio Giunta. There had been other editions of Mallermi's translation without cuts, and one by Jenson with six cuts probably intended as keys for the illuminator; but Giunta's edition is that whereby the work has won the attention of students of early printed books. About one-quarter of these tiny cuts are modifications of the swart massive cuts of the Cologne Bible and it is interesting to see how much lighter, more suave and tripping is the Italian idiom. The Italian versions show a more nervous type of line which is in admirable harmony with the fine roman types with which the Bible is printed. Many of the cuts are signed with a letter "b" which occurs also in the most famous of Venetian picture-books, the Aldine *Poliphilus*. The Mallermi Bible contains the first title-page with an architectural *encadrement* and its great influence made this and the use of small column cuts the two most characteristic features of Venetian books in the fifteenth century. The enthusiasm for Architecture, the great Art of the Renaissance, which preceded the minor arts and made them possible, the love of splendid tombs which grandees were ordering in all the great churches, are alike reflected in a humble way in the title-pages of Venetian books. There you will find cut in white line upon black or in frail nervous outlines the ornaments of such great tombs as that which Browning's bishop ordered for St. Praxed's, classical entablatures, pilasters, friezes, caryatides, medallions, swags and amorini:

> Some tripod, thyrsus, with a verse or so,
> The Saviour at his Sermon on the Mount,
> Saint Praxed in a glory, and one Pan
> Ready to twitch the Nymph's last garment off.

These Venetian title-pages are unequalled for lightness and grace;

for example, that of the 1494 *Herodotus* with its rich black border with white floral designs and its little picture of the writer at his desk garlanded by a beautiful youth. Another charming example is the first page of Guarino's Grammar (1488) with its delicate drawing of the schoolroom and one small boy hoisted on the shoulders of a larger boy to receive posterial castigation, while up one border children climb a Tree of Knowledge in pursuit of its fruits. Nor have we seen any frontispiece finer than that of the *Decameron* of the great printers de Gregorii. The border is enlivened

Medallion. From the "Vita di Sancti Padri"
(Venice, about 1500. 5¼" in diameter)

by amorini posing upon the bases of the columns and playing mock-tourney from either side of the blank shield which was a favourite ornament for the centre of the lower border. A cut at the top, of the width of two columns of text, shows the company seated in their prim garden telling their elegant tales of prurience among the flowers and peacocks.

The brothers de Gregorii are weighty names in a history of woodcuts, for many of the hundred Venetian *incunabula* which we owe to them are richly illustrated. We have spoken of the frontispiece of their *Decameron* which has in addition more than a hundred column cuts very neatly cut and designed. The *Fasciculo de Medicina* of Ketham (1493) from their press is dignified (and the verb cannot often be applied to incunabular illustrations) by the presence of four large and strong cuts showing physicians in consultation, students dissecting, and the like. Other notable books of this period are Lorenzo Giustiniano's *Della Vita Religiosa* (printed anonymously in 1494) and the

Vitae Patrum of Christopher de Pensis with about two hundred column cuts of the temptations, agonies and ecstasies of the saints.

The name of the great scholar-printer Aldus Manutius is rendered as illustrious in this as in other fields by his edition of the *Hypnerotomachia Poliphili* in 1499. This, the only illustrated book from the Aldine Press, is stated to have been printed at the expense of one Leonardo Crasso of

The Lover in the Wood. From the "Hypnerotomachia Poliphili" (Venice, 1499)

Verona. It seems almost an axiom in book-production that given a typographer of character the high standard of the illustrations is implied. At any rate, whoever it was that designed the 168 cuts for the Aldine *Poliphilus* they have never been surpassed in their kind.

"The Strife of Love in a Dream" (as the Elizabethan translator turned the title of the *Poliphilus*) is an eroto-architectural romance in the form of a dream-allegory full of the Renaissance enthusiasm for "sainte antiquité." The author, a Dominican named Francesco Colonna, has two main interests, the love-story (which has many luscious incidents despite the suspicion that the heroine, Polia, is really a personification of Antiquity), and the architectural setting to the characters, if characters they can be called who have no more life than those of *Euphues* or Sidney's *Arcadia*. The Renaissance discovery of the beauty of the human form, of a "bel corpo ignudo," gets prolix expression in the *Poliphilus* where the charms of the nymphs are catalogued with cloying gusto. There are of course pageants, of Vertumnus and Pomona and of the antique ladies

Venetian Woodcut, about 1500. From Pulci's "Driadeo d'Amore"

beloved of Jove, who were brought to bed of eggs and what not, and these provide the artist with admirable opportunities. The architectural interest of the author is even more conspicuous and he has described "cum elegante stilo, pyramidi, obilisce, ruine maxime di edificii, la differentia di columne," etc., with all the ardour of a Vitruvian.

The *Poliphilus* has all the elements that made for success in that age. It is euphuistic, luscious, pagan in sentiment and crammed with classical learning. Entertainment and instruction, love and archæology go hand in hand. It was translated into English and French. The latter version, by

Jean Martin and dedicated to Francis I., is a very beautiful book and affords an excellent illustration of the free translation of the book-style of one country into that of another which is so common at the time. Fifty years had elapsed since the Aldine edition first appeared and French printers had formed that consciously elegant style which is characteristic of all their subsequent productions. The page is higher and narrower, the type a fine italic instead of the Aldine roman, and there is a title-page with architectural entablature and caryatides where Aldus had only a colophon in majuscules. As for the cuts, the same translation into the later, more insensitive style is completely effected. The Aldine designs are taken one by one and gallicised, made "elegant." The shortish, stumpy, big-headed folk of the Venetian book are now endowed with long bodies, trailing limbs and small heads. The very trees writhe a little in the branches and have broadly-generalised clumps of foliage in place of the clusters of separate leaves which formed the earlier convention. In the Italian cuts something had lingered on of that older, more unconscious quality of style that we call naïve and associate with the Middle Age. At any rate, comparison with the French version shows that a new spirit is at work externalised in a style more confident and more exuberant, but somewhat tasteless and wanting in glamour.

So infectious was the Vitruvianism of Colonna that French buildings of the time are said to have been suggested by the descriptions and diagrams in the *Poliphilus*. The French artist may have been Jean Goujon or more likely Jean Cousin, some of whose designs in his books on Perspective resemble closely in style those of the French edition of Colonna. The authorship of the Venetian cuts is equally uncertain. As we have noticed above, the letter "b" occurs in some of these cuts, and some inquiring and ardent folk have found excitement in searching out contemporary artists whose names begin with that letter and balancing their possible claims to the authorship. There are, for example, Giovanni Bellini, Jacopo de' Barbari and Benedetto Montagna. However, it is much more likely that the "b" is the mark of an engraver's studio and that, since the same mark occurs in the cuts of the Mallermi Bible which is certainly not by the designer of the Aldine cuts, both sets were engraved in the same studio. The execution of the Mallermi cuts is decidedly inferior to those in the *Poliphilus*, but nine years had intervened between these publications, and the engravers in Studio "b" might have improved in craftsmanship by that time or risen to the height of the finer designs, or were dead and replaced by others more competent. However, it is a matter of little consequence, but, since we are upon this ground, it may be worth while to look at this statement from a *Vitruvius* printed at Como in 1521, and noticed by that great bibliophile the Prince d'Essling. The editor of this book expressly marks the division between designers and engravers when he writes, "non senza maxima impensa per molti excellenti pictori io ho facto designare e per non mediocri incisori ho similmente facto intagliare le affigurationi al circino perlineate et compassate" (Rivoli, iii., p. 91).

Aldus was a man with one great aim and ideal—the Spread of Humanism. To extend the study of the Greek and Latin classics Aldus de-

From the "Novella della Figliuola del Mercante"
(Florence, about 1500)

signed cheap octavos printed in the neat cursive script known as italic and said to have been based upon the handwriting of Petrarch. So great was the success of his enterprise that the popularity of the folio printed solemnly in double columns, which had been the ruling format in the fifteenth century, gave place to a taste for smaller editions. In Italy and France there arose a great demand for 8vos, 16mos and even 30mos, which changed the whole nature of book-decorations. If any designs were now wanted (and the scholarly printers like Aldus and the Estiennes did not want them), it is certain that they must be thin, elegant and small. More-over the triumph of cheap books (you could buy an Aldine classic for three marcolini or about two shillings) caused a decline in the standard of printing. In Venice other causes contributed. The Senate made interferences of a paralysing nature. There was a constant demand for cheap books for the populace, novelle, little books of piety, or romances of chivalry, and these were illustrated with the old stock cuts of the previous century or with the new shaded manner influenced by line-

engravings which was not only tasteless but more difficult to print. With
the cuts becoming greater in size and the engravers setting out to translate
into line the paintings of Titian and other masters, things got near to
the end in Venice. In 1514 Aldus died impoverished for all his industry,
and his body lay in state in the church at Carpi with his books all around
him, as a knight is panoplied with his arms. With him went the primacy
of Italian printing, the days of distinction in book-production. The stream
of popular books went on for a time, and printers poured out romances
and novelle with vignettes for each canto or chapter; but soon they all
began to glide underground into the shamefaced condition of chapbooks where in the seventeenth and eighteenth centuries you may still

discover impressions
from some very muti-
lated old block of the
best period, or borders
used once by a Grego-
rius or a Giunta and
now employed to pack
the title-page of a
pamphlet or to adorn
a broadsheet.

Though Florentine
woodcuts cannot be
compared to those of
Venice in variety or
number, they have a

From the "Novella della Figliuola del Mercante"
(Florence, about 1500)

charm quite of their own. The most salient feature of Florentine
cuts is the retention of black as the earth colour, broken up only
by horizontal white lines and dots. The figures and trees are
cleared out white so that they read in simple black outlines with
little or no shading. The borders are comparatively thick and black,
varied by a number of repeating devices. These cuts are generally
very small though a few are rendered larger by their inclusion in large
historiated borders. So close is the kinship in style and feeling of all
Florentine cuts that some critics (Mr. Berenson is one) claim that they
were all designed by the same artist. But it seems more likely that the
family likeness is due rather to their execution in one or two studios of
engravers, who were content to work with the roughest sketches of the

designers. These sketches by various hands may have been made on paper only, not on the blocks themselves, and they would then be translated into the style of the studio, which included white lines upon black grounds, a thing not likely to have been designed by an artist at that time unless Florentine artists were very singular among their kind. There is nothing of the manuscript tradition left in Florentine books; the black grounds are unlike anything in illuminated MSS. Moreover, they are never obscured by colouring and the fine taste of the Florentines forbade overcrowding of their books with cuts. The nature of these books was prescribed by the governing taste. The Medici, like other princely book-lovers, spent thousands of pounds on books, but not upon printed books. The scribes still had their day in Florence and, if they were distinguished scribes, their apartments in this or another palace. Indeed Vespasiano da Bisticci, called "Princeps librariorum florentinorum," in describing the library of Duke Federigo of Urbino says, "All the books were superlatively good and written with the pen, and had there been one printed volume it would have been ashamed in such company"

The printer, therefore, had to look to the lower classes for patronage and appealed to them by producing pretty little books of poetry or devotional works by preachers like Savonarola instead of great folios of exact scholarship. The words of the Florentine sacred plays or *Rappresentazioni* which were so popular on feast-days were printed in little books with tiny woodcuts full of reticence and taste, and usually prefixed with a title-page bearing a little cut of the Angel of the Annunciation, who acted as Speaker of the Prologue on such occasions.

Books like the *Epistole et Evangelii* cannot be too highly praised for their cuts. The little compositions here and there reminiscent of the works of the masters of Quattrocento Florence are all perfect. The type of line is light and gay, charming to express by a few flourishes the whirl of skirts in some nymph pursued or angel descending to the Virgin. There is not much variety in these cuts, to be sure, but the general standard is surprisingly high.

The white lines which serve to break up the black "terrain" never come right up to the objects represented thereupon, thereby leaving a sort of irregular black band round the objects, be they flowers upon the earth or dogs or anything. This yields a simple effect of great richness which modern engravers have been prompt to imitate.

From the " Libre de Cõsolat tractãt dels fets maritims" (Barcelona, 1439)

EARLY SPANISH BOOK-ILLUSTRATION

ALTHOUGH the incunabulists had been at work for some time there was no available monograph on the Early Book-Illustration in Spain until the publication last year of Mr. J. P. R. Lyell's work of that title. Vindel had brought together in his *Bibliografia Grafica* a large and amusing collection of woodcuts and copperplates from old Spanish books, but it was only a gallimaufry of decorations without any bibliographical arrangement. Mr. Lyell, notwithstanding his collector's ardour, makes a very un-Dibdinian invitation to students when he suggests that they will find these early woodcuts of "interest and often of considerable artistic merit." It is enough to deter the most hardened investigator.

The earliest printers in Spain were foreigners and they were responsible for at least two-thirds of Spanish *incunabula*. Although Lambert Palmart, a German and the first printer in Spain, used a roman letter in his first books, he abandoned it in favour of the massive gothic letter in which all the most interesting *incunabula* of that country are printed. The favourite format was the folio or quarto, double columned and heavily massed with borders and large initials to match the gothic type. This massive character with a sort of careless splendour is the main characteristic of Spanish art generally and is very noteworthy in Spanish books.

Art in Spain has always been derivative and eclectic. In the Middle Age the severe spirit of French Romance and early Gothic art was fused with arabesque luxuriance, while at the Renaissance Spain early adopted the pseudo-classical style which had originated in Italy. No country more feverishly exploited the Baroque until in its culmination, the Churrigueresque, it can show the most astonishingly skilful and the most atrociously overwrought style that Europe has seen. Indeed so normal is it for Spanish work to be overwrought and prodigal of ornament that the one style of building which has bareness and simplicity has been significantly dubbed "desornamentado"—the unornamented style.

The great Trade Route from Germany to Spain by the Rhine Valley and the Rhone Valley and through Basle and Lyons made easy the passage of itinerant printers and the purchase of German and French books and blocks. The Italian influence came early to Spain where the Kings of Aragon were also Kings of Naples, while, in the sixteenth century, the Spanish domination of the Low Countries brought Netherlandish influence to bear upon her book-production. These dignified volumes, of which about 900 are known, in at least 200 cases, contain woodcut illustrations. A favourite Spanish style of title-page is an enormous heraldic shield with the arms of the Catholic monarchs, or those of the author or the city or province in which the printer worked. These great trophies are often cut in white line upon a black ground and they completely swamp the mean strip of type beneath them which gives the title of the book. Another favourite style is the portrait perhaps of the author, or of a saint or hero in the book. But they are, of course, not portraits in our sense—*simulacra* rather. Equestrian portraits are common, of St. James, for instance, or the Cid, or Amadis de Gaul and other chivalresque worthies whose histories so fuddled the mind of the knight of La Mancha. They charge over rocky ground and lay low dragons or caitiffs while their great plumed crests float out behind them. Authors present their works to Ferdinand and Isabella, or sit stiffly at their scriptoria intent upon some mighty tome (as does "Tito Livio," that ancient historian), or sit expounding divinity to diminutive students. The actual title is a very secondary matter. It may be included on a scroll inside the design or it may be in bold xylographic black letter or even as a mean strip of type below, for not until the second half of the sixteenth century do we find the modern title-page. Where nowadays we look for the title and the imprint of the publisher we find in these old books a mighty decoration, and any information that the printer has to give is found in the colophon at the end.

The love of rich borders is there from the beginning, and in the *Tirant lo blanch* of Spindeler (Valencia, 1490) occurs a beautiful example which was subsequently used by Rosembach and other printers. The design of this border (which consists of four blocks of irregular width and by no means carefully joined) is of German extraction and the "verdure" through which enormous hares and other monsters are pursued by hunters reminds one of the German "Fabeltiere" tapestries of the fifteenth century. It is a metal-cut richly spotted in the manière criblée. There is a sumptuous quality about this border which has never been surpassed.

Title-page to the "*Libre de les Dones*" of Cardinal Ximenes
(*Barcelona*, 1495. 9½" × 6")

Though William Morris designed borders as heavy and more intricately patterned for his Kelmscott books he never attained to the same richness, and in comparison his borders are a little cold and mechanical.

We have said that Spanish art is nothing if not derivative; but it is equally true that it has a quality that is all its own. It borrows to transform; foreign motives become penetrated with the Spanish spirit and come out something new and strange, so that one would say, "Bless thee, Bottom! Bless thee! thou art translated!" The influence of the Parisian Horæ is early apparent, while Lyons, that busy centre, could not fail by reason of its situation on the Trade Route to influence Spanish printers. The great successes of the time are early found in Spanish garb. Breidenbach's *Peregrinationes* appears with several additional cuts, Brant's *Ship of Fools* and the *Stultiferae Naves* of Ascensius, with Sorg's *Æsop* and the *De Claris Mulieribus* also attract the attention of Spanish printers and are decorated with more or less free copies of the original cuts. But any immense quantity of pictures such as we have noticed in the Nuremberg books from the press of Koberger is not to be found in Spanish *incunabula*. On the whole their printers are more sparing of cuts than those of other countries. Nor have they produced any one illustrated book that can compare for number and quality of illustrations with the greatest achievements of Venice, Paris or Basle. Spanish printers preferred to make a bold display at the beginning and to content themselves, for the most part, with but few if any pictures in the text.

Such a book is the *Aureum Opus* of Diego de Gumiel (Valencia, 1515), with a title-page 242 by 162 mm. which bears the coat of arms of that city against a fretted background. It is boldly cut in white upon black and is so overpowering in its richness that one almost fails to observe the title of the book in a narrow strip of black-letter type below. On the next page is another splendid cut of St. James charging a dragon in a rocky place. As Mr. Lyell notices, the full resources of the cutter's craft are shown in the execution of the many textures in this design. There are black lines laid regularly like bricks and loosely as dashes or dots, white lines upon black, white lines laid across each other, white spots and even white triangular tool-marks. This is no mere facsimile. It is a piece of resolute and positive knife-work. Moreover it may be noticed that cross-hatching of black lines, requiring the painful removal of the interstices of crossed lines, is not yet required of the cutter, nor is his cunning yet sufficient to enable him to achieve it.

The books of the Barcelona printer Rosembach contain some memorable cuts in the massive style which is so eminently Spanish. Use is made of thick black lines very straight and uncompromising. The shading is of the most elementary kind, with regular comb-like lines leading off

Title-page to the " Lilio de Medicina" (Seville, 1495)

from some strong vertical in the drapery of a gown or some such object. His title-page for the *Libre de les Dones* of Cardinal Ximenes (1495) is remarkably massive in feeling. There is a total absence of perspective and the scale of the figures is entirely arbitrary. A hound in one corner in relation to the size of the chair by which he sits is no larger than a mouse. This freedom in the matter of scale is a circumstance in which

 Ureum opus regalium priuilegiorum ciuita
tis et regni Ualentie cum historia cristianissi
mi Regis Jacobi ipsius primi ɔquistatoris

Title-page to the "Aureum Opus" (Diego de Gumiel,
Valencia, 1515. 9¼″ × 6″)

modern artists are no longer content to *envy* the primitives of any period. They themselves enjoy the same liberty.

In his *Carcel de Amor* of 1493 Rosembach employs a beautiful cut of the lover approaching Love's fortress which is no larger than himself. Another charming cut is the title-page to the *Libre de Cōsolat tractāt dels fets maritims* (1493), which shows a galley powerfully and quaintly conventionalised, with a sailor swarming up the mast as though to exchange greetings with the Man in the Moon whose pleasant face beams in the sky above. Other title-pages that come to the mind at once are that to the *Lilio de Medicina* (Seville, 1495) which is Italian in its sweetness and grace, and that to the *Improbatio Alcorani* (1500) which shows a friar disputing with a body of heavily bearded heathens all of whom suffer from that homely shortness of limb to which the folk in primitive art are ever condemned.

Right into the middle of the sixteenth century, long after the Renaissance style had transformed the books of her neighbour France, Spanish books keep their archaic appearance, the massive incunabular quality which the gothic type imparted. But slowly and certainly the roman types began to oust black letter from the printer's trays and the decline of the gothic book in Spain is the decline of Spanish printing. New cuts are not commissioned. The old ones are used for a time alongside ornaments in the Plateresque style. Then, as in other countries, the vogue of the copperplate comes to the ruin of the old style of illustration. Updike in his authoritative book on *Printing Types* declares that the appearance of the copperplate coincides with decline in the quality of the book throughout, "because if the fashionable copper plates were supplied" (he writes), "printers seemed to feel that they could print as badly as they chose."

EARLY NETHERLANDISH BOOK-ILLUSTRATION

PRINTERS' MARKS AND INITIALS

In his first book, *The Woodcutters of the Netherlands in the Fifteenth Century*, Sir Martin Conway explored the field very thoroughly and carefully numbered and described all Netherlandish woodcuts in block-books and printed books; "but O what labour! O Prince, what pain!" His exasperation breaks out in such cries as this, "The figure of Christ is terrible, almost shapeless, the shade making it wooden; the thing is completely abominable"; or again, "The figures are ugly—frightfully ugly—there is hardly a nice face or a regular feature in the whole series." These descriptions wrung from him in the course of his labours have an odd ring to-day when some are not pleased without a "wooden" quality in a woodcut, and it is a mark of philistinism to talk of ugliness, nice faces and regular features. Nor have his groans deterred Mr. Schretlen and others from entering into the field of study and showing by their reproductions that things were not so "frightful" within as Sir Martin declared. Still it must be confessed that the woodcuts of the Low Countries in the fifteenth century are far inferior to those of France and Italy, even to those of Germany and Spain, although Caxton and Pynson and other early English printers paid them the homage of borrowing Netherlandish blocks.

We have said in an earlier chapter that the designers of the block-books which were in the main part of Netherlandish origin show the influence of the great school of painting then flourishing in that region. The art of the miniaturist reached its last stage of decadence in the florid, naturalistic style of the Low Countries, with their large borders of highly modelled birds and insects and flowers and their landscape backgrounds and placid skies. Sometimes the borders were divided into squares and lozenges of various sizes and different colours upon which realistic objects were painted. The earliest woodcutters carried this tradition over, and turned it as far as possible into design in terms of black

94

and white. Perhaps in the book-art of no country is the adherence to the manuscript tradition so close as in that of the Netherlands, and it is likely that the miniaturists gladly enough embraced this means of more easily multiplying their drawings (which could be coloured at will) or because they felt that their craft was threatened by the new developments. Even in the block-books we noticed a technique which for other

Medea. From the "Historie van Jason" (Haarlem, 1485)

countries came with the maturity of the craft of Woodcutting, namely the use of fine shade-lines. Draperies with hooked terminations are used to adorn the lean angular types common in Netherlandish painting. The outlines to the figures are firm and are strengthened by rows of shade-lines, like the teeth of a comb, impinging upon them. Objects are often shaded by divers combinations of dots and ticks as often as not unnecessary, badly placed and merely irritating. Rich decorative effects are obtained by the use of black-and-white chequered pavements for interiors, and of black grounds overgrown with white flowers of impossible luxuriance for landscapes. The characteristics of the Netherlandish school of painting are everywhere—in the angular forms, thin, hard and dry, the love of hushed woodland backgrounds, and the architectural settings in the late Gothic style like those in which the Madonnas of van Eyck or Roger van der Weyden are enthroned and suckle "the Desire of all the Nations."

Conway did his work so thoroughly that he reduced the band of anonymous woodcutters into some sort of order. All books with cuts having similarity of style which emanate from one city are assigned to a hypothetical artist who is dubbed "the Woodcutter" of that place or, if need be, the First, Second, Third or Fourth Woodcutter of that place. Thus there are four woodcutters at Gouda, one at Utrecht, three at Delft, and so on. Of all these hard-working cutters the most interesting belong to Delft and Haarlem. The latter worked for Jacob Bellaert, a printer of that city, and is responsible for the illustrations in *Der Sonderen troest* (an edition of the *Belial* of Jacobus de Theramo), published in 1484. A large cut shows several incidents in the Bible story, as the Fall of Lucifer, the Ark, the Passage of the Red Sea and the Baptism of Christ; yet all the scenes are so easily co-ordinated and so directly and blithely represented that it is worthy of high praise. The same volume has many combinations of three blocks arranged triptych-wise, with two narrow blocks around a central one. The walls of the buildings are carefully shaded with parallel lines and the pavements chequered in black and white and made to recede backwards from the eye. The style is that of the best block-books. One amusing cut shows the Eternal Father, a bearded old monarch, seated inside the Empyreal Castle, which a frill of clouds supports, and listening to the complaint of a bestial Lucifer who charges the Son with trespassing in Hell on the day of His awful harrowing.

But the *Historie van Trojen* and the *Historie van Jason*, both published by Bellaert in 1485, bear even more valuable cuts. In the former is a very decorative cut of Hercules slaying three lions. The hero in the armour of the period sweeps with a two-handed sword at the lions who seem to have come right out of a coat of arms. The combat takes place in a field the black ground of which is patterned with great white flowers. In the mid-foreground are trees from out of whose leaves peer spectators, while the farthest-off trees consist of arrangements of ticks without any line around them—the convention of the block-books. The *Historie van Trojen* contains another cut not unlike this but not so successful. The design is overcrowded by the number of warriors that are shown hacking and hewing at each other in such another meadow. At the risk of over-statement one might call these cuts gorgeous.

To the Haarlem woodcutter is also ascribed the very different kind of illustrations that is to be found in another book printed by Bellaert, namely the *Boeck van den proprieteyten der dinghen* of Glanville (1485). Chief among these cuts is a charming series of twelve little circular designs

Sir Hercules. From the "Historie van Trojen" (Haarlem, 1485. 5½" × 4¼")

representing the Labours of the Months. Tiny things as they are in size, they are big in spirit and the folk within them swing their limbs about in the most lyrical mediaeval fashion. We find it impossible to believe that these cuts are by the same hand as those in the other books here described. No artist until our own perplexed times worked in more styles than one.

The Delft woodcutter (there were three of them according to Conway) who illustrated Snellaert's edition of Ludolphus de Saxonia's *Leven ons Heeren* (1488) is perhaps the most interesting of all the brotherhood of the knife. The various incidents in New Testament story are freely

and ingenuously set forth. The decorative value of black is well understood and the variety of textures in the drawing of walls and other
objects is unusually large. These cuts are resolute pieces of knife-work,
full of vigour and sweep. To this cutter, whether or no he made his
own designs, the idea of a facsimile of a drawing had not occurred, or if
it had, was of little weight. The free use of the tool, the joy in mere and
sheer "cutting" seems to have dictated the treatment. There are seventy-

Herodias. From Ludolphus, "Leven ons Heeren" (Delft, 1488. 6¼″ × 4¼″)

five cuts in this Ludolphus, some folio, some half-folio and some quarto
so that they require to be padded out with factotum cuts to make them
half-folio in size.

Had this study been of a strictly chronological nature we would
have had to describe the *Dialogus creaturarum moralisatus* before these
other books. The *Dialogus* was published by Gerard Leeu of Gouda in
1480. It is thus one of the earliest illustrated books of the Netherlands
and one of the most popular, judging by the nine editions that were issued.
It contains 121 cuts (each 4 by 1¾ inches) of the animals, minerals, etc.,
of whose conversations the book consists. They are in pure outline and
are sometimes surprisingly full of character and always like the drawings

of a happily gifted child. It would be illuminating to know what the old cutter would think could he but read the solemn pages in which Sir Martin Conway analyses his style. It reminds us of that equally serious epic poet of the eighteenth century who began a canto with, "Now, Muse, let's tell of rats."

Colard Mansion of Bruges is dear to us as the master of Caxton. He was a calligrapher who like many at this time of transition turned printer, and published his first book in 1476. It was only in his last book that Colard Mansion employed woodcuts, but in some folios he had left blank spaces for the "hystoire" or illustration to be painted thereupon by the miniaturist. His *Metamorphoses* of Ovid (1484) has seventeen folio and seventeen quarto cuts which reveal the almost hopeless struggle of the artist to portray even the simplest objects. Nevertheless so pleasant is the spirit and so unexpectedly and felicitously placed the data that these designs are charming. The cutting is clean enough and firm enough to be adequate for the design, and the human details have all the mediaeval fragrance as in the cut of the Rape of Helen by that fifteenth-century knight, Sir Paris, where the lady's shoes have come off in the excitement.

The designer of the well-known set of illustrations in the *Chevalier Délibéré* of Olivier de la Marche is an artist of a maturer outlook than any of those we have noticed. He is a more skilled cutter, besides the fact that he has some knowledge of perspective and of the scale of figures in relation to their setting. He would never draw a man larger than the house beside him or a pavement that goes straight up like a curtain. But in Art (to risk a generalisation) the blessed are the pure in spirit, and knowledge and innocence of outlook are seldom lodged together in one head.

Olivier de la Marche was a favourite at the Burgundian Court and was alive when Gottfried van Os of Gouda published this edition in 1486. The *Chevalier Délibéré* is an allegorical poem, mercifully short but full of the personifications and other didactic apparatus of its dreary genre. The author is at pains to show how he wishes the illustrations done and writes a full account, of which the following is a sample: "The horse of the knight shall be black and on it shall be written in a conspicuous place in letters of silver, 'Trouble,' and his lance, which shall be white, is lying on the ground unbroken. And there shall be written on the plain in a conspicuous place in letters of azure, 'Time.'" It is obvious that Olivier

has got the miniaturist in mind not the woodcutter, but the passage is
of value as revealing the great stress laid upon the story-telling side of
mediaeval illustration. In his sixteen large cuts the woodcutter followed
out the instructions as far as his materials allowed. Very likely he followed
some manuscript pictures. Though these cuts have been greatly praised

*Christ before Pilate. From Ludolphus, "Leven ons
Heeren" (Delft, 1488. 5¾″ × 4½″)*

and have been reproduced one and all in the Bibliographical Society's
edition of Olivier's poem, they seem to us tired in feeling, while the
comparatively large amount of shading employed is neither fine enough
to charm by its delicacy nor strong enough to give form to the objects
upon which it is squandered. Their main interest is that by his maturity
of outlook this woodcutter foreshadows the development of the woodcut to its fullest range, seen in the Netherlands in the work of
Lucas van Leyden.

A few words about Printers' Devices. Readers of Dibdin's *Biblio-graphical Decameron* will remember with what quaint pedantry and charming hyperbole the reverend bibliophile treats of the marks of the early French and Netherlandish printers. The scope of this work does not allow of any detailed account of the hundreds of delightful devices with which the old books were decorated by their makers in the Heroic Age of Printing. From the simple device of two shields used by Fust and Schoeffer to the elaborate picture of a press used by Ascensius the humanist-printer of Lyons, the range and variety of the designs are vast and fascinating. Italians were fond of the cross as the central factor of their devices and they varied it endlessly with crosslets and circles and handsome initials upon or around it; all cut in white upon black or printed sumptuously in red. On the other hand the French were particularly fond of shields supported by heraldic beasts cut often upon metal against a spotted background. Kerver has unicorns, Vostre leopards, le Fevre bears, Pigouchet savage men. Often the device is of a punning nature, as in the knife of Gillet Couteau and the St. Anthony of Antoine Caillaut. The Netherlandish printers use devices no less quaint and delightful: Godfrey Back of Antwerp has a remarkable device of a bird-cage; Gerard Leeu and after him Thierry Martins use a device of Antwerp Castle; Bellaert has a unicorn, Eckert van Hombergh an eagle. Elephants with castles appear several times. They have trunks wrinkled superciliously and terminating like blunderbusses, and by the stiffness of their stance remind us that in the Middle Age the elephant was believed to have no knee-joints, and being born upon its feet, remained standing until its death. But two Louvain printers, the brothers John and Conrad de Westphalia, actually used their portraits as devices. These little heads, so small that you could cover each with a half-crown, are almost certainly likenesses of these humanist-printers. That of John de Westphalia which he describes as "suum proprium, suum solitum signum"—a shrewd white-line cut of a head in a velvet cap seen in profile—is the earliest dated woodcut in a Netherlandish book and is used as early as 1475. It fascinates us by its look of actuality and its rarity as the motive of a device out of all proportion to its value as a work of art.

.   .   .   .

And now, before we quit the subject of incunabular woodcuts for those which appeared as single-sheet prints, let us turn for a moment to the mighty harvest of Woodcut Initials. The early period of printing when its descent from the manuscript was most apparent was the most productive of fine initials. The manuscript tradition died very hard and survived for almost a century in isolated cases with the practice of adding the initials by hand with something of the splendour of the old illuminations. At any rate, for some time printers felt that their patrons might desire to have their books finished by hand, so that they often left a space for large initials and contented themselves with printing the initial in small as a guide-letter for the illuminator. Patrons must have been less particular than publishers thought, for in a great number of cases the guide-letter still has the blank space to itself.

From the beginning there is endless variety in the forms of the initials. Gutenberg printed a great letter in his Psalter in two colours from two blocks with wonderful accuracy of register. He was trying to emulate the illuminated initials of manuscripts, but later printers either left spaces as we have seen, or printed woodcut initials in black upon white or white line upon black. Those initials are best in which the letter partakes of something of the character of the floral or arabesque growths which penetrate or enclose it. Of course the varying manuscript tradition of each country suggested the character of these woodcut initials which are commonly about three square inches in size. Publishers had sets prepared for them which in course of time were sold or lent round to other firms for use in their books. Pictorial initials were popular from the first, but were of course larger and fewer than others. Sometimes the letter suggested the subject; for example an "A" might enclose a figure of Abraham, or a "B" of Balaam and his ass. But generally there was no restriction at all and you find the mediaeval types of subject frequently employed in large initials, as of the author on his knee presenting his book to a monarch or a pope, or seated at his scriptorium like the stone Aristotles on the fronts of Gothic cathedrals.

As the Renaissance reaches its height the pictorial character of the initials goes to extremes of elaboration and freedom. Great curly "Landsknechte" figure in these initials with prophets, sibyls, clowns, sileni, obscene and zoomorphic forms of every description. Children are represented ironically engaged in adult pursuits. Lovers embrace in the "Q" of a book of sermons and are attacked by pious readers. Sebastian sets his back against an "I" to sustain his burden of arrows. God the Father looks over a cloud, or Death leads on the Danse Macabre. Adam and Eve stiffly pluck from a "T" the fruit of Knowledge and Sin, or some of the infinite number of fools sail fatuously to Narragonia. If occasionally it pleases our sense of fitness to find in a Bible Jerome at work translating or David harping at the commencement of Psalms, we are just as likely to be startled by the discovery of an initial of quite indecorous nature pushed in by a printer with a scanty stock of cuts. For there is sad irrelevance in these matters in the old books and it is not impossible to find the amours of the Olympians enacted in the initials of a psalter and Leda invested by the Swan in the pages of holy writ.

Hans Holbein is credited with the design of three sets of initials famous for their delicacy—the Child Alphabet, the Peasant Alphabet and the Alphabet of the Dance of Death. The cuts are so very fine and the scale of the block so small that printing was rendered difficult. They were used, of course, irrespective of their appropriateness to the text they adorned, and as initials they are bad. A roman capital is super-imposed in white upon a ground animated with figures—an impurity of design, since there is no attempt at co-ordination of the two factors of the pattern.

THE DANSE MACABRE

Le squelette était invisible
Au temps heureux de l'art païen,

cried Théophile Gautier, thinking of the blitheness and repose of ancient
art as contrasted with the fear and pessimism of the art that grew up in
celebration of the Man of Golgotha. But it is the later Middle Age visited
by the appalling Black Death and worn out with terrible wars from
Cressy to Pavia that first is haunted by the Skeleton, inviting to the Danse
Macabre which each must join with the last steps of all. The change is
seen very clearly in the funeral monuments. The recumbent figures of the
thirteenth and fourteenth centuries have a calm and serene beauty.
Smiling, composed and wide-eyed they await the Day of Judgment without dread. But with the close of the fifteenth century comes a new consciousness of the foulness of life and the horror of death and corruption,
a morbid dwelling upon vermiculation which the earlier ages had never
felt. In the tomb of the Black Prince in the Choir of Canterbury, though
the effigy is of the most beautiful and serene mediaeval type, the lines
engraved around invite the spectator to think of dust and the worm.
"My great beauty is all gone," says the hero of Poitiers, "my flesh is all
wasted, and if you were to see me now you would not know that I had
been a man." But upon the tomb of the Cardinal Lagrange at Avignon
the after-state of the body is actually portrayed in its full horror.
Threatening verses are not sufficient now. It is no longer enough to remind
the passer-by, as a thousand inscriptions do, that what the deceased was
they are, and as the deceased is so will they be too; but the decaying
corpses are now represented, twisted around with snakes and riddled
through and through with worms. Death becomes the inspiration of a
great part of art and literature and the cry of terror is heard in every
Christian land: "Timor Mortis conturbat me."

The Danse Macabre is preceded by the story of the Three Dead and
the Three Live Young Men, which had been told in the thirteenth century
by Baudoin de Condé and Nicholas de Margival, but became very wide-

spread in its appeal at the close of the fourteenth. A hermit sees three gallants riding out with hawk on fist. One is a duke, another a count, the third a king's son. Suddenly they are confronted by three fearful figures, half-mummy, half-skeleton. Horror-stricken they try to flee; horses rear and hawks and hounds are released in panic, while with stinging eloquence the dead make out their claims. One had been pope, another cardinal, a third papal notary, and, with words that cleave the mind with

The Doctor and the Lover with their dead Selves. From Vérard's "Danse Macabre" (Paris, 1485)

despair as with a sword, they state their dreadful reminders. The cavaliers repent, the hermit himself is edified by their confessions. Such is the "Dit des Trois Morts et des Trois Vifs" which the art-loving Duc de Berry caused to be carved over the portal of Les Innocents in Paris to commemorate the murder of his uncle, and which is the subject of Orcagna's terrific fresco in the Pisan Campo Santo. The popularity of the story was enormous in the fifteenth century. In the French Books of Hours the "Dit des Trois Morts et des Trois Vifs" is the favourite illustration to the Vigils of the Dead, and its popularity is not entirely lost even with the flourishing of the fuller horror of the dance itself.

The derivation of the word "macabre" has excited the speculations of the curious for generations. Perhaps it is connected with the name of Macaire, a saint of the Thebaid who saw a vision of the living and the dead encountering before his cell. Perhaps it is derived from Maccabæus, the surname of Judas the Jewish hero, for "Macchabaeorum Chorea" is the Latin rendering of the name. But these are only the more reasonable of many explanations that have been urged. The Danse Macabre was probably a sort of "Morality" played by the people in the church, intended as an illustration in the round of a sermon on Death. The friars were great preachers of death and fond of driving home their texts with the aid of acting. Perhaps the actual dance originated in the church with the friars and later, as was the course of such things, became secularised and was represented in the street outside the church, or in the houses of the great. Thus we know that in 1449 the Duke of Burgundy caused it to be played in his mansion.

But the dance had been the subject of a famous painting many years before, for one chronicler under the year 1424 notices the making of the Danse Macabre in Les Innocents, the famous cemetery, and Guillebert de Metz remarks these same "paintures notables de la Danse Macabre." These were perhaps the canon of all subsequent paintings of the kind and were imitated all over the Continent; and in England there were Dances of Death at St. Paul's, the Tower of London and Whitehall. The Dance in the North Cloister of Old St. Paul's had verses by Lydgate, the monk of Bury, translated from the original verses which accompanied each pair of dancers upon the walls of Les Innocents. All traces of the prototypal dance and of its fellows have vanished and only woodcuts have retained their main features in a humbler form. For in 1485 the Parisian printer Guyot Marchant sent artists to copy these frescoes and the inscriptions which give them added meaning. Guyot's edition of the *Danse Macabre* was so successful by reason of its pictures that it was sold out in a few months. Another edition followed with additional dancers and there is no doubt that the subject was near and dear to the hearts of folk at that time. In these volumes we see all society brought into contact with the Skeleton: pope and kaiser, king, noble, soldier, bourgeois, peasant—each dances in his turn and the partner of each is *his* posthumous shape. For it is not the Arch-agent of Destruction itself who is personified but rather for each of the thirty dancers (in Guyot's edition) his own figure after he has put on corruption. This idea, however, of the partnership "d'un mort et d'un vif" is forgotten in the next

century and one terrible figure, LA MORT, does service for them all.
In Guyot's edition the dancers are represented under arcades, two pairs
of dancers to each arcade. In the series of Costiau and Menart that
followed his success a colonnette separates each of the pairs that figure
together on one block. These skeletons are full of atrocious gaiety. Their
victims are comparatively placid—they exhibit no disgust in the presence
of such hideous gambollings, no horror at the sight of their after-state.
At the most they go unwillingly or seem paralysed and unconscious of

*The Bride, the Daughter of Joy and their dead Selves. From Vérard's
"Danse Macabre des Femmes" (Paris, 1486)*

their fate, having no ear at all for the unearthly music to which their
ghoulish partners set their feet. The verses that accompany each figure
intensify the impression and are at times terrible and minatory, at times
fiercely ironical.

The success of Guyot's venture tempted him to a companion edition
in the ensuing year. This was a *Danse Macabre des Femmes*, and now the
skeletons perform with womankind from empress to peasant. The dance
could not fail to be popular with the people for whom Death is the great
equaliser of all classes and ranks of society, levelling in the common dust
slave and lord with equal nonchalance.

These woodcuts of Guyot's edition are near to the dance as it was actually enacted before princes and people in Court or church or market-place. Those who played the skeletons were draped in swaddling-clothes, five of which are yet to be seen in the Historical Museum at Berne. It would be thirsty work jigging about with the abandon with which folk did such things in the Middle Age and it is good to think of the kindly Minorite friars who at Besançon in France in the year 1453 distributed eight setiers of wine "à ceus qui ont fait la danse des Machabées dans l'église."

Holbein   *The Nun and Death*

But to most people there is but one Dance of Death and that is bound up with the name of Holbein. It has been reproduced innumerable times and is by far the most famous monument of Wood-Engraving. Many of the blocks used in this celebrated book are known to have been in existence for at least ten years before the Trechsels brought out their first edition at Lyons in 1538. The cuts in *Les Simulachres et Historiées Faces de la Mort*, as this elegant little book was named, are forty-one in number and each about two inches square in size. They appeared without the name of designer or engraver, but it is almost certain that Holbein was responsible for the designs, while the enormous class of people who abhor anonymous art as Nature abhors a vacuum have satisfied themselves that the engraver was a certain Hans Lützelburger. They have been congratulating themselves in weighty books for generations that the greatest designer for the wood-block here found for his reproducer the greatest master of the knife.

Who was this Hans Lützelburger, "Formschneider," about whom so much has been written? All that we know is that his name is printed under a large woodcut of a fight in a pine-forest between peasants and naked men. It also occurs alongside a tiny alphabet of the Dance of Death which is ascribed to Holbein, while "HLF, 1522" is found with another alphabet, "HL Fur" in a New Testament of the following year, and the monogram "HL" upon the bedside of the duchess in the great series in question. With this as skin, by taking breath and blowing, the learned have filled out some surprising balloons, as those who are curious of such achievements may see notably performed in Jackson.

The book-designs of Holbein are very dignified and thoughtful. Though best known by his Dance it was only one of many series which he designed for the great publishers of Basle, Frobenius, Amerbach and Wolff, Froschover (of Zurich) and others. He is responsible for about 300 designs for book-decoration, among them many elaborate title-pages in the heavy architectural style of the day with strap-work, medallions, allegorical and classical figures, grotesques and the like. All his work has a sobriety and restraint which is in marked contrast to the exuberant tasteless work of his German contemporaries. The designs for the Bible are so quiet that one is apt to overlook many indisputable qualities of drama and movement that they possess. Holbein uses shading with sureness and economy, and, without ever overcrowding his tiny designs, he is a master of significant detail. To say that he was fortunate in his engravers, in Lützelburger if you like, is not so likely to be true as to say that his engravers were lucky in having so clear and strong a draughtsman for whom to work.

Holbein   *The Kaiser and Death*

It is strange that folk should be amazed at the skill with which the faces are characterised in the Dance, for if the lines be equally clear and strong it is no more difficult to engrave a head than an involved drapery or an intricate arabesque or anything else.

But the genius of Holbein served to reduce the whole conception of the Dance of Death from tragedy to tragi-comedy and even farce. The Dance of Guyot Marchant is stark and almost hieratic. It has no realistic background to detract from the whole height of each protagonist alone with his Fate. Holbein introduces a hundred little touches of shrewd observation bringing the conception down to a more human level. By gaining in breadth it loses in intensity.

The nun enjoys the company of her lover in her cell. As she turns to him from off her knees, Death quietly snuffs the candles on the altar. It is in the delineation of such gestures, fearful in their quiet gaiety, that the great wonder of the series lies. The Skeleton acts the tirewoman to the countess and decks her with a chain of vertebræ. He climbs the pulpit behind the preacher and lightly arrests his attention. He shuns the agonised beggar clamouring for an end to his misery; but seizing the lance of the knight he drives it sheer through his body. He is gentle with the good bishop and the good pastor and aids the wretched peasant to plough his land; but he snatches the shield of the tyrannous count and hurls it derisively to the ground.

Holbein   *The Abbot and Death*

In the hands of the woodcutters, variations of the Death theme are endless, but never again is it touched upon with the same subtle spirit as that of Holbein. The older formal Dance of Death with victim after victim each typifying a class of his subjects is no longer seen. Mockery is sometimes present but generally a sick terror is the main emotion with which the theme is dealt. The skeletons hunt in pairs or groups or even in legions. In the famous painting of Breughel, himself a designer upon wood, a whole army of skeletons invade a helpless world. It is the Ragnarok of Humanity. Death is the first-born of the world and is that very tree which bears "the crude apple that diverted Eve." Its arms are branches, its limbs the trunk around which the Serpent twists. The ubiquitous Skeleton is there at the expulsion from Eden and runs gleefully alongside our first parents as they cower before the flaming sword. When Adam digs the ground it lends him its aid to uproot a tree. It bursts into the crowded places of the world to claim its victim, be he seated on the Chair of St. Peter or upon imperial throne hedged round with spears. It strives in the press and hurls down the "Landsknecht," or leads the charge upon the barricades.[1] It is not always raging, but its

[1] Death upon the barricades, Death as the Sansculotte, is the dominant theme of Rethel's famous series of woodcuts, published at Leipzig in 1849 with verses by Reinick. There had been bloody insurrections in Germany, and, in the year before, barricades had been set up in the streets of Paris. So that Rethel's severe and noble designs had a message for the times. His is the most genuinely inspired of Danse Macabre sets of cuts in modern times; but even it is not "popular" in sentiment. It is not, like the old versions, the expression of the popular fear of Death; but the broodings of an individual artist on human folly and wickedness and human fate.

rage is the least of its horror. It can be bashful, it conceals sexual characteristics that it does not possess. It is full of badinage or meretricious wiles or even of a mockery of sorrow and tears. At times it claims all mankind as it does in Breughel's awful painting—it leaps from Hell's mouth on its charger with scythe and coffin in its arms and crashes over the prostrated world, or treads the nations under the hooves of the black oxen that draw its chariot of triumph.

DÜRER

The life of Dürer was one of unremitting industry in the city of his birth, varied by three expeditions to other lands. Born in Nuremberg in 1471 he was apprenticed to his father, a goldsmith, with whom he continued until the age of sixteen when his great desire to be a painter constrained the unwilling father to place him under Michael Wohlgemuth to learn that craft. There he continued for three years, and afterwards in the course of his "Wanderjahre" possibly went as far as Venice, and certainly saw Basle and Strassburg. In 1494 on his return he married Agnes Frey, a barren wife, none too pretty in her youth and by all accounts hard and avaricious in later life, though whether her greed for money drove her husband to overwork and consequently shortened his life will never be satisfactorily shown. She had probably all the domestic virtues of a Nuremberg "Hausfrau" and cannot be expected to have been an intellectual companion for such a man as Dürer. In 1506 the artist visited Venice where he remained for more than a year and wrote to Willibald Pirkheimer, his life-long companion, several delightful letters, happily preserved, from which a very genial human personality emerges. We find that the profound and gloomy artist whose beautiful head we know so well could be merry and facetious, had his little vanities and vexations like other people.

His reputation had preceded him to Venice where he was well received by Giovanni Bellini who praised him highly, though others (says Dürer) criticised his work as not done in the antique style and therefore no good. "I have become a *gentiluomo* at Venice," he wrote to Pirkheimer; and again in the very famous words, "How I shall freeze after this sun! Here I am a gentleman, at home a parasite." Pirkheimer writes saying that if Albrecht doesn't hurry home he will make love to the Dürerin, and Albrecht laughs and warns him not to try: "A big fellow like you would be the death of her." Altogether these bright letters should be read by all who are interested in two of the most outstanding men of that day.

In 1511 Dürer returned to Nuremberg, to his great disappointment having failed at Padua to meet Mantegna whom he admired above all contemporaries. In 1511 his four woodcut books saw the light. Henceforward his life was one of unbroken productivity until 1520 when, on the completion of his work for the Emperor Maximilian, he set out on a journey through the Netherlands of which he has left an itinerary of great interest. But the interesting things in the itinerary are only incidental. They are strewn here and there throughout tedious accounts of pennies saved and curios collected, and we are faced by the ironical fact that a brilliant man with all the scientific curiosity of the Renaissance, a man numbering among his friends the greatest minds in Germany, delights to enumerate among the main interests of his journey just such objects as the vulgar pay their pennies to see to-day, monsters with two heads and a liberal supply of legs, bones of a giant eighteen feet high, a bed that held fifty men, a fish-bone a fathom long. He comes back laden with elks' feet, hats of elder bark, fish-scales, snail-shells, wooden weapons from Calicut, parrots, buffalo-horns and what not. But it is absurd to be indignant with Dürer for not recording what *we* want to know, and along with the dross we get much real gold. For example this from Antwerp, August 1520: "On Sunday, it was St. Oswald's Day, the painters invited me to the hall of their guild, with my wife and maid. All their service was of silver, and they had other splendid ornaments and very costly meats. All their wives were there. And as I was being led to the table the company stood on both sides as if they were leading some great lord." Surely we can envisage the scene from this, and, with the aid of the great self-portraits, see Dürer in all his beauty and dignity, with that brooding forehead, those eyes of extraordinary depth and clarity and the long precious hair, fine hands and sumptuous clothes. No great lord ever graced the table in that guild-hall with greater ease and assurance—of that we can be sure. Here was a man whom all men in his day recognised as a great man and who received him as such wherever he went, and he knew it himself but it could not make him vain. He goes on calmly and as he proceeds enters in his book what towns he visited, what receptions he got, what drawings he made, how many prints he sold or exchanged, how he admired the shoulder-blades of the Giant of Antwerp, how Erasmus sat to him once again, how he bought a red woollen shirt or crossed a ferry without payment. His calm irritates us across the gulf of the centuries. "Has the man no sense of values!" we exclaim, who want to hear what Erasmus said, and not to learn how many times he dined with Fugger's agent at such and such a town. Only twice does he seem stirred, and perhaps one may be pardoned for quoting these passages; the first describes the procession at Antwerp and shows how near at hand and how beautiful were the subjects of the designers of religious woodcuts; the second is the outburst of the artist on hearing of the supposed betrayal and capture of Luther whose opinions he shared enthusiastically, with his friends and all folk of enlightenment at the time.

Among sights so many "that I could not write them in a book" (Dürer admires), "the company of Prophets on their order and scenes from the New Testament, such as the Annunciation, the Three Magi riding great camels and other strange beasts very skilfully arranged, and also how Our Lady fled into Egypt—very conducive to devotion.

". . . Last of all came a great dragon which St. Margaret and her maidens led by a girdle; she was extraordinarily beautiful. Behind her followed a St. George with his squire, a very fine cuirassier." But when he learns of Luther's capture he forgets whales and giants and red woollen shirts and writes at length and with indignation and sorrow. He appeals to God and man against this shameful wrong. (As a matter of fact Luther was not betrayed at all, but captured lest others should capture him—a ruse of his protector, the good Elector of Saxony.) "Oh, Erasmus!" (cries Dürer), "where wilt thou stay? Dost thou see how the unjust tyranny of worldly power and the might of darkness prevails? Hear, thou Knight of Christ,[1] ride on beside the Lord Jesus, guard the truth, win the martyr's crown. Thou art already only a little old man (*Du bist doch sonst ein altes menniken*) and I have heard thee say that thou givest thyself but two more years in which thou mayest avail to accomplish something. Lay out the same now well for the Gospel and the true Christian Faith." But alas for Dürer and perhaps for mankind at large, the "little old man" did not covet the martyr's crown, and the Reformation, instead of being the work of men of intellect, of "sweetness and light," was carried through in a flame and welter of mob passions, peasants' revolts and intolerant Anabaptist doctrine so that in a few years wise men were shaking their heads with Pirkheimer at the realisa-

---

[1] "Erasmus gave the greatest vogue to the notion of the Christian knight by his *Enchiridion Militis Christiani*, first printed in 1502, but the book did not achieve real popularity till translated into German in 1502" (Campbell Dodgson). In calling Erasmus the "Knight of Christ" Dürer is surely referring to that writer's creation of the great type.

Dürer

Full-size Detail. From the "Apocalypse," 1498

tion that "the Evangelical knaves make these Popish knaves look pious by contrast."

In the eight years that ensued between his return from the journey to the Netherlands and his death in 1528 Dürer was busy for the most part with his books upon Proportion, Measurement and Fortification. Of his opinion on the antique theory of a Canon of Human Proportion, revived by the neo-classic tastes of the Renaissance, perhaps it is not irrelevant to speak in a history of Wood-Engraving as it serves to explain in some measure the schematic beauties of his Madonnas and Personifications and the like which contrast strangely with others of Dürer's figures; for example the dramatis personæ of the *Passions* or *The Life of the Virgin*, where Dürer shows himself a continuator of the old German style of figure-drawing and employs types grimacing, vital, almost caricatural and more remarkable for grotesque vigour than for any formal beauty. But Dürer, we must always remember, stands with his feet in two worlds, belongs to two traditions and two ways of thought, the one mediaeval, the other of the Renaissance. According to Vasari, Raphael said that if Dürer had been acquainted with the antique he would have surpassed them all. But the style of the pupil of Wohlgemuth and the creator of the *Apocalypse* and the *Melancholia* was in the main untouched by Renaissance ideas though they penetrated his thought, as well they might since he numbered among his friends some of the greatest humanists of Germany.

"The sight of a fine human figure" (says Dürer) "is above all things the most pleasing to us, wherefore I will first construct the right proportions of a man." To do so he had to trust largely to his own observations and intellect. Of feeling for the voluptuousness of the female figure no artist ever had less than the engraver of the *Great Fortune* or the *Eve*. It is characteristic of Dürer's Germanic pertinacity that he should thus sit down to work out mathematically a recipe for human beauty as for the proportion of a letter. North of the Alps there was no one to help him. Vitruvius, it is true, had made a few suggestions which excited humanists greatly. "Howbeit" (says Dürer) "I can find none such who hath written aught about how to form a canon of human proportions save one man, Jacopo de' Barbari by name, born at Venice, and a charming painter. He showed me the figures of a man and woman which he had drawn according to a canon of proportions and now I would rather be shown what he meant than behold a new kingdom." In search of types Dürer

frequented the baths at Nuremberg and made drawings of the nude.
The same curiosity made him press close at the entry of Charles V. into

Dürer   *The Four Angels. From the "Apocalypse,"* 1498 (original 15½″ × 11¼″)

Antwerp where lovely girls figured almost naked in mythological scenes.
The chaste grandson of Maximilian did not suffer his eyes to dwell long
upon their beauties; but, "being a painter" (Dürer says), "I looked about

me a little more boldly." Sad end to all Albrecht's researches for a Canon of Human Beauty! We remember him as the designer of the amazing *Great Fortune*, that big-bellied old hag who is borne aloft on a globe over the beautiful Franconian landscape.

In April 1528 Dürer died at Nuremberg from a disease which he had contracted at Zierikzee in the Netherlands. He had been drawn to the place in the hopes of examining a great whale which had been washed up in a storm. "No one in Zeeland has ever seen one even one-third as long and the fish cannot get off the land. The people would be glad to see it gone, for they fear the great stench." In his attempt to examine it he had a narrow escape from drowning and contracted a fatal disease.

His domestic life seems to have been uneventful and he never speaks with affection of his wife; but his relationship with his parents was far different. His great love of them and his sorrow at their death are extraordinarily well described in his literary fragments. His description of his mother's death is made with such amazing force that one cannot refrain from quoting it here, throwing as it does so vivid a light upon the artist and his age. "She feared Death much, but she said that to come before God she feared not. Also she died hard and I marked that she saw something dreadful, for she asked for the holy water, although for a long time she had not spoken. Immediately afterwards her eyes closed over. I saw also how Death smote her two great strokes to the heart and how she closed mouth and eyes and departed with pain." At what other period could these lines have been written? It is like a pictured Triumph of Death. This man, his head full of Renaissance pedantry, sees yet with the haunted eyes of the Middle Age; a dreadful figure enters that chamber and before Dürer's eyes smites his beloved mother to the heart.

Though among the world's greatest draughtsmen, the peerless delineator of things seen, Dürer was not a great painter. He owes his lasting fame to his engravings and it is by these that he has exerted the greatest influence. While apprenticed to Wohlgemuth he probably began to design for the block, but the unsigned works ascribed to him upon the evidence of style are not interesting enough to compel our attention here. In 1498 appeared the first famous woodcut series—the *Apocalypse*, with text printed in a type of Koberger. We believe that we are right in refraining from a description of each illustration. They are the best known of his works and far too much rhetoric has already been outpoured about the imagination which devised the designs. People who write thus seem to be grossly ignorant of the art that preceded Dürer and fail to see the artist in relation to his age, his contemporaries and his predecessors.

Dürer   *Adoration of the Three Kings* (11½″ × 8½″)

Dürer invented no new motives, saw nothing in the preternatural world unseen before him. He had the clearest, bitterest vision of things as they are, but was no seer, mystic or poet. He inherited the whole stock of con-

ventional subjects and their treatment from the late Middle Age and what
he added was not so much personal as derived from new reservoirs of ideas,
from the Italy of the Renaissance which he had visited, and which was
visiting Germany personified in such artists as Jacopo de' Barbari. Dürer
takes the old stock-in-trade of religious art and brings to bear upon it
the new plastic conception, gives it body, solidity, richness, greater
naturalism and at the same time loses something of the old sweetness
and simplicity as well as of the old terror. His version of the Vision of
St. John is stronger and clearer than any that preceded him, the bizarre
details are not so much symbolically as literally realised by his powerful
hand and his knowledge of the superficies of nature. He has made the
very apocalyptic dragons into articulated credible monsters. It remained
for Dürer to give the old tradition its final expression; and although an
artist of the Transition, Janus-like looking both ways, he speaks here as
a representative of the Gothic tradition and is its last authentic voice.

One other point: Conway admits that Dürer's apocalyptic designs
were not altogether original, being based upon those in the Cologne Bible
published by Quentell, but he claims that they were the first designs
aimed at the Church of Rome, the Whore of Babylon. Yet he seems to
have overlooked the fact that popes are prominent among the damned
in Quentell's designs just as they are in mediaeval church sculpture. In
fact it is absurd to call this a "Reformed" version of the apocalyptic vision,
for whatever Dürer's later opinions were upon Popery he is merely following
mediaeval tradition in these designs.[1] "Young Albrecht evidently lacks
neither courage nor scorn," says Conway, remarking the Pope whom an
angel is slaying in the foreground of one design, but the bearer of the
triple hat undergoes just such a fate in Quentell's version, and as for courage
and scorn, why the risk was small enough—think of Dante's simoniac
Pope head-downward in the flames of Inferno two centuries before.

Dürer, indeed, takes Quentell's crude and stammering cuts as a
basis and clothes them in the rich rhetoric of his style, just as Shakespeare took a wooden stumping chronicle-play and transmuted it into
the tragedy of *King Lear*. Here and there, however, we observe debts to

---

[1] Dürer was too busy with his art to get into trouble for Reformed opinions. There is nothing
fanatical about his character; but it is interesting to note how his pupils, the brothers Bartel and
Hans Sebald Beham, and Georg Pencz, got into serious trouble for their sympathy with revolu-
tionary ideas. His "Formschneider," Jerome Andrea, had the same fate. Mr. Sturge Moore makes
the quaint suggestion that Jerome's rebelliousness may have been due to "the pitiless tyranny
of the Master's [Dürer's] will for perfection."

maturer sources. The Michael who triumphs over Satan is derived from a copperplate of Schongauer, and those who know the works of the Masters E. S. and of the Amsterdam Cabinet realise how much less than is commonly suspected was the great Dürer the creator of his types.

In 1511 Dürer published a third edition of his *Apocalypse* and with it three other woodcut books, each with latin text, namely, *The Life of the Virgin* and the *Great* and *Small* woodcut *Passions*. These books and the numerous single-sheet prints from wood-block or copperplate were Dürer's main means of a livelihood. They were offered for sale at the fairs in Frankfort, Nuremberg and other places and were widely disseminated, making him famous as far as Rome where the great Raphael was among his admirers, while Marcantonio Raimondi was a shameless plagiarist of his designs. He took a large stock of books and prints with him on his journey through the Netherlands and presented, exchanged or sold them as occasion arose.

We have already spoken of the *Apocalypse*, and the other books will not detain us much longer. *The Life of the Virgin* illustrates the main events in the lives of Our Lady and of her parents, the lack of information about whose careers was readily made good by the imaginative Middle Age. Throughout, of course, honest German folk in the costume of the day enact the sacred scenes, set for the most part against rich architecture in the style of the German Renaissance, and (very happily) in ruined barns. The soundness and style of the drawing of the background to the *Nativity* and the *Adoration* show Dürer at his best, while the landscape in the distance of his *Visitation* is lovely. *The Flight into Egypt*, while it has none of the frail exquisiteness of Schongauer's version, charms in the treatment of the trees and foregrounds.

Such richness of detail, knowledge of natural forms and power of handling is so remarkable that it is little wonder that Dürer made so great a reputation in his day and has held it ever since. Wood-Engraving had known nothing like this before, both in the power of the drawing and the unprecedented skill of engraving. These qualities are equally apparent in the *Passions*, *Great* and *Small*, as in all signed works where he doubtless personally supervised the engraving of his drawings, so that at the best one could only pick out in each one or two cuts that seemed happier than the others. What strikes one most in these cuts of Dürer's is his exceptional knowledge and confidence. No designer upon wood before him had shown half this vigour and certainty of hand. Every line is a clear statement and has a swinging vigour of its own. The engraver had something definite here which demanded to be preserved in facsimile and the artist probably was a tyrannous taskmaster and, being himself of tireless industry and sleight of hand, must have demanded from the others all that he knew himself to possess. The employment of cross-hatching begun by Reuwich is brought to maturity by Dürer and perfectly reproduced by the cutters of his blocks. So wonderfully is the intolerable task performed in such blocks as the *Trinity* that Bewick (who was so convinced that cross-hatching was more trouble than it was worth that he only once used it) had a theory that these parts of Dürer's designs were obtained by printing from more than one block and in his last work he set out to demonstrate how it could be done. The pity is that Dürer did not himself engrave upon wood. If he had been obliged to do so he would not have made his designs upon wood merely less intricate copper-engravings, for the great labour entailed in the clearing of the grounds would have driven his inquiring mind to work out a technique more suitable for creative woodcutting and more consonant to the call of the material. As it was, he trained or found trained in readiness a body of men skilful enough to reproduce his intricate pen-drawings. And indeed all sense of the medium is lost in the brilliance of the execution, so that when we look at Dürer's woodcuts we look at facsimiles of his strong and facile pen-drawings.

With his eye on the subject he is an amazing draughtsman, but in that other kind of drawing which is evolved from the inner consciousness and is synonymous with linear design his talent is not of the highest. "Dürer's hand became so disciplined" (says Conway in reference to his line-engravings) "that it has been reckoned he could lay a line accurately within the thousandth part of an inch." Yet his very sleight of hand and his very knowledge and inventiveness are the cause of some of his defects and end in mere virtuosity on one hand and redundancy of detail on the other. He cannot conceive of a limb without tasteless indentations and convexities of the contour for each muscle that his knowledge of anatomy and his mathematical preoccupation with form taught him should be located at a certain place. In his free pen copies after Mantegna's engravings and Italian "tarocchi" cards it can be seen how the continuity of line is lost by his insistence upon fact and his greater knowledge of form, so that much of the charm of the originals vanishes in his versions. His certainty and power seem to us often mere frigid brilliance and lack of taste, and it is quite maddening in looking over any number of Dürer's cuts to see how he cannot resist the temptation to give each line a flourish. His woodcuts show none of the felicity in the loose juxtaposition of data that is the charm of mediaeval design—ease, blitheness, good taste. He was too learned and ingenious an artist for that. Unerring, untutored instinct for style was as far from Dürer as any artist of the Renaissance, nor had he mastered the classical conception of composition which his Italian contemporaries had reduced almost to a science. So that as a composer Dürer is not among the elect. He packs his designs with data till essential unity is lost in the wealth of elaborated details, of draperies wonderfully studied and insane with hooks and crinkles, or landscapes all crag and tree and curly weed in rank recession.

His drawings upon wood which Jerome and others rendered in fac-simile are merely necessarily simplified variations of his procedure in his original line-engravings. They are elaborately cross-hatched and flecked with little curly lines so that they attain to a limited range of colour. The histories say that Dürer first makes woodcuts free from the need of colour. To be sure, for no colour could be bright and pure over designs so grey and closely shaded. But there is no virtue in that, for open wood-cuts are exceptionally charming with the addition of bright colours as modern French publishers have realised; nor has Dürer "engraver's colour" to the same degree as the designers of the criblé plates, not to mention what has been done in the century or so since Bewick's time.

From 1512 for about a period of ten years Dürer expended consider-able energy in the huge woodcut schemes of the Emperor Maximilian. As these schemes embraced the work of Burgkmair, Schaufelein and other designers of woodcuts, we have chosen to treat of them as a whole and merely signify as we pass what share each designer had and where. In reward for his services Maximilian settled upon Dürer an annual pension of 100 florins and the position of Court Painter. In 1518 Dürer attended the Augsburg Diet as one of the three representatives of his town and there, "in his little chamber high up in the palace," he made a drawing of the emperor from which he subsequently made a large woodcut design. In the next year, however, Maximilian died and the pension went with him. Dürer's letters show how he worried, used all his influence, presented the Duchess Margaret with many works and at length succeeded in obtaining from Maximilian's grandson and successor to the imperial sceptre a confirmation of the grant which he enjoyed for the eight years of life that remained to him.

THE WORK FOR THE EMPEROR MAXIMILIAN

MAXIMILIAN was by far the most magnificent patron that Wood-Engraving has ever had. Descended from Rudolph of Hapsburg he was full of pride in a race of emperors, warriors and saints, and full too of a self-pride which is characteristic of the man and the period, brimming over with energy and vigour and free from all meanness and vanity. The son of a miser, Max was prodigal and impecunious all his reign. Imaginative, gifted and full of stupendous ideas he was ever retarded by his lack of money. A great hunter, justly celebrated as the "last of the knights," victor in many dangerous single combats, full of majesty and bonhomie, the most spirited of his race, he spoke seven languages and abandoned fourteen mistresses. In a life given up to wars Max gained more by marriage than by invasion so as to deserve the epigram of Matthias Corvinus:

> Bella gerant alii, tu, felix Austria, nube:
> Nam quae Mars aliis, dat tibi regna Venus.

Towards the end of his reign, this princely patron of the Arts and Sciences conceived of the idea of celebrating the events of his life and the glory of his race in a great series of wood-engravings which enlisted the hands of the best designers of Nuremberg and Augsburg. The main scheme consisted of a great Triumphal Arch with a Triumphal Procession and a Car of Triumph made up of large numbers of blocks printed together. In addition to this the emperor planned a series of illustrated books, the *Theuerdank* to celebrate in the thin disguise of allegory his early manhood and pursuit of a bride, the *Weisskunig* which treats of his parentage, upbringing and the events of his reign, and the *Freydal* which illustrates the many varieties of jousting in which he engaged and invariably emerged the victor.

The Triumphal Arch or "Ehrenpforte" is a monstrous structure, 9 by 10½ feet, consisting of 92 blocks having as basis the arch of Cæsarean Rome but distorted and obscured by Venetian details, the castellated style of the German Renaissance and a whole gallimaufry of undigested symbols and motives pagan and Christian, mediaeval and ancient, brought together by pedantry with a passion for allegory. It has, as Conway says, "the scale of a modern street advertisement and the minute finish of a *Punch* cartoon." There are three gates respectively of Honour, Praise and Nobility, a central tower with the genealogical tree of the Hapsburgs and over the side gates twenty-four compartments illustrating events in the reign of Maximilian, with busts of kings and kaisers on one side of each gate, and of Max's kinsmen on the other, the whole flanked by round towers and bedizened everywhere with ornaments of obscure symbolism. The literary supervisor was Stabius, a Professor of Astronomy at the University at Vienna, of which Conrad Celtes was the intellectual head; the architect (if the word be pardoned for such a structure) was Kolderer; the main embellisher was Dürer, and the scutcheons of the three are placed on the steps at the right of the Arch. Altdorfer, Springinklee, Wolf Traut, and Hans the brother of Dürer were also employed upon some of the ninety-two blocks which were splendidly cut by Jerome Andrea of Nuremberg and his assistants. Frigid competence in the outpouring of tasteless ornament—that is the main thought that arises from the contemplation of this baroque monument, the work of years and perhaps the most eloquent evidence of the taste of the age of Maximilian.

With the Procession, however, of which the Arch was probably intended to be the termination, the exuberance and delight of the authors found a more suitable outlet. The tiresome conceits which the emperor's humanist advisers so loved could find little place here, where the appeal is altogether to the splendour-loving eye. *The Triumph of Maximilian* is the most grandiloquent expression of the art of engraving. As many as 138 blocks were employed, peopled with hundreds of figures each about sixteen inches high. The whole procession when the prints are pasted together on one scroll extends to a length of about 200 feet. There is truly no limit to the wealth of sumptuous invention expended upon this baroque triumph, crowded with swaggering warriors, caracoling horses, rococo chariots, heraldic achievements, which with its rant and "superbia" makes the triumphs of the ancient Cæsars as we imagine them chill and restrained in comparison. The Procession is heralded by a naked man perched upon a prodigious griffin and blowing a horn of uncouth shape. Then come Landsknechte leading horses that support a great tablet which should have boasted (but none of the inscriptions were ever cut) the titles of the Emperor Maximilian. Then follow musicians, falconers with their hawks, hunters of the chamois, the deer, the boar and the bear, each leading the animal of which he is a skilled pursuer and preceded by the principal master of each sport bearing an ornamental tablet as a standard. Elks and bisons drag chariots of musicians; a boy rides a fantastic dromedary; fools, preceded by the

Burgkmair   *Griffon. From the "Triumph of Maximilian"* $(14\frac{3}{4}'' \times 13'')$

imperial favourite, Conrad von der Rosen, are drawn by donkeys in a car. Then march out the picked fighters, jousters with flail and lance and halberd, and knights distinguished in the tourneys of the last great patron of Chivalry. Banners of the utmost splendour of florid design denoting the hereditary realms of Austria are carried by knights on horseback. These are followed by fifers four in line, and then more knights ride past with garments amazingly ringed and slashed who bear the banners of the Ducal House of Burgundy. The achievements of the kaiser in war and marriage are displayed emblematically upon cars fantastically propelled by grave Landsknechte. Artillery, treasures, sepulchral statues follow, and groups of prisoners encircled in chains like the damned upon a mediaeval church front. Men carry statues of Victory with curly palms. Trumpeters and timballers, heralds and arquebusiers ride or tramp along the weedy path, and pikemen proud as turkey-cocks, fiercely and luxuriantly hirsute, thrust out their great limbs, gesticulate and shout. Savages of Calicut troop along to denote the extent of the imperial influence and then the "Tross" or train of camp-followers brings the procession to a close. With the "Tross" the serried order of the Triumph gives way to a loose advance through a landscape with a background of firs and pines and distant villages. The whole nature of the Triumph is changed. Men and women, dogs and goats, carts and packmules straggle along behind the clear regulated progress, so that if they were not all wreathed we would be tempted to doubt their right to a place in the scheme.

Schaufelein's hand can be detected in part of the designs for the Triumph and Dürer is responsible for the historiated chariots; but the main credit for the work rests with the Augsburg painter, Hans Burgkmair, who is certainly the author of sixty-seven of the blocks (including numbers 1 to 56). The knights who bear the banners of Burgundy and Austria are drawn by yet another artist to whom Mr. Dodgson also ascribes the concluding blocks of the series and calls him the "Master of the Tross." It has ever been our way to leave the discussion of subjects of attribution to the learned, and it is sufficient to say here that the so-called "Master of the Tross" works in the style of the Danube School and is a little reminiscent of Altdorfer and Wolfgang Huber. The woodcuts were based upon a written programme illustrated with miniatures, but these were transformed with the utmost freedom. The engravers were numerous, their names are preserved and the numbers of the particular blocks they finished—all but three of these are preserved at Vienna. Two names of engravers are worthy of remembrance, Jerome Andrea and Jost de Negker.

In addition to the small Triumphal Car celebrating the marriage of Austria and Burgundy which has its place in the Procession, Dürer designed a large Triumphal Car which he published in 1522. It is one of his show pieces devoid of feeling, a *tour de force* exhibiting all his resources of manual dexterity and fecundity of invention. Personifications of Victory, Temperance and the like, dull schematic figures in crinkly draperies, flourish garlands or run alongside the rearing horses that draw the rococo chariot of the emperor. The very reins are emblematic of Nobility or Power and the wheels are surcharged Dignitas, Gloria or the like.

The *Weisskunig* was a picture-book on a most ambitious scale planned by the emperor to commemorate and glorify the history of his reign. The scheme was so involved and the allegorical apparatus so delicate that many hitches took place in the production, so that Max did not live to see its publication. Two hundred and thirty-six of the blocks of this folio exist at Vienna, but it was not published until as late as 1775. The designers were Burgkmair, Beck, Schaufelein and Springinklee, and a considerable standard of florid, decorative excellence is kept throughout, but the *Weisskunig* is somehow a tired performance. There are few blocks which one can pick upon as unexpectedly and inevitably beautiful in design.

The *Theuerdank*, a long allegorical poem shadowing forth the courtship of Maximilian and Mary of Burgundy, was written by an imperial courtier called Pfinzing and published in 1517. A remarkable black-letter type with great flourishes was cut especially for the book and there were scores of competent designs chiefly by Schaufelein. This artist had learnt the style and artistic conventions of his day very thoroughly and had considerable facility of design and drawing; but being without the knowledge of and reverence for all kinds of natural objects, such as Dürer and Holbein possessed, his work is monotonous and somewhat unconvincing.

The schemes of the Emperor Max gave an importance and dignity to Woodcutting which it never had before nor perhaps since. The most famous engraver of his day, Jost de Negker, left Antwerp and came to Augsburg in 1508 to supervise the cutting of the blocks for Maximilian. Among the many assistants of de Negker was Hans Lützelburger, the cutter of Holbein's designs. In a letter which exists de Negker begs permission from one of the imperial officials to employ assistants in the cutting of the blocks for the *Weisskunig*. He promises to go over the whole work and trim it up himself so "that the engraving shall appear to be by one hand, and no one be able to know that several have worked upon it." In addition to the *Weisskunig*, Jost de Negker is believed to have had a very important share in the cutting of the *Theuerdank*, of the Procession and of the Austrian saints. He was also a publisher and famous for his colour-prints.

There is contemporary authority for the belief that a certain Jerome

Resch or Andrea was the engraver of most of Dürer's designs. Among the master's drawings in the British Museum is one of the head and bust of a blooming young woman. "1525 Fronica Formschneiderin" is written in capitals across the top of the drawing. This Fronica the Formschneider's wife is almost certainly Veronica, wife of Jerome Andrea of Nuremberg. In the year when Dürer drew his wife, Jerome suffered imprisonment for sympathising with the revolted peasants and the reformers of religion. In 1542 he was exiled for the "sinful words" which he used to a councillor of Nuremberg. He was buried in 1556 in his native town and upon his tombstone were engraved the date of his death and the words "worshipful Jerome Andrea, Woodcutter, to whom God be gracious. Amen."

THE GERMAN PAINTER-ENGRAVERS OF DÜRER'S TIME

In the early decades of the sixteenth century in Germany nearly every artist of eminence made designs for the woodcutters. From an art practised by anonymous artisans it had become one honoured by imperial patronage and attracting all the greatest painters of the German Renaissance. Dürer at Nuremberg, Burgkmair at Augsburg, Altdorfer at Ratisbon, Cranach at Wittenberg, Holbein at Basle, Baldung at Strassburg, Lucas van Leyden and Jacob Cornelisz in the Low Countries—these were the artists constantly employed in making drawings for the block to be reproduced as book-decorations, single-sheet prints or series of pictures like the *Apocalypse* or *Passions* of Dürer. Indeed, as Mr. Dodgson remarks, only the painters of Cologne, Schaffner and Grünewald, are not responsible for designs of this nature.

Dürer had made no colour-prints, but about 1508–10 Cranach, Baldung and other artists began to produce woodcuts in which a second block with a light tint was superimposed over the "drawing." High-lights were cut out of this tint-block so that you had three tones, the black, the tint and the white high-light. The practice doubtless arose out of the drawings that these artists loved to make upon tinted paper, light green or brown, heightened here and there with white paint for the purpose of suggesting relief.

When judging of the merits of Cranach as a designer of woodcuts it is necessary to put as far as possible out of one's mind his achievements as a painter and draughtsman. Obviously a different type of design is necessary for each. For example, Cranach's woodcuts of *Jerome in Penitence* or *The Flight into Egypt* which get the traditional landscape background are so crowded with interest—hills, trees, cities, shields, birds or weeds—that all sense of organised design is lost in the welter of undigested data. In paintings of such-like subjects this unpleasantness is not apparent for the simple reason that tone is employed and one gradation of green or grey in the distance can bind together a multitude of detail which would be incoherent if translated directly into line. Cranach,

Albrecht Altdorfer   *Lovers in the Forest*

then, did not realise sufficiently the limitations of his medium and the consequent demand for a strong pattern and clarity of statement. Nor are these details of which I have spoken designed with taste and pleasant in themselves as is so often the saving grace in Dürer's backgrounds, for Cranach, charming artist as he is, has none of Dürer's reverence for natural things nor his power of construction. The huge woodcuts of *Tournaments* which he designed reveal a complete absence of feeling for pattern.

Let us look for a moment at his well-known *Judgment of Paris*, a favourite subject of the time, and one which he has painted with exquisite grace more than once, giving his nude figures just that touch of naughtiness, as though they were roguishly conscious of being without their cumbrous gowns, which is endlessly fascinating. The scene is a woodland glade receding romantically past ruins and rivers to far mountains seen between two flanking trees of curliest wriggling shape conceivable, from which are suspended the electoral arms of Saxony. Paris, a bearded knight, is awakened by a rap on the breastplate from Mercury, a venerable mailed figure who introduces him to Frau Venus. Before him stands Divinity disrobed except for head-gear and neck-chains (German ladies would have felt indecently naked without these), and very unbeautiful Divinity it is, their figures (to borrow a description of Mr. Sturge Moore) being "warped and water-logged like the contours of a sleepy pear." A horse occupies one corner and is interesting to us as evidencing the agelong German identification of Wotan (who rode a horse) with Mercury, which is made by Cæsar and Tacitus. Altogether, so much fact is assembled here that all salience of the pattern is obscured and the eye pestered by the multitude of little lines with which the designer endeavours to give form to his objects.

Cranach was Court Painter to the Elector of Saxony whose arms he places almost without fail upon his designs. He was forced at times to earn a living by other means than painting, was at one time a druggist and found his position as Burgomaster of Wittenberg a difficult one in the stirring days of Luther and Reform. He supervised, as master, a sort of factory for producing pictures and perhaps it was only necessity that drove him to design upon the wood-block.

Another engraver and painter, one who has received especial attention of recent years, is Albrecht Altdorfer, chief artist of the Danube School, a citizen of Ratisbon, architect to the municipality and a member of the Inner Council of that town. Altdorfer is a painter of outstanding personality, imagination and charm. He has a sense of the mystery of deep forests and the glory of sunset skies which is modern and makes a great romantic appeal. But he has not the instinct of the engraver, the sense of the right use of line. He is sketchy and suggestive where he should be firm and explicit, nor has he a nice sense of the juxtaposition of figures and the evolution of expressive pattern. Altdorfer carries the swirly curvilinear mannerism of the German School to its utmost limits. With difficulty you will find a line that does not swerve and flourish in his drawings.

His woodcuts deal with the same subjects as his paintings. Lovers caress in the depths of German forests where pine-trees writhe and twist their branches to vertiginous heights. Into such Altdorferan forests must St. George penetrate to transfix the Dragon. Massacres of Innocents or Visitations of the Virgin are enacted among ruins from which great weeds trail dankly like hair, or bushes curl furiously. Paris is awakened from his slumbers by the hoary Mercury to view the beauties of the Olympians and award the prize to the most fair. Out of a cloud spluttering like flame issues Cupid the archer. Trees and enormous weeds sway here, there and everywhere behind the nude goddesses who are as unattractive as only German ladies of this age can be.

Altdorfer is an architect and loves to build elaborate structures in his paintings and designs. St. John the Baptist is beheaded under arches which recede accurately in perspective and are shaded with elaborate hatchings to get engraver's colour. When Jael hammers the nail into the head of sleeping Sisera, or Thisbe stabs herself sentimentally over the corpse of Pyramus, the new interest in foreshortening is shown in the way the opportunity is snatched for projecting the prostrate forms in violent perspective, while if an angel descends now to deliver a message to mortal he plunges head-first down as they do in paintings of the Italian Cinquecento.

Altdorfer has done a series of forty tiny cuts on the Fall and Redemption of Man where his gentle nature, his love of the picturesque and the mysterious are well displayed; but unfortunately it is almost impossible to get a good impression of such tiny blocks. The lines are laid-in so closely together and the cross-hatching so fine where he wants to convey the gloom under a vault that the cutter's skill was overtaxed as well as that of the printer. He never employs a pure black no matter how near his closest hatchings approach to it, and thus he never attains to the utmost of the dramatic effects at which he aims, while the poor Formschneider with his knife has to peck out the minute interstices between his lines

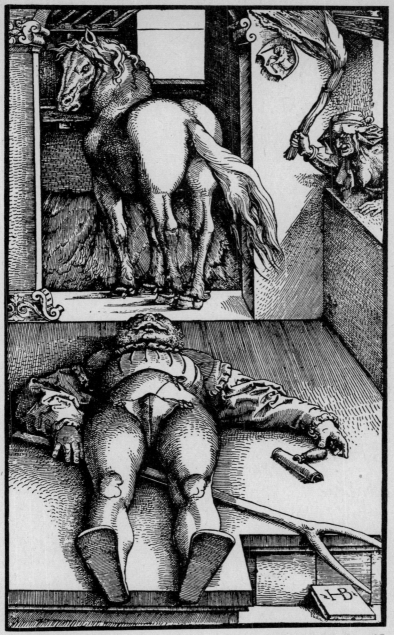

Hans Baldung Grien   *The Groom Bewitched* (13″ × 7¼″)

which had far better been left uncut. When Mr. Sturge Moore writes that Altdorfer "evidently made his designs with more appreciation for the capacities of the medium" than Dürer and other German artists, we have to rub our eyes and look again. That anyone who (to quote Mr. Moore again) "probably knew and practised engraving enough to enable him to go over the work of his assistants" should have designed on so tiny a scale, employed so many curly lines and so much cross-hatching seems to us fundamentally absurd. Even so hard a taskmaster as Holbein in the cuts of the *Dance of Death* is lenient compared to Altdorfer, his lines are straighter and more open, and of course he had Lützelburger as his cutter, while Dürer's designs for the wood are always on a larger scale and consequently offer far less trouble to the cutter.

Of all these vigorous artists Hans Baldung Grien is the most dæmonic. He has affinities with Matthias Grünewald, most poignant and colourful of German religious painters. All his work is pervaded with a feeling of diablerie, of Walpurgis Nacht. He has a grasp of form unknown to Cranach and Altdorfer and only inferior to Dürer's; but in everything he is violent and exaggerated except in his religious subjects where he seems ill at ease and subdued. He loves to represent naked pulpy women in indecent attitudes and in his best-known woodcut witches ride on goats, and sit among bones, excrement and cats, while, from an opened jar which one of them holds, whirls out a coil of smoke with lizards and filth far into the night. Death is never far away from his creations. In his painting at Basle Death seizes the maiden and ravishes her in his fatal embrace. The pine-woods of the Rhineland are behind his religious groups and hoary larch-beards trail behind his Parcæ who mind the threads of Life in all their coarse Germanic nakedness. He has left three cuts of wild horses fighting in a forest, rearing and kicking and glaring with hunted eyes. His Sebastians pierced with arrows or Christs at the Column show no triumph of the soul over the body's agony—they writhe and cry aloud in their awful suffering. No other designer of the time has such power. In his cut of the *Conversion of St. Paul* the composition admirably conveys the catastrophic effect. The Redeemer appears suddenly in the sky among great bellying clouds, and light flames forth upon the terrified cavalcade as though to strike them off their horses. His *Deposition from the Cross* is more poignant than any of the period. He has indeed more "fire in his belly" than any of his contemporaries. His portraits are the best woodcuts of their kind and school—full of character and drawn with less bravura than those of Dürer and with hardly less mastery.

If more folk were aware of his cut of *The Groom Bewitched*, Baldung might take the place beside Dürer long due to him as a creator of sinister and recondite design. Perhaps no other German of the time could have kept the design so simple and stark or so powerfully have realised the conception. The groom has been currying the horse's flanks and has been outstretched upon the ground by the maleficent power of the witch who bears a torch in her hand. His figure lies strongly foreshortened towards the stable where the restless horse throws back its head as though conscious of the spell.

We have already seen how large a share Burgkmair took in the enormous woodcut projects of the Emperor Maximilian, and indeed they are his most notable works. Beginning in the service of Ratdolt, the great typographer, Burgkmair did a vast number of drawings for the illustrated books of Augsburg printers. He is not a designer of much distinction. He has neither the felicity of Altdorfer, the intellectuality of Dürer, nor the macabre power of Baldung. His work is very uneven though at its best it shows great facility of handling and fecundity in the outpouring of florid decoration. Of the vast amount of Saints, Holy Families, etc., that he designed few are more than commonplace, but in his set of woodcuts illustrating an expedition to the Portuguese Indies fitted out by the Fuggers and other great merchants he is very charming. One large cut of aborigines in Arabia, "Das Gros India" and other places reminds us of the groups of Calicut natives in the Imperial Triumph. Another shows the King of Cochin carried in procession by his warriors. The xylographic text which accompanies the groups is happily placed and on the whole there are few prints of the time more decorative. In 1529, two years before his death, Hans Burgkmair painted a picture which, unlike most from his brush, is more than merely capably drawn and modelled. The artist and his wife look out at us: she holds a mirror in her hand inscribed "Erken dich Selbs" wherein the pair are visible as grinning death's heads. They are no longer young, their eyes are dazed, their mouths droop. Hans Burgkmair, who lives forever in the baroque splendour of the Imperial Triumph with its lustiness and arrogance, turns to the future sick at heart and makes a gesture of dismay.

"O if you were only here" (cries Dürer in one of the merry letters that he wrote to Pirkheimer from Venice), "how you would admire the fine

Hans Baldung Grien

Aristotle and Phyllis (12¾″ × 9″)

Italian soldiers! How often I think of you! Would God that you and Kuntz Kamerer could see them! They have scythe-headed lances with 218 points; if they only touch a man with them he dies, for they are all poisoned. Heigho! But I can do it well, I'll be an Italian soldier." But Urs Graf the goldsmith-engraver of Basle, of whom we now must speak, *was* a mercenary soldier. He led a wild life, "marched through the country with market-women" (says Richard Muther), "served as a Landsknecht in the murderous battle of Marignano, was warned in Court to cease the licentious life which he had openly and shamelessly led with strumpets and had to promise that he would henceforth neither jostle, pinch nor beat his lawful spouse." Graf's output is very considerable; he produced hundreds of borders, initials and other book-decorations for Frobenius, Amerbach and other Basle printers, but none of them is designed with taste and distinction. Art ever seems to forsake the

Urs Graf   *Standard-bearer of Basle*

picturesque haunts of Bohemians and come more naturally as the solace to those who court it in homes of bourgeois routine and industry. But Urs Graf is interesting as the designer of white-line cuts upon the plank. These spirited drawings with the pen were cut out in intaglio upon the block and when printed in the ordinary way read of course as white upon black.

They represent the standard-bearers of the Swiss cantons, men of that terrible infantry which had overwhelmed Charles the Bold and had been irresistible everywhere until Marignano.

But rival infantry had now arisen to these men of the hills, the men of the plains or Landsknechte, of all secular subjects quite the most popular with the German artists of the time. Jost de Negker, the famous engraver, made a great collection of cuts from the designs of Burgkmair and others of the Landsknechte who descended on Italy to fight for the Emperor Charles V. in his campaigns of 1525.[1] These insolent soldiers, their costumes amazingly slashed, knotted, ringed, feathered, padded, puffed and striped in all manner of shapes, strut around and thrust down their sword-hilts or bear great flapping banners. They push out their stomachs and trail their great limbs with cod-pieces which would have excited the admiration of Panurge. They "display the posterial luxuriance of Hottentots." Never were men more frankly dressed as men, nor the trulls that often accompany them, as women. It is the age of Rabelais.

Love is another favourite subject of these artists, and no longer does it bear the ethereal disguise or make the parade of chivalry and courtesy wherewith the craving of the Middle Age was so exquisitely obscured. The "Liebesgarten" of the German Renaissance is no mediaeval Garden of the Rose where the lover before he plucks the flower (symbolical of mere physical consummation) is beset by one personification after another. There is no shame now, no thought of allegorising appetites. Lovers sit fondling each other on flowery banks, in garden-closes to the sound of music and fountains, in the depths of Altdorferan forests. They bathe together in pools or sit at banquets. He dives into her bosom, "and that scarce honestly sometimes" as Burton the Anatomist would say. She meanwhile looks out vacantly with a flower in her hand or caresses a tiny hound on her lap. Sometimes the gloomy nature of the artist makes its comment as when the "Liebespaar" are between Death and the Devil. Sometimes it is not love but a horrid mockery of love, as in the common subjects of old women caressing young men and old men young women. In each case the young folk want money and the old lechery. Sometimes the ubiquitous skeleton plays the lover and fondles the breasts of the maiden; sometimes he seizes the gallant as he quits his mistress's bed.

---

[1] They have been reproduced in a folio by Graf Breünner Enkevoerth, *Römisch Kaiserlicher Majestät Kriegsvölker in Zeitalter der Landsknechte: in facsimilirten Nachbildungen gleichzeitiger Holzschnitte* (Vienna, 1881–3). Inferior pieces both of design and of cutting, they form a fascinating gallery of military types.

Or the theme is developed as the "Influence of Women over Sages and Heroes." David watches Bathsheba and Solomon is idolatrous through the influence of his wives. The favourite subject of lovers in a garden gets added point if it is called "Samson and Delilah." Samson is a Landsknecht of advanced age. He dozes in Delilah's lap with the jaw-bone in his hand. She coolly snips off his hair while behind great leaves creep on the Philistines. Prime favourite of all is the "Lay of Aristotle," or the "Subjugated Husband." The greatest of philosophers crawls on all-fours and often in complete nudity through a garden. Phyllis, a buxom beauty, drives him by a bit and reins, and whips his withered flanks.

ON THE WOODCUTS IN HERBALS AND OTHER SOURCES CHIEFLY IN THE SIXTEENTH CENTURY

WITH the mid-sixteenth century came a new style of ornament called "Strapwork" which requires our attention since it was widely exploited by wood‑engravers and endured for more than a century. The name is derived originally from leather‑work and later extended in use to all those forms of ornament in which the ends curl or bend outwards. The exuberant designers of the Baroque decline of the Renaissance loved all twisting curving forms, and soon the ornamental cartouches and frames were made to bend and curl at the ends. Before long designers varied and pierced and twisted the edges of the cartouches and shaded them up to get a semblance of

Jost Amman. Imprint Device of Sigismund Feyrabend of Frankfort, 1574 (7½″ × 10½″)

plastic relief. Then figures and grotesque motives were thrown in, and the openings in the panels peopled with nymphs and saints and

144

personifications of the Sciences, or enriched with swags and cornucopias. In the hands of skilful designers (and in mere executive ability perhaps no artists have equalled the Baroque) the whole panels writhe with ordered animation. Through the apertures in the strapwork nymphs push their heads or hands or breasts, cupids crawl, or athletes support swags. Used with some restraint there is no form of ornament with more capacity for varied delights. Used by the appallingly facile artists of the decline, like Jost Amman and Virgil Solis of whom we are about to speak, it disgusts more by its tasteless exuberance than it delights by its vigour and richness.

Jost Amman, whose designs for the books of the great house of Sigismund Feyrabend, publisher of Frankfort-on-Main, show the intricacy of the new style of ornament at its richest, was born at Zurich but passed his life at Nuremberg where he died in 1591. A designer of amazing fecundity, everything comes easily to his hands. He pours out brilliant little compositions and wonderfully elaborate ornaments as though he

Virgil Solis   *Diana and Actæon. From the "Metamorphoses"*
of Ovid (Frankfort, 1567)

kept them "on tap." His emblematic title-pages for Feyrabend's editions of the classics compel our unwilling admiration. Never was there so facile a designer on the wood. He pierces the strapwork structure with circular panels representing scenes from Roman or sacred history. He understands the whole business of fashionable ornament and his restless pen sweeps all forms into life. He has a formula for making book-decorations and never requires to wait and think. Jost Amman in his great strapwork title-pages for Feyrabend and his dozens of vigorous variations of that publisher's "Fama" imprint is merely doing upon wood what was already being done with much greater delicacy and richness by skilled copperplate engravers like the ever-delightful Theodor de Bry. And before long the masters of the burin won the title-pages for themselves entirely, although woodcuts being cheaper held their own for a time in copiously illustrated books. Two memorable books of this sort were produced from the designs of Jost Amman—the *Theatrum Mulierum* (1586) with quite charming cuts of the women of Europe in their national attire, and the famous *Panoplia omnium artium* (1574) which portrays very realistically the craftsmen of the day engaged at their work, among them the Form-schneider cutting his block.

Virgil Solis was born at Nuremberg in 1514. A little master, his work is not unlike that of Sebald Beham and their Lyonnese rival and contemporary Bernard Salomon. The "unique" Virgil (as his nickname goes) also worked for Sigismund Feyrabend in his copiously illustrated books. A *Metamorphoses* of Ovid with 179 small cuts is a good example of his elegant style. Like Amman and Salomon he imparts to his figures a baroque theatricality, full of vigour but monotonous, since without any reference to nature. His figures are always poised on one foot and in their restless gestures ever seem to be making over-statements. Always the same rhetoric, never anything but rhetoric, driving into our minds the truth of Pascal's thought, "La vraie éloquence se moque de l'éloquence."

In sixteenth-century books it is very often the case that mere diagrams with little or no æsthetic pretensions are vastly more charming than illustrations by the fashionable draughtsmen of the day. The little books of patterns for embroidery, *Patrons de Broderie* or *Livres de Dentelles* as they were called in France, are full of very charming suggestions. Indeed, considered merely as book-decorations by reason of their weight and colour they could not be excelled. The books on Perspective and Architecture are full of splendid diagrams which might profitably be rifled by modern cubists. Serlio, architect of Francis I., published a *Traité de Perspective* in 1545 with most distinguished and scholarly designs, and the same is true of Cousin's book on the same subject which it inspired. It would be difficult to find any designer of sufficient zeal, learning and distinction to do so splendid a book of diagrams to-day.

In this century the passion for antiquity gave rise to the publication of numerous books with medallions of Roman emperors, each accompanied by a short biography in prose or verse. The portraits were more or less carefully derived from ancient medals. Beginning in Italy, the fashion for this kind of book, of which the half-pagan Cardinal Sadolet is said to have written the first, spread westwards, and transalpine imitations are prompt and many. Soon the plan was extended to collections of heads of kaisers or kings of France, and in course of time the medallion portrait was exchanged for others of less cramping dimensions. Francis I., in whom

The Emperor Maximilian. From " Imperatorum Romanorum Imagines" (Zurich, 1559. 16″ × 12¼″)

the new ardour burned with its first and fiercest intensity, appears in a hundred French woodcut representations as a garlanded and grotesque Cæsar.

The first French book of the kind that I have examined is the *Illustrium Ymagines* (8vo. Lyons, 1524), which bears the imprint of Francoys Juste;

each page is printed within woodcut borders with little medallions cut in white upon black and an explanatory text. There is seldom anything to remark in the designs for this or other books of the kind that I have seen, but there is a cumulative effect through the harmony of types and decorations, and an unfailing sense of the *mise-en-page* that makes them all desirable possessions. But in 1559 a really superb example of this sort of picture-book was published at Zurich by Gessner. This is a great atlas called *Imperatorum Romanorum Imagines* with portrait heads by Wyssenbach and Schweitzer, borders by Wyssenbach and Deutsch, and arabesque panels by Peter Flötner. Here a rigid order is kept of portrait medallions on recto page and biographical sketch on verso. The borders are sumptuous but commonplace, the arabesques are among the most ingenious of this century, where alone the arabesque was understood in its rigid logic, and the portraits are often remarkably designed, with the greatest freedom and rare tact in the use of conventions for hair, beards, garlands, etc.

Where the likeness of the Cæsar is well known, because of the number of busts or medals that exist, the designer does a vivid portrait, and when he approaches the German kaisers like Maximilian or Charles V. he excels himself. Few picture-books are so delightful to turn over as this great work. It has such an outstanding unity of design throughout and so superb a sense of style that of all the old woodcut books this is the one that we most desire to possess.

Even schoolboys who would "duck" Macaulay's fourth-form boy as a "weed" and a bookworm have heard of Beza's *Icones* because of the well-known portraits of the Reformers that it contains. These joyless soldiers of the faith look out at us through heavy garlanded frames. There is a good deal of close hatching on their images, but, at this size —it is octavo—wood-engraving cannot compete with the copperplate. De Bry proves this beyond all possibility of dispute in his collections of portraits of illustrious men of letters and of the sultans of Turkey.

We come now to a class of books notable for the exceptionally large and beautiful sets of cuts which they contain. These are the Herbals or Histories of Plants with their medicinal virtues which appeared in the sixteenth and seventeenth centuries. The men who wrote the herbals were of great learning in their day but they were hardly botanists in the modern sense. What chroniclers like Holinshed are to the modern historian so are herbalists like Gerard to the botanist of to-day. The really regrettable thing is that the more botanically valuable the illustrations of plants become, by so much the less are they interesting to the lover of design.

There had been herbals at an earlier date than those which we are about to notice and most of them had woodcuts of a very elementary description. The *Ortus Sanitatis* (Mainz, 1475), for example, was a popular book with many cuts, but like mediaeval plant-drawings they are "quite ideographic" (as Hatton observes) "and not in any sense imitative. Usually they present four or five leaves of the form supposed to be characteristic of the plant, arranged in symmetrical fashion upon an upright central stem."

And although the practice of plant-drawing had been brought to a high degree of perfection by artists like Leonardo da Vinci and Albrecht Dürer, there were no botanical diagrams with careful representations of plants before the publication of the *Herbarum Vivae Eicones* of Brunfels in 1530. Brunfels, says Johnson, the editor of the celebrated Gerard, "was the first that gave the lively figures of plants." There are 288 diagrams in this small folio, of which the greater number are full-page with very little shading and no cross-hatching of lines. These grey, open cuts were designed by Hans

Upas Tree. From the "Ortus Sanitatis" (Mainz, 1490)

Weiditz, and the great realism of the series is shown by the presence of dead and torn leaves in the diagrams, which proves that the artist, for the first time in a herbal, drew from an actual plant. The Herbal of Brunfels is also notable for two beautiful woodcut borders with medallions containing heads of kings. The title-page has a large woodcut border, not of much interest however. Had the volume appeared a few decades later the title-page would almost certainly have been from a copperplate. Upon these beautiful title-pages the authors are usually represented—sweet-faced old men with flowers daintily held in their fingers—in the company of the great botanists of old, historical or legendary, Theophrastus and Dioscorides, Solomon and Diocletian, Ceres and Pomona, Mithridates, Lysimachus, Artemisia Æsculapius or Adam. Of course all these worthies will not be together upon one page, but one may be sure of some of them posturing heroically with plants in their hands; and perhaps a medallion, set in the strapwork or architectural framework which supports them, will show Eden or the Garden of the Hesperides.

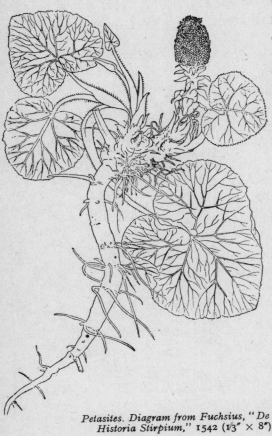

Petasites. Diagram from Fuchsius, " De Historia Stirpium," 1542 (13" × 8")

The next herbal of importance was published at Basle in 1542 by Fuchsius and entitled *De Historia Stirpium*. The title-page is not interesting, but on the page behind is a full-length cut of Dr. Fuchsius himself dressed in the broad cloak and scone hat associated from our school-days with King Henry VIII. It is good to see the likeness of so beautiful an old man. He has a mild, serious face framed with a curly beard and bears a flower in his hand, but not the fuchsia as we would like it to have been. So large are the 516 figures in the folio of Fuchsius that the plants disdain to observe the proper margins of the text and stretch themselves out gaily to the utmost limits of the page. Often they have to bow their heads in order to include their full length on the page. These great cuts are so clear and thin and grey, so devoid of all engraver's "colour," that Fuchsius must have meant his readers to colour their copies. In the copy in the Library of the University of Edinburgh this has been carefully and skilfully done by a hand long since at rest. Fuchsius was proud of his book and delighted to honour his coadjutors. We have noticed in a previous chapter how he has included in his book, on the last page, the "Pictores Operis"—the artists who adorned this the most beautiful of all herbals.

In his Introduction Fuchsius makes the following interesting statement: "We have purposely and deliberately avoided the obliteration of the natural form of the plants by shadows and other less necessary things by which the delineators sometimes try to win artistic glory."

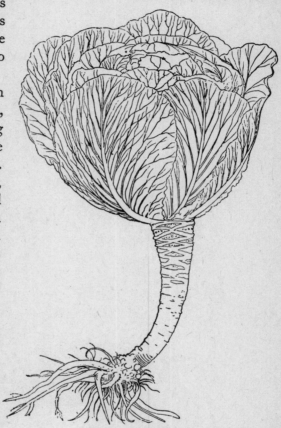

But Matthiolus, an Italian commentator on Dioscorides, employs very careful shading in nearly a thousand of the cuts which decorate his book. The artists that he employed, and whom he praises with all the hot-blooded enthusiasm that savants had in store in these days, aimed at rich effects by close and searching hatching and cross-hatching. Some of the sprays of pine and fir are most painstakingly followed needle by needle, and the hundreds of facets in the cones are searched out with equal honesty of purpose and power of realisation. The *Discorsi* of Matthiolus on the text of Dioscorides contains a full-page

Cabbage. From Fuchsius, "De Historia Stirpium" (13″ × 8″)

portrait of the author with a Latin conceit appended, and 957 large and very noble diagrams, all of which show a sense of pattern which seeks every opportunity offered by the subject and gives it decorative value. Thus for example the snakes, on whose medicinal virtues Dioscorides insists, are twisted into bold interlacing patterns with no loss to the value of the diagrams as such and of considerable decorative quality.

The *Kreuter Buch* of Hieronymus Bock is another German herbal distinguished for the excellence of its cuts. The artist was a young man of Strassburg, David Kandel, with considerable talent, though on the whole his cuts are not so important as those in the three sets already

Rowan Tree. From Matthiolus, "Commentarii in Libros Dioscoridis" (Venice, 1565)

noticed. Kandel varies his drawings of plants with little groups of figures —for example the vine yields a pretext for a little picture of the drunkenness of Noah and the misconduct of his sons thereby occasioned; children climb the cherry-tree in search of fruit, and a swineherd watches his swine beneath the oak.

The three herbalists of the Low Countries at this time all placed their books under the care of the great Antwerp printer, Christopher Plantin. These men, Dodoens, de l'Ecluse and de l'Obel, more or less "pooled" the blocks which were made for their books. Rembert Dodoens published his Dutch Herbal in 1560 and it was Englished by Henry Lyte in 1578. Lyte's *Niewe Herball* has a really beautiful woodcut title-page with nymphs, cornucopias, Apollo, Æsculapius and a view of the Orchard of the Hesperides. On the back of this is a great full-page coat of arms of the translator, and a few pages on, an excellent portrait of Rembert Dodoens himself in a fur coat, with a flowing beard and of course a herb in his hand. But the cuts of plants themselves are thin, meagre affairs without the bold decorative quality that such things generally have in this century. Lyte got his cuts from Dodoens who for the main part borrowed from the octavo Fuchsius, and of the 870 figures in his book only thirty are new.

Yew Tree. From the second (Johnson's) edition of Gerard's "Herbal," 1633

Mention of Dodoens brings us to the best known of the herbals, at least of those in English—that of Gerard. There are about 1800 cuts in Gerard taken from the *Eicones* of Tabernæmontanus, the blocks of which the printer acquired from Frankfort. It is painful for those of us who have read snatches of Gerard and handled his book to learn that this delightful man was unscrupulous in his ways of business. Not only did he borrow all his blocks (that was too common a thing to be an offence) but he did not even write the book. A certain Dr. Priest had translated Dodoens, but Death interrupted his labours when they were nearly ended. Gerard, who took this work and published it as his own in 1599, was not really a botanist but a working-gardener and superintended Lord Burleigh's gardens in the Strand and at Theobald's in Hertfordshire, as well as a famous garden of his own "in Holborn within the suburbs of London." In his account of the water dock he confesses that certain learned matters are "farre above [his] reach, being no graduate but a countrey scholler, as the whole framing of this Historie doth well declare."

Banana Tree. From the second (Johnson's) edition of Gerard's "Herbal," 1633

In 1633 another edition of Gerard's Herbal was published, greatly enlarged and corrected by another London gardener, Thomas Johnson. An ardent Cavalier, Johnson was killed at the defence of Basing House in the Puritan rebellion. His edition of Gerard, which is more valuable in every way than the first edition, has 2850 cuts from the series belonging to the great publishing house of Plantin of Antwerp. It is a large folio of 1630 pages printed in two columns and illustrated with extraordinarily decorative diagrams wherein the roots are given as well as the blossoms, and the whole is drawn with so sure a sense of the character and growth of a plant that no diagrams could be more lucid. In this enormous collection of cuts the level of skill in drawing and engraving hardly ever flags, but if the writer be pardoned for giving his own preference he would suggest that the cuts of conifers and the few amazing exotic trees that are included give the most delight.

Not a little of the decorative charm of the diagrams in the herbals is due to the stern rectangular shape to which the boundaries of the wood-block confine the irregular outwrithings of plant-growth. As Mrs. Arber says in her thorough and fascinating book on Herbals, "It was impossible for the artist to be unmindful of the boundaries of the block, when those took the form, as it were, of miniature precipices under his hand."

A third herbalist who had a famous garden in London was Parkinson. For his *Paradisi in Sole Paradisus Terrestris* (1630) he commissioned a

set of cuts crudely imitated from many sources with a new arrangement
of four specimens together on a full-page diagram within double rules.
It is not, however, a happy departure, for full-size details of a poppy-
head cannot compare in beauty or utility with a complete diagram of the
plant with roots and all. His engraver, Switzer, was well known in his
day. He has signed his name at the foot of the delightful title-page which
is in the form of a folio-cut of the Garden of Eden. In his enormous
Theatrum Botanicum (1640) Parkinson competes unsuccessfully with

Porcupine. From Gesner's "Icones Animalium" (Zurich, 1560. 8½″ × 6″)

the second edition of Gerard. The blocks were derived from Low Country
sources.

Mrs. Arber finds only five collections of cuts of any importance.
Already we have noticed those of Brunfels, Fuchsius and Matthiolus;
Plantin's set was used by the three great herbalists of the Low Country
as by Johnson, Parkinson and others. Of the fifth set, made from the
drawings of Conrad Gesner the learned Swiss naturalist, and used by his
literary legatees, the writer cannot speak as he has not yet encountered
the works that contain them. There were, of course, other and minor sets,
such as that used by Castor Durante, the Venetian, and Chabræus
of Geneva.

We have also looked over the works of Bauhin, Daléchamps, Turner and many others without many pleasurable surprises. The natural history of the New World was then exciting much interest. Clusius translated the Spanish work of Garcias ab Orta and Christopher Acosta on the medicinal properties of plants of the Indies, and Francisco Hernandez compiled a great history of Plants, Animals and Minerals of Mexico (Rome, 1651), illustrated with cuts of grotesque animals with impossible names, and long-billed fowls called zytachoitzitzilin or tozcacozhoitzilin, who look as though they took their names to heart.

The Elizabethan Frampton translated the history by Nicholas Mon-

Camel. From Conrad Gesner's "Icones Animalium" (Zurich, 1560. 11″ × 6″)

ardes the Spaniard in 1577, giving it one of the most tempting titles in an age of charming titles, *Joyful newes out of the newe founde Worlde*. The literary side of these books is as delightful as the decorative, but the limitations of this subject oblige the writer to move reluctantly on in search of other cuts.

Nothing could be more natural and inevitable than the step that leads from the Herbals to the Histories of Animals, of which by far the most famous was published in 1560 at Zurich for the learned Swiss, Conrad Gesner. Gesner's *Icones* (as this book is called) consists of three parts, Fishes, Beasts and Birds, with a goodly company of monsters of the best ancient brand, some of which the author approves of and seriously discusses, while others being suspect (but not proven fabulous) are included with a caution and with their likenesses in little.

The book is a tall narrow folio beautifully printed; but the blocks are so large that to get them on to the page many had to be printed sideways-up, so that you have to turn the book to see a great number of the cuts. The frankness of the expedients to get these awkwardly large birds and beasts on to so narrow a page is most engaging. Yet the printer would not for anything have sacrificed an inch of the most distressingly long tail. The ichneumon, for example, has to have its tail amputated; but the severed portion is printed as well, so that to get the complete quadruped you merely have to make a mental addition of the parts.

The learned Gesner has a very grim array of sea monsters. When they are particularly ugly he always takes shelter behind the authority of a certain Olaus Magnus who had studied their habits in the northern ocean. We have searched out this great Olaf and found that his book is a sort of dictionary of general information about the northern countries of Europe and the islands towards Ultima Thule. Olaus Magnus was Bishop of Upsala, and his Latin folio is plentifully illustrated with worthless column cuts, from which Gesner landed his strangest sea monsters —great fish like monks or mitred bishops, and others with heads of oxen or unicorns.

In Gesner you find unthinkable whales engaged in aquatic battles or chasing a brig whose mariners bait them with empty barrels or lull them with the sound of trumpets. Even Leviathan is there, and the sailors have anchored their ship [1] by his side from the tempest, thinking him an island. Two mariners have landed on his back and are boiling a cauldron; but Leviathan's patience seems about exhausted. A shocking hippo is nipping the tail of a stiff, indignant crocodile, and there is even a *Hydra monstrosa* with seven heads. The quadrupeds are very beautifully designed in large open lines. There is a delightful camel and a rhino copied from Dürer's famous version, while Breidenbach supplies not only the goats but the missing link and the salamander. The birds are solemn and gawky. They are placed any way except head-downwards, but never lose their dignity. They are amply taloned and stride out with the most supercilious, high-stepping airs. All the drawings are admirably bold and decorative and yet the characterisation of the different species is in most cases thoroughly grasped.

[1] "Nautae in dorsa Cetorum, quae insulas putant, anchoras figentes, saepe periclitantur" (Gesner, p. 177).

The Cosmography is another kind of book in which woodcuts of great abundance if of poor quality are to be found. Editions of Ptolemy,

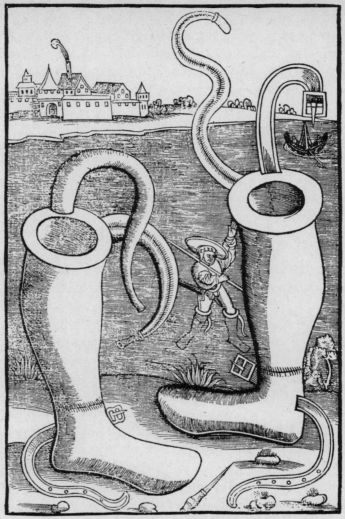

Diagram of Boots. From Vegetius, "De Re Militari"
(Basle, 1532)

Strabo and Pomponius Mela the ancient geographers were among the earliest books to be printed and were in great demand. We have noticed above the woodcut maps in Holl's beautiful edition of *Ptolemy*, and we are now going to glance at a famous cosmography of the mid-sixteenth century whose great popularity makes it representative of the taste of the time. This is the folio by Sebastian Münster published at Basle in 1550 and giving an account of all peoples, sects, customs, religions, rivers, animals, etc., of the world. Münster, who is portrayed with a scone-shaped hat and a two-days' beard, dedicated his great work to the Emperor Charles V. In addition to hundreds of coarse cuts of various sizes, ranging from four-sheet folding maps to small single figures, Münster gives two pages of Hebrew type from the writing of Prester John. The seas around the countries in his maps are the playing-ground of terrific whales and incredible sea-serpents like those described by the great Olaf. The erudite Sebastian has a childish love of mirabilia. Out of Pliny and Pomponius Mela he gets tales of African mirabilia and illustrates them with a cut of cynocephali, monoculi or anthropophagi. The pygmies war on cranes as they did in Homer's time, and there are creatures called sciopodæ who have only one foot, but that generously planned and affording ample protection from the rays of the sun!

Many of the blocks in Münster's Cosmography are printed several times, and one, at least, upside-down. Chatto is right in remarking that technically the woodcuts in Münster are no better than those in Holl's *Ptolemy*. But Münster's cuts show one interesting feature in that the Formschneider is no longer obliged to cut out his letters upon the block. Instead of that, the names of towns and countries, etc., are now printed from types by inserting them in holes bored into the block.

Another popular kind of book in the mid-sixteenth century and for some time later is the Collection of Emblems. The most famous of emblem writers was Alciati, and many editions of his conceits with woodcut vignettes were published. But the most charming emblem-books that we have seen bear the imprint of Denis Janot, the Paris printer whose *Hecatongraphie*, *Tableau de Cebes*, *Théâtre des bons Engins*, and similar books written by Gilles Corrozet and others, are delightfully decorated with arabesque and ornamental borders and tiny vignettes, each accompanied by quatrains in italic. The *mise-en-page* of these books is so charming, and the harmony of the cuts and the type so exquisite, that we are reluctant to admit that the vignettes are a little commonplace and lacking in "salt."

But the vogue of the small book with the grey roman or italic types was unfortunate for Wood-Engraving. It was obvious that the capacity for much greater delicacy inherent in the rival method would lead to the decline of the woodcut in finely printed books. For some time, as we have observed, the two methods existed together. A large and splendid copperplate generally prefaces the herbals, for example, while the diagrams inside are printed one and all from wood-blocks. But Plantin in some of his Horæ actually knits them closer by enclosing copperplate pictures inside woodcut borders. Only its cheapness kept the older method alive. You cannot print a copperplate at one impression with type as you can a woodcut. Anyone who has seen Theodor de Bry's truly amazing *Book of Voyages* with its hundreds of exquisitely designed and engraved copperplates (published at Frankfort-on-Main in 1590) will realise sufficiently why the woodcut declined.

During the seventeenth and eighteenth centuries Wood-Engraving was alive only in the popular pamphlets and broadsheets. In the year 1755 an edition of the *Fables* of La Fontaine was published at Paris with decorations by Oudry engraved on wood by Le Sueur and that Papillon of whom we have already spoken and will presently speak again. These were so excellent that the publisher feels it necessary to point them out as a novelty. This art (he writes) which once served as a means of expression to all the great artists, serves no longer except to disfigure books and to introduce "un certain goût gothique qui tient de la barbarie des premiers siècles." So that publishers are obliged to employ etching instead of the woodcut which is the real ally of Typography. However, says the writer, the cuts in this edition have been done in a manner that avenges the art from the discredit into which it has fallen.

This shows us how unusual it was for the wood-engraving to be considered seriously as an object of beauty by the middle of the eighteenth century. Being divorced from fine printing it sunk until by that time it was used only for the humblest purposes, for bill-heads, wall-papers, and funeral cards. And yet here and there throughout these centuries of decline it had been employed occasionally by famous artists. We must now look at some of these cuts, which were made for sale as single-sheet prints.

About the year 1566 Titian got interested in the art to the extent of making a number of designs for reproduction by skilled engravers like Nicolo Boldrini, Domenico delle Grecche, Andreani and others. In 1519 delle Grecche cut a huge *Submersion of Pharaoh* upon twelve blocks clamped together as one, and later a *Martyrdom of Ten Thousand* which required eight blocks. Things like these are of little or no artistic value, but they show how the Italian mind was haunted by the thought of immense wall-paintings.

The Paduan painter, Domenico Campagnola, is another maker of single-sheet prints. Perhaps a pupil of Giulio Campagnola, the exquisite translator into line of the glamour of Giorgione (for there was no blood relationship between the two), and certainly the assistant of Titian, Domenico made several large woodcuts from the designs of the great Venetian artist. Titian's drawings upon the block have not the line-by-line deliberation of those of Dürer or Rubens. They are loose, quill sketches so that they do not lend themselves very readily to facsimile engraving. In fact, to envisage a Campagnola woodcut, think of a Titian landscape-drawing without its sweep and without its nerves.

One might have expected light and witty drawings from a master with so charming a name as "IB with the Bird"; so that it is a matter for gloom to discover that he is just another capable designer of the High Renaissance, influenced by the tradition of line-engraving begun by Mantegna, and clearly cognisant of the prints of Albrecht Dürer. His subjects are the commonplaces of the Paduan School, arid landscapes out of which queer piles of rock ascend, with Sebastian or Jerome posing somewhere in the foreground. He is responsible for ten large cuts each signed with the initials IB followed by a little figure of a bird. The most interesting of these is a design of the *Three Graces* which has been borrowed by Mr. Charles Sims in one of his plates. The nude figures are shaded with lateral hatchings in the manner of a Mantegna engraving, but in their sweet voluptuous postures betray the influence of gentler masters like Botticelli or Piero di Cosimo.

Jacopo de' Barbari or Jakob Walch (the Italian) was the artist who so influenced the young Dürer. He is memorable in a history of Wood-Engraving for his immense Panorama of Venice as it was in the year 1500, which is nine by four feet in scale and is composed of six blocks. Every house is drawn in by Jacopo and carefully engraved; which can hardly be said to be the case in his other cuts—combats or processions of naked men—which are crudely rendered as well as being dull in composition.

Giuseppe Scolari of Vicenza is another Italian artist who has left a few large single-sheet prints. Scolari belongs to the latter half of the sixteenth century and is notable for the use of white-line work without any cross-hatching. He was almost certainly the engraver as well as the designer of his prints which look like coarse graver-work and are quite modern in feeling. In his *St. George, St. Jerome* and other prints the rocks are drawn and the clouds swung in with white lines of varying thickness.

Vasari claims that Ugo da Carpi (1455–1523) was the inventor of chiaroscuro prints; but it is probably more accurate to say that he was the first to make them in Italy, although Germans like Cranach had used them many years before Ugo's first dated print which is *The Death of Ananias* (1518). We have given some account of the method in our chapter on Technique. Ugo worked largely from the designs of Raphael but his prints have little æsthetic appeal. Other chiaroscuro woodcutters of the period were Andrea Andreani, Antonio da Trento and Giuseppe Vicentino, while about the end of the sixteenth century Hendrik Goltzius was producing important prints at Haarlem and Abraham Bloemaert at Utrecht.

Lucas van Leyden is more famous for his line-engravings than for the thirty woodcuts which he designed, which are not unlike the productions of his German contemporaries but are more Italianised and on the whole less skilfully cut: Jakob Cornelisz, another Netherlandish artist of Dürer's time, has a fine grasp of character but is also distinctly inferior to the great German woodcutters to whom his work bears much resemblance. His most important achievement was a pageant of noble riders, *Les Preux à Cheval*, which suggests a comparison with the Processional cuts of Burgkmair or Dürer which it cannot in any way sustain. His cross-hatchings are plentiful but unskilfully laid in, and the lines are cut in a ragged way. Although born in 1480, nine years after the birth of Dürer, his work is in some ways nearer in quality to that of Reuwich.

The Netherlands produced three outstanding woodcutters in the first half of the seventeenth century—Christoffel Jegher the brilliant cutter of several tremendously virile drawings by the great Rubens, and Jan Lievens and Dirk de Bray who each left a few brilliant portraits. Otherwise there are no names to check us in our scurry through this dreary period until we come to that of Jean Michel Papillon, who was born in 1698 and lived until 1776. When Papillon as a young apprentice-engraver tried to find some treatise on his craft to guide and instruct him, he searched all Paris in vain and had only derision for his pains— so low was the prestige of the craft. That young enthusiast having devoted a lifetime to the practice and study of Woodcutting and being exalted in his calling, published in 1766 the result of his labours. His *Traité historique et pratique de la Gravure en Bois* is the funeral monument of the old school of wood-engravers.

Papillon's grandfather was a "cartier" (or engraver of playing-cards), and his father, a one-time student of Cochin the Elder (the famous master of the burin), was well known later as an engraver of *chinoiserie* patterns for ladies' dresses. So that his passion for engraving was pre-natal. Papillon was the author of about 5000 pieces, mostly small book-decorations, headpieces and *culs de lampe*. The best that can be said for them is that they are pretty things and skilfully cut, for Papillon was ever engaged in pursuit of improvements in craftsmanship. It is unkind to laugh at one whose passionate love of a craft in which "sa savante main enfanta des merveilles" (so runs a line of contemporary verse in his honour) led him into the wildest irregularities of misstatement. He insisted that all the great artists were engravers upon wood, and Wood-Engraving the oldest and most honourable of crafts. And since evidence was lacking he let imagination supply the want. In his old age he was mentally deranged for a time and some of his statements are quite reckless. He is the last of the old tradition of woodcutters to achieve any fame, though knife-work was the sole means used in France until 1816 when Charles Thomson introduced the technique of Thomas Bewick.

POPULAR PRINTS OF THE SEVENTEENTH AND EIGHTEENTH CENTURIES

We have noticed more than once in the course of these chapters that the woodcuts in the *incunabula* preserve the last vestiges of the mediaeval tradition of book-decoration. The advent of artists like Reuwich the Flemish painter and Tory the French humanist meant the end of that tradition in the printed book. But the tradition is not and could not be killed, though it be sadly discredited and, like Lazarus, cast out, for it is the tradition of the people, the natural means of expression of the people who remain untouched by academic culture.

The popular prints of the seventeenth and eighteenth centuries which we now intend to survey show astonishing spiritual survivals of the tradition of those of the fifteenth century. They are simple, crude and ineloquent, but always direct and to the point, always decorative, bright in colour and charming in sentiment, though it must never be forgotten that good popular artists are quite as rare as good trained artists, and nothing is duller and more stupid than bad primitive art, for the scope thereof is the narrower. Gothicism, swept underground by the Renaissance, survived in the pamphlets and broadsides for the people prepared by obscure, illiterate and overworked artisans, and sold to the poor at prices within their reach. Conservatism of thought and expression, impermeability and repugnance to change, is a main feature distinguishing popular art from that of the schools. In Catholic countries, Christ and His saints still resist the invasion of the Olympians into the minds of the unlearned and the nine mediaeval worthies still mean more to the poor man than the heroes of Plutarch. In treatment as in spirit there was no change.

Certain subjects are common to most countries and never seem to weary the people. The Wandering Jew like a mediaeval pilgrim with scrip and burdon wanders on until our father's times over all lands and seas.[1] The Struggle for the Breeches between Man and Wife ("La Lutte

---

[1] The Odyssey of Ahasuerus, the Wandering Jew, is perhaps the favourite of all the subjects of popular prints. For striking Christ on the road to Calvary he was condemned to wander the earth awaiting the Second Advent. Each time that he reached the age of a hundred he was seized

pour la Culotte") had been the subject of a dotted metal-cut and is popular until the end. The tale of Pyramus and Thisbe, that "very tragical mirth," had vastly appealed to the "rude mechanicals" in Shakespeare's time and in its chapbook shape in later times doubtless excited the same terror and pity in its readers as it had done in the minds of Bottom the weaver and his brethren. In Protestant countries, of course, the tradition of religious broadsheets ceased almost as soon as it was born, but in countries unsubdued by the Reformation the style of the earliest wood-cut "Heiligenbilder" continued without a break. Popular revisions in

La Bête de Gevaudan. From a broadsheet (Rouen, eighteenth century. 5¾" × 12")

chapbook form of the adventures of Robinson Crusoe and Lemuel Gulliver were very popular in France and the Netherlands, as were subjects of a superstitious, portentous nature. The people in the centuries before Waterloo would as gladly exchange a copper for a broadsheet or pamphlet of a horrible nature as folk do to-day for a sporting paper. Everybody loved a good monster. There was one more dire and thrilling than all others, the famous "Bête de Gevaudan," who terrorised that district in France for many months in 1775. The broadside *Complaintes* published contemporaneously describe its ravages in piteous rhymes

with a painful illness from which he recovered aged thirty—the number of years of his life when he was cursed by Christ. Like the eagle, he continually renewed his youth. During the course of his wanderings, Ahasuerus, or Isaac Laquedem as he is sometimes named, was frequently seen. Pious men, who had conversed with him and had been edified, told the English monk Matthew Paris about him in the mid-thirteenth century. Much later he passed through France. Rahier, the "'imagier'' of Orleans, published a broadside with the title " Le vrai portrait du Juif-Errant, tel qu'on l'a vu passer à Dijon, le 22 avril 1784." To a bourgeois who spoke to him the Jew explained that he had been wandering for two thousand years!

and portray it in rude woodcuts so that it almost seems a survival of some monster of the bestiaries, though it is believed to have been but a wolf. Autolycus, the Shakespearian chapman, had a ballad, it may be remembered, which an egregious fish sang "against the hard hearts of maids," and, two centuries later, folk in the neighbourhood of Chartres were buying for a sou an exact description of an amphibian "cast up by

French popular Cut used for illustrating Murders (about 1840)

the sea on the coast of Provence" which had a mighty appetite for human flesh. This man-eater is represented in the woodcut as a Chinese dragon, and the designer, wishing to give it a form worthy of its character, copied it (we suspect) out of some *chinoiserie* of the period.[1]

Autolycus, too, that cunning fellow, had another ballad also of a very popular nature, that celebrating prodigies, wonders of wonders,

[1] An amphibian which was cast up by the tempest on the shores of Provence on 4 March, 1817, devoured a child on landing, pillaged a cemetery to consume the corpses, and was slain by a regiment of English soldiers who were passing through the neighbourhood. A broadsheet published "chez Rahier-Boulard" at Orleans commemorates the event. Rahier, according to Desnoyers who knew him, was a thoroughly sincere man.

miracles of miracles. It was set, of course, "to a very doleful tune" and describes "how an usurer's wife was brought to bed of twenty money-bags at a burden, and how she longed to eat adders' heads and toads carbonadoed." Ashton in his collection of chapbooks has a parallel prodigy of the eighteenth century. It tells with the aid of a shocking cut of the accouchement of Sarah Smith, daughter of an Essex farmer, the result of which was a monster with many heads, part dragon, part eagle, part calf. The chapbook is advertised as being "very fit and necessary to be had in all families for a warning to disobedient children." It is a relief to find that Sarah's baby was "by the command of the Magistrates knock'd on the head," for if it had lived (to judge from the woodcut) it would have come to no good.

The "black-letter ballads," so called from the gothic types in which they were printed, were very widespread in the sixteenth century in England, and in the seventeenth century the Civil Wars fostered their growth. People like Mr. Pepys were sufficiently above their intellectual and social plane to find them quaint and amusing and it is in collections like his that they are preserved. The nearly complete disappearance [1] of this and other classes of popular print is easily accounted for. An odd collector like the fun-loving and widely sympathetic diarist might think them worthy of preservation, but, in the main, such "trash" ("slovenly stamps" as Horace Walpole called them at a later time) disappeared naturally as the daily papers disappear in the house to-day.

The black-letter ballads were seldom decorated, but the broadsides and chapbooks, whether of political, satirical, romantic, superstitious or any other nature, were generally decorated with cuts—all more or less "comic cuts," though they were that by accident, certainly not by intention. Chapmen, or "flying stationers" as they were called, peddled these prints all over the countryside, generally along with knick-knacks of all sorts. In the cities, however, there were street singers who went around offering for sale the rhymes they sang. Country pedlars radiated round some centre like Chartres or Newcastle where popular prints

[1] Cheap and popular things always tend to disappear easily. The broadsheets were put into the hands of children or nailed up on the walls of houses. Garnier says that the large sheets that his parents produced illustrating the Creation of the World, the Prodigal Son or other favourites were called "tours de cheminées" through the practice of sticking them up over the fire-places as decoration and recreation. No wonder few have survived. The blocks have suffered a similar fate. Rahier at Orleans inherited from the "imagiers'" who preceded him a vast hoard of wood-blocks, which occupied so much space in his workshop that he eventually burned them all. At Chartres the Garniers did likewise with their great store of ancient blocks.

were made. All those connected with the manufacture were of the artisan class. They were "rude mechanicals," quite unschooled in design as in letters and unconscious of the simplest rules of perspective or advance in the technique of Engraving since the block-books. They worked as family circles, often prolonged into dynasties. Duchartre says that the

French popular Print of the seventeenth century.
Provenance unknown (7″ × 6″)

Chapoulards of Limoges were "imagiers" from 1607 to 1804, and the famous house of Pellerin at Épinal lasted for a century and a half.

Woodcutting was the main means of multiplying images for the market, though later on Line-Engraving and Lithography were employed. The treatment is, as I have suggested, incunabular or even more immature. There is no cross-hatching. The pattern is bold and decorative and the woodcutter was almost without a doubt the designer. Hand-colouring was almost a necessity and the people rejoiced in bright colours. The thick black outlines of the cuts when filled in with gay reds, blues and yellows yield a decorative effect of much splendour, reminding one of the glories of mediaeval stained glass. And, like the men who made the stained-glass windows in the Gothic churches, they cared little or nothing for natural truth in their colouring. Men with red beards or blue beards, red asses or blue trees are as common in popular broadsides as in mediaeval windows. Children were employed to do the colouring. Dibdin, who visited the workshops of Picart-Guérin at Caen in 1819, saw a merry band of children seated each with brush in hand and saucers with colours before them. When each did one colour alone they could easily attain to the automatic facility of a machine without its monotonous exactness. Sometimes stencils ("patrons") were used, a practice which has been brought to an amazing degree of proficiency in the "pochoir" system of French illustrated books. Most print manufacturers kept a press and types, but this was forbidden to the French "imagiers" until the Restoration, so that blocks had to be printed "au frotton," by hand-friction in the ancient manner. Garnier, who came of a famous family of "imagiers" in Chartres, tells us in his valuable book how laborious was the life of his parents. The Garniers slaved from five a.m. to eight p.m. each day to get their modest profits—so low was the selling price of their prints. "A diligent worker" (says he) "gained from 7 livres 10 sous to 9 livres a week."

The French popular prints are by far the most beautiful that I have seen. This may have been due in part to the unbroken tradition from the earliest Burgundian cuts of saints and incidents of the Passion of Christ—a tradition unbroken by the Reformation. French peasantry wanted cheap prints of a religious nature and these are frequently of a very high decorative quality. A popular type was the "Cantique spirituel" with a folio-cut of a saint above or girt around by thin bands of verses in small type. The saint parades surrounded by his emblems. The colours are exceedingly boldly and often very felicitously placed, with no attempt at gradations or care for naturalistic standards. Clouds yellow, blue and red in colour cluster together in the sky like the balloons that children love, and a great splash of green covers the bundle of leaves which is always the primitive version of a tree. The saints were noted for their intercession for the poor and wretched--Roch, for example, who healed the diseased; Nicholas who loved the young, and Margaret who succoured women in travail.

Another type of print common in France and the Netherlands showed the traditional arrangement of the Crucified Christ surrounded by the symbols of the Passion. It was cut rudely enough but often with much feeling, and showed the same attention to all the details of the Day of Golgotha that the mediaeval tradition demanded. Nothing is omitted; the sponge is there, the dice, the sun, the moon, the handkerchief of Veronica, the spear of Longinus. The cock that gave the lie to Peter is perched upon the column of the Flagellation; but the great difficulty of

Cavalry. Block used at Rennes, 1830 (8″ × 12″)

the craft as practised by these humble artisans obliged them to omit the symbols of the kiss of Judas and of the sword-stroke of Peter. This adherence to the tradition of the Middle Age makes it a very difficult thing to reckon the date of a print. But the triumph of the ideologists of the Revolution substituted Reason for Christianity as the state religion of France, and the "imagiers" were ordered to destroy all blocks representing "the mummeries of a religion which Philosophy and Reason have annihilated for ever."

It is vastly intriguing to find the successes of Vérard and others of the early French publishers enduring for centuries among the people. The *Kalendrier des Bergers* of 1480 appears as late as the last decade of last century and has not been altered out of recognition, and even Guyot Marchant's *Danse Macabre* of 1486 is reproduced in 1641 by Garnier of Troyes. Other popular subjects which occasioned delightful cuts are the Æsopic Fables, the Land of Cockaigne, Bluebeard, Credit is Dead, The Folly of Man or the World Upside Down, and The Four Verities.

Copyright was undreamt of. Any successful venture was promptly pirated. Nor were the methods too intelligent. Blocks were recklessly thrown in regardless of their appropriateness as illustrations. Portraits

The Royal Martyrdom. From a Ballad of 1648

are still *simulacra* and are used time and again for different persons.[1] A cut of Bonaparte as First Consul with Joséphine de Beauharnais is used later as the likeness of the emperor with his Austrian bride, and one marshal becomes another by changing the title underneath the cut. There was a considerable industry in military prints, particularly of types of the French army. You could buy battalions at the cost of a sou per soldier and colour the uniforms yourself. These prints emanated largely from Strassburg. When France embarked upon the great campaigns which finally terminated at Waterloo the "imagiers" poured out military prints of all descriptions, from the simple "soldat d'un sou" to the representation

---

[1] Van Heurck shows that a block of Mary Stuart, wife of the Stadtholder, William of Orange, was used turn by turn for all the princesses of Orange until the Revolution.—*Histoire de l'Imagerie populaire flamande.*

of some incident of the war, such as the planting of the standard upon the bullet-swept bridge of Lodi by the young Napoleon.

All these types of prints are illustrated in the work of the Pellerins of Épinal. The house of Pellerin began in 1750. By 1845 it employed 80 to 100 workers and the editions of impressions mounted to hundreds of thousands. One of their woodcutters, Reveillé, had served under the emperor and lost a leg at Essling, and Georgin, who became the best of the "imagiers" of Epinal, inspired by the veteran, assisted to build up "la légende du petit caporal"—the Napoleonic legend. Before the house of Pellerin came to a close late in the last century it had almost "cornered" the whole output of popular prints in France. In its earlier period the Épinal prints are among the finest of their kind, simple, vigorous and decorative, but latterly the immense popularity of their productions and the over-work that ensued caused the development of the family workshop into something like a modern printing-works. One of the designers, Pinot, was even a medallist of the Salon and a pupil of Delaroche! Well may we groan, "que diable allait-il faire dans ce galère?" But Pinot's work was very successful—commercially.

Long Meg of Westminster. Chapbook Cut, from "Ashton"

The practice of engraving in facsimile the drawings of a skilled designer is the antithesis of the tradition of popular Woodcutting. Before long came Chromo-Lithography and photo processes, and the place of the popular print upon the walls of French houses is now occupied by the supplements of illustrated magazines.

The popular prints of Italy show the almost complete decay of the minor arts that set in with the High Renaissance and the Cinquecento. The Arts flowed into the Baroque, that extraordinary style at once the product of and the excuse for exhibitions of tasteless virtuosity; but the Baroque, being the style of the virtuoso, is the very antithesis of the style of the people. Hence the popular prints of the sixteenth and seventeenth centuries in Italy are for the great part identical in spirit and technique with the woodcuts of the earliest Venetian and Florentine printed books. The huge and pretentious woodcuts made by skilled workers like Boldrini or Andreani after the drawings of Titian, or the efficient blocks of artists like the master IB with the Bird, have no influence at all upon these popular prints. Blocks once used by a Giunta or a Pacini may be found a century or more later bruised and warped by constant employment in the pamphlets of the poor. But disfigured as they are, these cuts in the old style retain in their humble circumstances something of an "air," something of the dignity of the great artistic period from which they come.

The Florentine convention for the ground—a black passage scored with rows of horizontal white lines—is retained into the late seventeenth century. Cross-hatching and the use of rounded, fluent contours, which was the style of knife-work at its fullest development, is not to be found in characteristic examples of the popular pamphlet. But of course we must not look for purity of style in these cheap publications, wherein inconsistencies abound. For example, in the pamphlets giving the text of the Florentine *Rappresentazioni* of which we spoke in another chapter, the Angel of the Annunciation is now of a more florid

Chapbook Cut. From "Ashton"

type, and is surrounded by a garland of bumpy-contoured clouds in strange stylistic contrast to the title-block of the older tradition which accompanies it.

English popular prints are more interesting to the historian and the collector than to the lover of woodcuts. The industry never yielded such charming results in this country as in France, and the interest which artists of our own day have evinced for these productions is rather more due to the weariness bred of the technical triumphs and pathetic tameness of the tradition of reproductive Wood-Engraving which replaced them than to their own intrinsic merits as designs. Unlike Germany and France, England never had what the older books call a "Golden Age" of Wood-Engraving. The cuts used by Caxton, Pynson and the other early printers are almost always borrowed or at least derived from foreign sources, just as was the case at a later time with famous sets of cuts like those in Gerard's *Herball* or Topsell's *Natural History*. The preference of seventeenth-century publishers was mostly for handsome copperplate title-pages, and if there were cuts inside they were seldom original or ambitious. There are, of course, exceptions, and one English printer of the sixteenth century, John Day, did commission a dignified and large set of woodcuts in a mature style with cross-hatchings. But this book, the well-known edition of Foxe's *Book of Martyrs* (1563), serves but to show the extreme paucity of its kind in England. Indeed there is no period in the history of the craft in England comparable to that in Germany when the foremost painters of the day were everywhere making drawings upon the wood-block which were reproduced in great fidelity by brilliant craftsmen. So that the popular woodcutter in England has few highly

Robinson Crusoe. Chapbook Cut, from "Ashton"

trained rivals of the same calling and the "slovenly stamps," as Horace Walpole calls the woodcuts of his day, are almost all that this country has to show of Wood-Engraving before the days of Bewick. These "slovenly stamps" carry on the tradition of Caxton's time with no advance in style, knowledge or technique. They fall into two main groups: illustrations in chapbooks and embellishments of broadsheets. The latter are of a political, satirical or criminal nature for the most part and are often very happily arranged with the types and borders of *fleurons*. A common form of broadsheet was the ballad referred to above, and in the *Compleat Angler* we read how Piscator conducts his friend to an "honest ale-house," where they would find a cleanly room, lavender in the windows, "and twenty ballads stuck about the wall." But wide as was the range of these subjects, the broadsheet is perhaps better known to us as the forerunner of the sensational Sunday newspaper of our own days. For selling purposes the printers of broadsides loved nothing so much as a sensational murder giving "exact descriptions" of the revolting circumstances and a portrait of the criminal. But rapes, suicides, and mon-

Miss Davies. Chapbook Cut, from "Ashton"

strous births were also good sellers, and there is one class of print which made a peculiar appeal. This purported to give the confession of the condemned man in his last hour and was arranged in piteous and highly edifying doggerel with little vignettes and often a final cut of the gallows, the victim and the crowd. An unscrupulous

Northumbrian, Jemmy Catnach of Seven Dials, with the aid of the wretchedest denizens of Grub Street and obscure, untrained, wood-cutters, contrived to make considerable profits by the sale of such prints. Indeed he is said to have disposed of as many as 2,500,000 single broad-sheets dealing with a certain enthralling murder of the times. Jemmy Catnach died in 1842 and the industry may be said to have died with him, for the jolly broadsheets published of recent years by the Poetry Bookshop are antiquarian revivals and, far from being "popular" in spirit, are precious and designed for a coterie. These charming things look admirable upon the walls of Montessorian class-rooms and "arty" tea-shops in Bloomsbury or Chelsea. The poorer classes who put out their pennies for the old-time broadsheet know nothing of them.

English chapbooks are mostly octavo and duodecimo in format and are illustrated very fully with little woodcuts. Some of these are not only decorative and illustrative but are really charming designs. It is surprising how much variety can be obtained by such means and it is not uncommon to find the woodcutter turning a design by an artist of the day into popular form and wonderfully improving it in his broad unrhetorical version. The heroes of the chapbooks are the bold outlaws who oppressed the rich and benefited the poor—Robin Hood, Claude Duval, Turpin, King and others of that chivalrous fraternity. The "mirabilia" of the romances of Guy of Warwick or Bevis of Hampton are not too broad for the quite mediaeval credulity of the purchasers of chapbooks. The superhuman patience of Grissel and infrahuman fatuity of the Wise Men of Gotham are alike unable to arouse criticism and are fair specimens of the popular taste in literature in the century of Pope and Johnson.

At the same time there was a large output of illustrated books for children, very tiny in size and amusingly decorated. We have examined about 200 of the booklets, alphabets, hornbooks, etc., sold for the use of the young at a penny or twopence at the beginning of last century, and, though there are few very delightful surprises, they keep a high level and are certainly far superior to the grotesque hobgoblinish style of book-illustration which is supposed (we believe erroneously) to delight the children of to-day. A great number of these little books were produced in Northumberland where the interest in them lingers long; but the chapbooks proper of the eighteenth century were printed in nine cases out of ten in London and published by the very prolific Dicey at Aldermary Churchyard in the city.

After the epoch-making innovations of Thomas Bewick the old traditions died away. The pupils of Bewick, who were as skilful with the graver as their master, came south to London and set up shops. Fashionable designers were called upon to make drawings upon the blocks and these were slavishly reproduced. A great seriousness set in, and, with the astonishing feats displayed by these engravers to all the world, the "slovenly stamps" were soon forgotten, or remembered by the refined with horror. Jackson says that no apprentice of his day would dare exhibit such incompetence at the end of his first year of service as that apparent in blocks of the chapbook tradition still employed by humbler printers of Newcastle.

But the whirligig of time brings in its revenges, and an affectionate memory for chapbooks, not merely antiquarian but æsthetic, was not long in showing. In the 'eighties of last century, that is in the very dark void and abyss of the night of Victorian reproductive engraving, when proud and generously whiskered masters of the burin were everywhere translating paintings in all their tonal variety into wonderful systems of line and tick, a native of Newcastle,

Chapbook Cut

Joseph Crawhall, published from "Ye Leadenhalle Press" a series of extraordinarily jolly, fat and light-hearted books loaded with "comic cuts" in the chapbook tradition. Because of his blithe and care-free outlook, his undeniable instinct for book-production and gift for engraving bagatelles, Crawhall's books are eminently refreshing. His delight in the old ballads and tales of the chapbooks is great, and he reprints them with free adaptations of the woodcuts which accompanied them. Crawhall is the first engraver to be artfully naïve and deliberately unaccomplished. As though Bewick had never existed, he goes back to the "slovenly stamps" and pounces upon their quaintness and felicities of ingenuous statement with the delight of a folklorist who is also an artist. His candour and childlike gaiety disarm criticism and even his little affectations like the spelling of his book-titles, as *Olde ffrendes with newe faces* and *Impreses quainte*, seem to add to his charm where with most users they merely irritate. But it is not only from the popular prints of the North Country that Crawhall finds the sources of his "sculptures," but from mediaeval glass and MSS. and even from the designs of William Blake.

Crawhall has a very pretty sense of design and his books are admirably produced. The types are chosen for their heavy and clumsy appearance and the *mise-en-page* is always admirable. Moreover his books are fully coloured by hand in the old ways and the broad use of yellows and reds and greens among the heavy-lined cuts yields a jewel-like effect. His collection of angling poems called *Izaak Walton, His Wallet Booke* (1885) is full of the jolliest cuts of sheep and cows and anglers and beetles and flowers borrowed from the popular prints and made bright and even witty in his versions. Old Joe Crawhall deserves to be better known. His unpretentiousness in an age of swollen solemnity is not his only charm. It is sad that he should be best known as the father of Young Joe Crawhall, the able and superficial brushman whose sketches of birds and horses may be seen in many public galleries. Publishers of light-hearted books for the young of all ages could do no better than to consult his publications from " Ye Leadenhalle Press."

But Crawhall was no artisan-engraver. He was not of the class that produced the popular prints of the previous century. He approached them with the curiosity of a cultivated man with a *flair* for the quaint and homely in art. His limited editions of hand-coloured books were soon forgotten, but his influence upon artists of our own day like William Nicholson, and, through the latter, upon Gordon Craig and the late Claude Lovat Fraser, is considerable and not sufficiently realised. Nicholson's charming coloured woodcuts are in no way Japanese in style as is often stated, and they could hardly have originated at all without the influence of Old Joe Crawhall.

BEWICK

THOMAS BEWICK was born in 1753 at Cherryburn near Newcastle of small-farmer stock. He was sent to school at Mickley where his father had a small coal-pit, and later was removed to Ovingham where the rector kept a small private school, and where he was more distinguished for mischief than for any love of books. No thrashing could repress his innate propensity for drawing, which overflowed into his exercise books, and from there to the church porch, the gravestones, and even to the flag-stones of his father's hearth, where the fire used to scorch the face of the young enthusiast. At length a compassionate person gave him pen and ink and paper and he soon made a name for himself among the cottagers, drawing with ardour those birds and trees and hunting scenes whereby his name has become a household word. When not at school or playing truant he worked in the fields in all weathers, or engaged in the wild escapades of healthy, adventurous boyhood. Indeed, the recollection of these early years made the old man's heart to swell when he sat down to pen his *Memoir*, and sixty years and custom lay upon him with a weight

heavy as frost and deep almost as life.

At the age of fourteen he was bound apprentice to Ralph Beilby, copperplate engraver, and, heartbroken, said good-bye to his care-free boyhood, the whins and the open air. Beilby kept a shop in Newcastle where he performed all kinds of engraving but very little upon wood. Indeed Bewick was kept at the "coarser kind of engraving," door-plates, clock-faces, sword-blades, mourning-rings, pipe-moulds and the like, until, as he tells us, "my hands had become as hard and enlarged as those of a blacksmith." However, when a little wood-engraving came his way he did it so cleverly that Beilby found him more and more to do. He is said to have invented a labour-saving tool, and doubtless made many experiments and learnt much from the cuts in the popular tradition that he did during his apprenticeship. It was at this time that he won a medal from the Society of Arts for a woodcut of *The Huntsman and the Old Dog* for an edition of *Æsop's Fables*. And that the Society should think it a very meritorious piece of wood-engraving is a pretty good illustration of the depth to which that art had descended, and from which it was Bewick's life-work to raise and adorn it. Indeed that phrase of Johnson's about the debt of our literature to Dryden, that he found it brick and left it marble, might truly be applied to Bewick and Wood-Engraving.

His bondage over, Bewick with three guineas sewed in his belt set out on a walking-tour. By way of Carlisle

Bewick

Sheep

he tramped right into the Highlands of Scotland, all of which he has described, not without didacticism, in his *Memoir*. The "Wanderlust" still on him, he left Newcastle shortly after his return and came to London, where he lived for a twelvemonth working at his profession. Refusing a tempting offer of work, for (as he said) "I would rather be herding sheep on Mickley bank top than remain in London although for doing so I was to be made the Premier of England," he returned to

Newcastle and the weekly visits to thrice-beloved Cherryburn which he continued to make until his parents died.

Through the agency of their friends it was soon after arranged that Bewick should enter into partnership with his former master. As Beilby had an apprentice, Bewick, to square matters, took his seventeen-year-old brother John as his apprentice. Thereafter for many years his life was industrious and uneventful. With his brother's assistance Bewick engraved the designs for two editions of *Fables* which show an

Bewick

Cur Fox

amplitude, richness of texture and fineness of execution which were little known at that time, but which will not compare with his later works. The *Select Fables* of 1784 are to a large extent merely copies upon the boxwood of Croxall's edition, and he cannot be said to have done much more than refine the already pleasant enough designs, although his treatment of animals shows a knowledge and vigour which are not to be found in the originals.

In the following year Bewick began a task which he had long had at heart and which appeared in 1790 under the title of the *General History of Quadrupeds*. In this famous book we find the mature work of the master, and its appearance marks an epoch in the history of Wood-Engraving.

Bewick   *Vignette for Somerville's " Chase "*

At the risk of repeating much of what we have already written about the white line of Bewick, a word about technique may be appropriate at this point. Bewick is often credited with innovations which he did not make and which were undoubtedly known to the engravers of London whose acquaintance he made when exiled in that city. But it is true to call him the first *great* exponent of the new method, for it was due to the success of his work that the use of the graver upon the cross-section of boxwood became the most popular method of wood-engraving. As he was for the most part the designer as well as the engraver of his work, the choice of line was left to him, and Bewick chose to make his engravings consist as far as possible of white lines and to get his effects by variations on the width of these lines rather than by cross-hatching. He never made a serious practice of drawing the lines in black and then reproducing them, for he wisely refrained from imitating the black line of copper-plate engraving, which proved such a fatal temptation to many of his successors. His main technical characteristic, then, is his use of white lines infinitely varied to express all manner of textures and tones.

We have spoken above of the practice of "lowering" and "overlaying" wood-blocks, so we will not define them again. Bewick was wonderfully skilled in these practices, which he perfected, if he did not actually discover for himself. Certain portions of a block where he wanted to display markings and yet which required to be printed very light (for example the breast of a bird) would be lowered below the surface of the block and then engraved by a tool with a slightly turned-up belly. As though these precautions were not enough, "overlays" might be used to "bring up" the main darks and prevent over-pressure on the greys, and the very

Bewick   *Vignette for Somerville's "Chase"*

delicate part (the downy breast of the bird) might even be slightly wiped with a rag by the pressman after each inking and before each impression. For Bewick not only performed feats of delicate engraving in advance of his generation, but he trained pressmen to print them. It is to his personal supervision of the printing of his books that we owe their admirable impressions. He preferred a rich brown print which allowed every hair-line to read, to a full black one with the inevitable risk that some of the lines should become charged with ink and the lace-like and all-over quality be lost in consequence.

The success of the *Quadrupeds* was due not only to the delicacy of the engraving but to the remarkable truth and vigour of the representations. These qualities, however, are far more apparent in the diagrams of British animals, for these he drew from nature, while, for the foreign animals, he was dependent upon the plates in Buffon, Goldsmith and other writers on Natural History. Bewick's engravings of dogs and deer and foxes and sheep are superb. By means of brilliant graver-work he gives us the ripple of the loose skin over limbs, or the fleeciness of coats or the leatheriness of hides. He has an unerring eye for the character of every animal, its shape and temper, and his backgrounds are not only exquisitely patterned but brilliantly conceived as settings for the species.

The literary part of the book was the work of Bewick's partner Beilby, who was of a bookish turn of mind and who, with the aid of Dr. Smellie's *Abridgment of Buffon* and other histories, compiled the verbal descriptions. Bewick helped him with his own knowledge and personal observations in the cases of animals of our own country and was careful in "blotting out in his manuscript what was not truth." Most of the work for the *Quadrupeds* was done after the partners had closed their shop for the day. Bewick was sometimes entertained, while he engraved, by his friend the Rev. Richard Oliphant who was kind enough to read aloud the sermons which he had composed for the following Sunday. Such are the main facts concerning the *History of Quadrupeds*, a book which can easily be procured for about a guinea or a smaller sum. A plain, sober, unpretentious volume, it is delightful to handle and to read, as well as to rejoice in continually for the beauty of the engravings.

In 1789 Bewick engraved his best-known work, the *Chillingham Wild Bull*. It was one of a herd of wild Highland cattle of a type almost extinct, which was kept by a Yorkshire squire, Marmaduke Tunstall. Though celebrated as a technical triumph (as for its day it undoubtedly was) and in size only second to his last work, the *Waiting for Death*, there is little in the *Chillingham Bull* to interest us to-day. It is too rich in texture, deficient in colour and obvious in pattern. Whether Bewick himself negligently laid the block upon the window-sill (as his own silence suggests) or whether drunken pressmen were responsible (as his pupil Charlton Nesbit told Chatto) seems of little consequence to this writer; but it remains a fact that the block split through the heat before more than a few impressions had been pulled and it has given to these impressions a great fictitious value.

An old Newcastle friend of Bewick had settled in London where he was exercising his trade of printer to the admiration of all lovers of fine books. This man, William Bulmer, was determined to show what could be done at The Shakespeare Printing Office which he managed, to demonstrate what modern Printing, Type-founding, Engraving and Paper-making were capable of. He therefore called in the aid of John and Thomas Bewick to engrave designs for a quarto edition upon What-man paper of *Poems of Goldsmith and Parnell*. Thomas Bewick does not appear in these as an original designer, but he engraved all the thirteen

Bewick   *Swan Goose*

embellishments from drawings by Westall and Robert and John Johnson, his pupils. These designs, among them a large *Sad Historian* engraved from his own drawing by John Bewick, were considered triumphs of delicacy and refinement, and the delighted Bulmer hurried out another fine edition, this time of Somerville's *Chase* (1796). But in the meantime John Bewick had died. He was buried in Ovingham churchyard, leaving drawings for the edition of *The Chase*, which Thomas Bewick completed and engraved. *The Chase* is very much superior to its predecessor. The designs are in the vignette shape which was so well suited to the peculiar gifts of the artist, who in the earlier volume not only did not engrave from his own drawings but was obliged to work within a rectangular border. The designs are bigger in treatment than is customary in Bewick's work and there are more passages of undisturbed black. These and a certain glow and freshness of spirit point to the influence of the designer, as they are not to be found elsewhere in the works from the graver of the elder brother.

John Bewick left no monument to his talents more enduring than this. After serving a five-years' apprenticeship to his brother he came south to London where he executed many comparatively uninteresting children's books. His health necessitated several returns to his northern home, and consumption carried him off at the age of thirty-five. He had given some anxiety to his austere brother by his gayer mode of life. We understand that he sang and caroused and swaggered a little! It is idle to dilate upon his mediocre children's books or to wonder what he might have achieved had he lived much longer. It is given to few artists to leave behind them designs as admirable as *The Dawn* or *The Fox Hunt* in Somerville's *Chase*.

Bewick followed up the success of the *Quadrupeds* by the publication of the *History of British Birds* which absorbed his spare time for six years. The first volume, dealing with *Land Birds*, was published in 1797 and Beilby again contributed the written descriptions. The second volume, of *Water Birds*, followed in 1804, after Bewick had severed his connection with his former master and partner, and was written by Bewick himself. In these two famous volumes there is the same knowledge and sympathy resulting in consummate representations. As the birds were entirely British and therefore not derived to any extent from other drawings, there are none of the defects which were unavoidable when Bewick had to engrave animals he had never seen. The British Museum preserves many water-colour studies of birds from which these cuts were made, often by merely tracing them on the block. They are extraordinarily searching drawings and in the feeling for the main shapes, the intense realisation of all details of claws and beaks and plumage remind one of the occasional studies of this nature made by Dürer and other German masters of the Renaissance. There is knowledge behind every line of pencil or graver, and this knowledge is so well digested and borne so easily that it does not result in mere diagrams of markings or contours. The lines are swift and essentially vital, life-giving.

In the case of the commoner birds Bewick needed no models. His amazing memory was enough; but rarer specimens were studied at Wycliffe in the museum of Squire Tunstall, owner of the Chillingham herd. The wretchedness of taxidermy at that day is revealed in a letter written to Beilby from that place: "I can only pay attention to the beak and plumage—they are so distorted and unnaturely stuck up, that, as faithful representations of them as I can do, appear stiff as a poker." Bewick's admirers, however, helped him and all over the country birds were shot and sent off to him to be used as models. There is certainly room for wonder that he imparted so much life to his representations when we consider the circumstances under which they were made.

To every new edition Bewick added birds or vignettes or replaced old cuts by new, or plugged and re-engraved a portion which had been damaged in the press. Thus Hugo in his *Bewick Collector* observes that the blackbird has had his beak replaced six times. And as the blocks in the

main were not worn out despite the eight editions to which the books ran, it is wiser to get the later editions as these have the most pictures. The "life" of one of these blocks would be at least 900,000 good impressions. The engraver tells us this himself in his *Memoir*. On being

Bewick   *Vignette, "Windy Day"*

asked one day how many good prints could be taken from a block before it began to betray signs of wear, Bewick bethought him of a little cut he had done for a local newspaper. By calculating the number of times that paper had appeared bearing the cut and the number of each edition, he was able to state that after 900,000 impressions the block was none the worse for wear.

How that country round Newcastle looked in Bewick's time and what manner of folk tramped or drove along those roads we can see very clearly in these hundreds of vignettes and in the backgrounds to bird and beast, and we know that all this must be true. As his daughters used to say, he went out and saw things, and came back and drew them. Those weekly walks of his to Cherryburn were not spent merely in revolving schemes for self-advancement, but must have greatly enriched his knowledge of natural things. No artist ever knew the face of nature more certainly, for he had studied and reverenced natural objects during all the rich seed-time of his boyhood. The Newcastle of his apprenticeship was not the great squalid spreading place we know, but a trim old-fashioned town pleasantly diapered with gardens, where crows came yearly to nest on the weather-vane of the Exchange, and beyond the mediaeval walls the pleasant common began at once, where townsfolk grazed their cattle and whence the cries of the corncrake were audible.

Few of his vignettes are merely decorative. Wherever it is possible he packs them with literary significance. He preaches a lot, for there is much of the Hogarthian in Bewick, and he can give you a *Rake's Progress* or an *Idle Prentice* in a nutshell. But in the main he is a detailed, keen, unsympathetic observer of life. One suspects that the sound virile intelligence is turned a little sour, that he cannot suffer fools gladly, that these mischievous, often malicious and even indecent vignettes are revenges upon the dullness of a workaday world. We are told that the vignettes gave him more pleasure than any other work, and they are in our opinion his most remarkable achievement. Within the limits of his

Bewick

Vignette, "The Blind Man"

own experience, from which alone he derived, his fancy and ingenuity are inexhaustible. He would sit for an evening in his domestic circle with the glass in his eye elaborating a tiny block with the graver in his great blacksmith's hand. When he lay dying someone asked of what he was thinking. Smiling, the old man replied "that he had been devising subjects for some new tailpieces."

Things are generally going badly for the inhabitants of this vignette world and the old and infirm are particularly the victims of circumstances. Poor withered old crones hobble about like witches, half-mad and pitilessly tormented by geese or curs or unfeeling urchins. If they make to cross a stile a bull looks menacingly over, or men drive a mad dog round the corner into their arms, or curs steal their meals reckless of brandished toast-bracket. Nor is there any mercy for the blind. Careless urchins lead them about, heedless of warning signs, or the wind removes their hats while the rain is pelting down, or they are led vainly fiddling with only a dog for audience. Old men are buffeted by winds which whisk away their hats, while they dare not dismount from their Rosinantes for fear of displacing eggs and ducks and other impedimenta. They are usually engaged in pointing out the monuments of very famous victories to the little Peterkins of the North Country, or reading "Vanitas Vanitatum" upon a gravestone or moralising in the storm about the prodigality of youth. Disgusting fellows over-eat or over-drink in cellars, vomit, perform physical necessities, hang cats or dogs, or lie thrumming drunkenly under a hedge upon the king's birthday. A hulking artisan watches boys tormenting a dog by the can-and-tail torture. Brutal fellows thump their over-laden and broken-kneed jades and in the background (to point the moral and reveal their end) you can discern the gallows. Disappointed beggars go off leaving the gate open, and into the neat garden stream hen and cock and pigling and last of all the great sow to befoul the washing on the lawn. A sheep caught in a thicket is stripped of half its fleece; a dog is left

Bewick   *Headpiece to Introduction, the " Land Birds"*

lying with legs tied together. Human footsteps lead away from it in the mire and already the corbies are gathered round. The same kind of grim suggestion finds its way into the backgrounds of the birds and quadrupeds. The spruce magpie is waiting to make its dinner of the old horse left to die in the background. The red-legged partridge will take another step and dogs will raise it for the gun. Away in the grey of the vignettes little death-dealing sportsmen move about. In the famous tailpiece of hare-hunting in the snow you are made aware of the chill by the way the tiny figure carries his gun under his coat to avoid the burning cold of the barrel. To shooting and angling, however, a score or two of delightful designs are dedicated which are comparatively free from the ironic comment so often made in these vignettes.

In these epitomes of his world Bewick has not forgotten the old soldiers who delighted his youth, the battered veterans so full of camaraderie over their ale, so full of tales of Minden and Lord George Sackville, and how in that general's absence "they shook hands the whole length of the line, vowing to stand by each other without flinching." In his vignettes we see them tramping the weary moors in the sleet, or stumping over stiles, or greeting old comrades with glee, and the old red coat which was riddled by French shot at Minden and other fields is hung at last upon a "tattie-bogle" and is less potent to scare crows than it was in its prime to scare Frenchmen.

For an illustration of the compendiousness of these engravings and of Bewick's power of concentrating a world of fact and suggestion into a space little larger than a postage stamp we need only look at the head-piece to the Introduction of the *Land Birds*. Let Chatto describe it for us: "Everything is true to Nature; the birds assembled near the woman seen winnowing corn, are, though on a small scale, represented with the greatest fidelity; even among the smallest the wagtail can be distinguished from the sparrow. The dog, feeling no interest in the business, is seen quietly resting on the dunghill; but the chuckling of the hens, announcing that something like eating is going forward, has evidently excited the attention of the old sow, and brought her and her litter into the yard in the expectation of getting a share. The season, the latter end of Autumn, is indicated by the flight of fieldfares and the comparatively naked appearance of the trees; and we perceive that it is a clear bright day from the strong shadow of the ladder projected against the wall, and on the thatched wall of the outhouse, a heron, a crow and a magpie are perceived nailed against the gable end of the barn; and a couple of pigeons are seen flying above the house. The cut forms at once an interesting picture of country life and a graphic summary of the contents of the work."

The twenty years that remained to Bewick between the publication of the *Birds* and his death were not remarkable for any new development or achievement comparable to that of his middle age. Doubtless he was busy all the time doing what was demanded of him in what we call the commercial line, in that trim and well-swept workshop in Newcastle. The one work of importance that he was to produce was hindered by occasional ill-health. This was the final *Æsop's Fables* of 1818. We will spare our readers the tedium of a bibliographical account of this edition or of those which had preceded it, namely the *Gay's Fables* of 1779 and 1788 and the *Select Fables* of 1776 and 1784. None of these works is of sufficient artistic value to warrant our dwelling at length upon the subject. The designs for the 1818 *Æsop* are similar in shape to those of the preceding editions, in every case, that is to say, an oval containing the illustration is enclosed within a rectangular decorated frame. In few, if any, cases are they engraved by Bewick who contented himself with drawings upon the blocks which were cut by his accomplished apprentices Temple and Nesbit and by Robert Bewick, his only son. These designs are richer and fuller developments of those of his early versions, which were based upon the woodcuts, or "cuts upon metal in the manner of wood" (as Bewick declares them), from that very popular book *Croxall's Fables*, and these in turn were copied (and thereby reversed) from the line-engravings of Sebastien Le Clerc, whose *Æsop* was published in 1694. The *Fables* of 1818 disappointed the admirers of the artist who had expected wonders from the author of the *Quadrupeds* and *Birds*, and, indeed, if the cuts are richer and more elaborated, they are much less spirited than those in the aforesaid volumes. Bewick was in the later sixties when they were done, but that is no explanation of the sugariness of the textures: every space is broken up into charming but essentially otiose and insignificant detail, and the lines are comparatively flaccid and spiritless. In the tailpieces there are joyful "magots" still, but too much preaching, while the habit of engraving moral tags gets irritating. Bewick's Olympians, however, his Apollos, Jupiters and the like, are delightful because they so persistently refuse to be classical. Something genuine and clownish is mixed with the ichor of them so that they remind us of the delightfully "Gothic" Olympians of the mediaeval artists and poets, of Chaucer's "Dan Phoebus and his Cart."

We know a great deal about Bewick, for he became famous in his own lifetime and people of his own town or who visited him on their way through Newcastle thought him a man whose words and appearance were worth perpetuating in writing. Of these, Audubon's description of a few days spent with Bewick in 1827, the year before his death, is perhaps the most illuminating. With this and other pen-pictures, the anecdotes told by his daughters and the numerous portraits and busts, we can create a tolerable likeness of the old man. He had been "bonny" as a boy, but he was a hard-featured man, with a prominent nose and eyes placed unusually far apart. He was pock-marked, had prominent veins on the temples, tufts of hair in his ears, and constant "chewing" had produced a prominence under the lower lip behind which he used to lodge the quid. In stature he was six feet tall and sturdily built, and his careful rules for diet and exercise kept him in perfect vigour and health. As he was bald and did not wear a wig, he protected that part with a "smoke-grimed cotton night-cap." His mind was powerful and keen and he loved to ventilate his opinions. In old age he became garrulous and when he came to write the *Memoir* these opinions, slowly formed, tenaciously

Bewick   *Vignette for Somerville's "Chase"*

held, and already fully clothed in words by constant conversation, over-flowed into his pages. These streams of didacticism, of moral disquisition, sturdy animadversions upon war and Mr. Pitt and the "shape-destroying dresses" of young women, or exhortations to the young men to seek for sound qualities in a wife, to choose her at least as carefully as one might do a horse or a dog, or to women to give up frivolities and turn to horti-culture—all these outpourings we must be prepared to wade through in order to understand the man, and must be traversed in our journey between the idyllic passages and those brief and consequently precious pages in which the craftsman discusses his craft. We hear a lot of his niggardliness and he was undoubtedly keen with money, but he had to be keen for the work was wretchedly paid. Bewick got nine shillings each for the blocks of his *Select Fables*. His brother John for facsimile engravings of the Holbein *Dance of Death* got only six shillings a block. In spite of this, by his industry and talent, he was able to leave a fortune of £2000 to his spinster daughters. There can be little doubt that he amassed this sum by industry accompanied by a lifetime of frugality. He had at various times sixteen apprentices who became the most brilliant engravers of their generation and he must have profited very much from their talents. But the benefits were mutual. He seems to have been more just than liberal in his treatment of some of them, but there was never any question of their respect and admiration of their master. In an age that worshipped Bacchus he drank water, in a town of good fellows he was only once known to sing, and he never smiled. Like Franklin, whom he resembles remarkably in the broad outlines of his character, he became the leading spirit of a club of respectable townsfolk with philosophical tastes, where every member paid fourpence an evening and that sum covered the expenditure on drink. He had all the domestic virtues. So attached was he to his parents that he resolved never to marry in their lifetime and kept his word. A man of such economy and mental stability was not likely to make a failure of matrimony when the time came. Bewick would see no "Helen's beauty in a brow of Egypt." He chose his wife, we presume, as he chose his boxwood, with an eye to present soundness and capacity for standing time and wear. He was a doting father and his children cherished his memory fondly. There is a letter of his in which he describes how he loved to work "at my happy fireside surrounded by my wife and girls at work and cheered at intervals by many a wild tune on the Northumberland pipes."

The woodcuts of the chapbooks and broadsheets were well known to Bewick as a boy. "The house at Ovingham, where our dinner poke was taken care of when at school, was hung round with views or representations of the battles of Zorndoff, and several others; also the portraits of Tom Brown the valiant Grenadier, of Admiral Haddock, Admiral Benbow . . . Captain Coram" (whom Hogarth painted)—and the like. "In cottages everywhere were to be seen the *Sailor's Farewell* and his *Happy Return*, *Youthful Sports*, and the *Feats of Manhood*, *The Bold Archers shooting at a Mark*, *The Four Seasons*," etc. These have gone out of fashion, Bewick says, which is a pity, "as whatever can serve to instil morality and patriotism into the minds of"—and so on. At any rate Bewick was determined to produce a picture of an edifying nature to be multiplied and sold at low prices for the cottage. He had, moreover, seen the colour-prints, each made from several blocks by John Baptist

Jackson, and was minded to try the experiment of printing two or more blocks severally for the production of one print "so that a greater and more natural effect—as to colour and softness—may be produced." He essayed this in his last days but did not live to complete even the first or main block. This is already so elaborated that it is difficult to see how much more he could have done to it by cross-printings. The subject is an old horse waiting for death in a bleak northern landscape realised with all Bewick's verisimilitude. This, his largest block, was to have been dedicated to the Society for the Prevention of Cruelty to Animals, and was accompanied by a lengthy verbal description of Man's inhumanity to animals that give their lives to his service.

Only a few impressions had been pulled from the first block of *Waiting for Death* when the artist himself was arrested by that fell sergeant. Thomas Bewick was laid to his last rest by the side of his brother John in Ovingham churchyard in November 1828—good times and bad times and all times got over, as he had commented upon the tombstone of a characteristic tailpiece. He died babbling of the green fields of Cherryburn, his birthplace and the beloved playground of his childhood.

REPRODUCTIVE ENGRAVING OF
LAST CENTURY

THE achievements of Bewick triumphantly demonstrated the possibilities of Wood-Engraving as a means of illustrating books. Not only was it a cheaper method of illustration than Copperplate Engraving but in the hands of Bewick and his pupils it was seen to be almost as elegant and delicate. From this time an enormous impetus is given to the development of the art. We have seen how low Woodcutting had declined all over Europe. So obscure were the exponents of the art in 1776, the year of Papillon's death and when Bewick was already twenty-three years of age, that in the Parisian *Almanach des Artistes* for that year Courboin finds only five names of woodcutters, and of these, three specialised in lettering. Equally significant of the humble status of the art at that time is the offer of Papillon to sell fine proofs of no fewer than 5000 of his cuts for two louis d'or. But with the attention drawn to Wood-Engraving by the books of the Newcastle master things developed rapidly. Collectors soon began to scramble for fine proofs of Bewick's works and Hugo was not the only enthusiast who devoted a lifetime to the collection of his engravings.

Bewick's pupils proved themselves worthy of their master. Robert Johnson, William Harvey, Charlton Nesbit and Luke Clennel were all accomplished engravers and draughtsmen of no mean quality. Coming south to the metropolis these men, with John Thompson and John Branston who were already resident there, raised the prestige of the art very high in the first half of the nineteenth century. In the histories of Jackson and Linton, themselves professional engravers, these men are upheld as the highest ornaments of their profession. With the knowledge born of years of experience Linton and Jackson discuss minutely the methods of Nesbit for representing flesh or of Branston for foliage, indicating their achievements to the young engraver as the *ne plus ultra* of perfection.

The Newcastle men carried on the white-line tradition of Bewick, but Branston, a self-taught engraver and no draughtsman, was more dependent upon others for preparing drawings for reproduction and was influenced by the black line of the copperplate. A fashionable illustrator and line-engraver of the day, John Thurston, was much employed by them in making drawings upon the block. Thurston was very highly feed for his help, but, as he was a line-engraver, the wood-engravings after his drawings tended to a large extent to resemble the rival method. A sense of inferiority to the copperplate has all along dogged Wood-Engraving banefully and rendered it false to its own genius.

William Harvey having served his apprenticeship with Bewick came down to London and studied drawing under Haydon. During that time he spent two years upon an engraving after Haydon's historical painting, *Dentatus*. Rightly acclaimed by the older writers as a masterpiece of engraving, full of resource and variety of line, the *Dentatus* is almost painful to us who can only think of such enormous labour and skill misdirected in the effort to make Wood-Engraving yield the qualities peculiar to the copperplate. Bewick, it may be remembered, disliked and avoided cross-hatching except of white lines, but Harvey in this work first of all laid in his lines with a pen in the manner of a copperplate, and then, with infinite labour, picked out the interstices between them. The same effect could have been got with infinitely less trouble by arrangements of positive white lines.

Clennel, Nesbit, Branston, and others were the engravers of a book called for the sake of convenience *Ackermann's Emblems* (1809). Thurston supplied drawings in a sweet academic manner without any real intensity; but so charmingly did the engravers do their work that this is one of the most notable books of the century. To carry the craft of Wood-Engraving farther than was done in *Ackermann's Emblems* was to lose all boldness and clarity of line and to sacrifice form for colour and trivial detail. This, however, was done by the next generation, with such results as we shall see.

The following passage from Jackson's *Pictorial Press* (cited by Gleeson White) throws a very pleasant and interesting light upon the condition of Wood-Engraving about the year 1825. "Illustration was so seldom used" (says Jackson) "that the preparation of even a small woodcut was of much interest to all concerned. I have heard William Harvey relate that when Whittingham, the well-known printer, wanted a new cut for his Chiswick Press Series, he would write to Harvey and John Thompson, the engraver, appointing a meeting at Chiswick, when printer,

Millais   *The Prodigal Son. Engraved in facsimile by the Dalziels*

designer and engraver talked over the matter with as much deliberation as if about to produce a costly national monument. And, after they had settled all points over a snug supper, the result of their labours was the production a month afterwards of a woodcut measuring perhaps two inches by three. At that time perhaps only a dozen persons besides Bewick were practising the art of Wood-Engraving in England."

At the risk of constant repetition it cannot be too strongly stressed that the engravers of last century were for all the world mere "Formschneider," only their equipment was vastly fuller. They copied pen-drawings in facsimile, and what little chance for brain-work or originality entered, was where they had to translate washes or tints into the hard uncompromising medium of line and to choose their own linear arrangements to match a tone. As the century wore on the demand for wood-engravings grew greater and greater. Not only the illustrations in books but those in periodicals like *Punch* or *The Illustrated London News* were cut upon wood. Considering the shortness of the time at their disposal and the inconsiderate treatment meted out to them by publishers and artists alike, it is wonderful how successfully they performed their tasks. Herbert Furst in his book on *The Modern Woodcut* says that the artists were continually protesting against the "mutilation" of their drawings by the engravers. There is some evidence for the statement, and Rossetti certainly wrote a letter to W. B. Scott which contains the following passage: "I have designed five blocks for the Tennyson, some of which are still cutting and maiming. After a fortnight's work my block goes to the Engraver, like Agag delicately, and is hewn to pieces before the Lord Harry.

ADDRESS TO THE DALZIEL BROTHERS

O woodman spare that block
O gash not anyhow
It took ten days by clock
I'd fain protect it now.

Chorus: Wild laughter from Dalziel's workshop."

But Rossetti's effusion is more amusing than reliable. Rossetti liked writing such things.[1] Besides these same "woodmen," the Dalziels, in the *Record* of their life-work published in 1901, reproduce two autograph letters from the artist expressing himself as highly delighted with the execution of these very blocks. And not only Rossetti but dozens of artists the most famous in their day, Leighton, Millais, Tenniel, Walker, Gilbert, Pinwell, Sandys and others, submitted their designs to the care of the Dalziels and were completely satisfied with the result.

[1] For a discussion of the whole matter, see Gleeson White's *English Illustration ; the Sixties*, p. 158. Rossetti was too difficult to please and did not understand the nature of Wood-Engraving. As Gleeson White says, "no craftsman who ever lived would have been absolutely successful." Rossetti later found in Linton a more sympathetic translator of his elaborate drawings which were full of subtleties of touch almost impossible to retain in an engraving.

There is no lack of good critics to contend that the work of the above-mentioned artists makes that period of the last century roughly called the "'sixties" the greatest period of English book-illustration. There was Sir John Tenniel, for example (for whom the Dalziels and Swain laboured), who made with Lewis Carroll a happy combination which occurs only once in a generation. What Phiz did for Dickens, Cruikshank for Harrison Ainsworth, and Leech for Surtees, so did Tenniel for the creator of Alice. Marriage of author and illustrator made without a doubt on Parnassus! Only Mr. Shepherd and Mr. Milne have been so happily joined in our own time. Then there was the great project of the Dalziels for the illustration of the Bible, which was a financial failure but which contained nine remarkable drawings by Leighton, and many by Madox Brown, Holman-Hunt, Poynter and others, full of distinction and thoroughness. Millais and Sandys were never so happy as when designing for book-illustration, and Pinwell and Arthur Boyd Houghton, if not quite in the same class, brought great knowledge and feeling and imagination to bear upon all their illustrations. Rossetti, Burne-Jones and Arthur Hughes all contributed to raise the standard of periodical illustration to a height of seriousness and distinction which has never been equalled since. And in these works there is no doubt that the medium plays a considerable part. It would be absurd to claim that the engravers "improved" in their facsimiles the drawings of these artists; but it is surely significant that with the advent of photographic methods of reproduction the state of book-illustration and especially of magazine-illustration has become absolutely tragic.

During this time the most resounding name in the history of French Wood-Engraving is that of Gustave Doré. Of the dozen and more engravers who were kept in constant employ by this fervent artist the Pannemakers and Pisan are the most notable names. In his prodigious career Doré illustrated 119 books and refrained from no subject sacred or profane. To universal applause he set to work on the Bible, Milton, Dante, Cervantes, Chateaubriand, Ariosto, Rabelais, La Fontaine, Münchhausen, and even planned an attack on the works of Shakespeare. This writer has had no wearier experience than a fortnight in a Moray-shire manse where the rain poured unceasingly outside and the only books were Commentaries on the Bible and two great volumes of a *Gallery* of Doré illustrations. Doré in his sublime vein is more than dull, he is even painful, and he considered the sublime his fittest vein. But the Doré who illustrated with fiery and grotesque pen-scribbles the hearty animalism of Rabelais and the rollicking sensualities of the *Contes Drôlatiques* of Balzac is a less known but really brilliant man. But of course the *Galleries* that our fathers loved contained little of the vital and Rabelaisian and no end of the frigid and pretentious type of his work. Mr. E. J. Sullivan in his *Art of Illustration* points out an amusing instance of the servility of Doré's engravers. In a headpiece to a story of Balzac the overworked artist, tired of putting in all the windows in a vast building he had drawn, contented himself with scribbling "etc.," meaning the engraver to complete the fenestration himself before engraving. But that plodding fellow without a thought engraved the block just as he found it, so that in the impression you find the "etc." reversed and no additional windows.

Doré's rival in Germany and a much more important artist was Adolf von Menzel, whose great set of illustrations to Kugler's *History of Frederick the Great* was wonderfully reproduced by the graver [1] of Unzelmann. Menzel had no quarter for his engravers. Every scribble had to be translated with complete self-effacement by the executant. Neither Menzel nor Doré had any sense at all of the decorative illustration of books, but in that, of course, they were the children of their age.

The full-page drawings in weekly papers like *The Graphic* or *The Illustrated London News* were reproduced in this manner: A large block was prepared by the amalgamation of many pieces of boxwood riveted carefully together. The artist then spread the thinnest film of white paint over the surface in order to get a crisp ground on which to make his pencil or pen or washed drawing. The drawing being complete, the block was sent to the workshop of the engraver where it was broken up into its component parts, and skilled men set to work each upon a section. If one man made a speciality of lining-in skies, to him any portion containing sky was entrusted. If another were expert at faces or a third at trees, to them would be given such parts to engrave. Almost certainly they would be rushed for time. Breathlessness has ever been the normal condition of editors and publishers. If this were especially the case, then each engraver would take home his section in his pocket and sit up during the night until it was complete. Upon the next morning all the parts would be assembled, fitted together and bolted up. Then the master engraver himself would take a fine tool and go over those parts where

[1] According to Mr. Dodgson, Unzelmann used a knife in his reproductions of Menzel's drawings! (Note in the *Catalogue of Early German and Flemish Woodcuts in the British Museum*.)

were the junctions of the blocks, smoothing off the work, running one line sweetly into another, until all evidence of the junctions was removed. And so to press.

In this way the British public week by week received its cartoons in *Punch* or its pictures of Derbies or Crimean battlefields in *The Illustrated London News*. The procedure was like this until the close of the century, although sometimes printers preferred to print from electrotype casts of the blocks rather than from the originals themselves, wood-blocks being easily damaged in the great machine-presses of recent times. Up to his death in 1901 Tenniel had all his *Punch* cartoons reproduced by the prolific engraver Joseph Swain or his employees. Apprentices served long and arduous apprenticeships in cutting tints by the means of parallel lines of varied thickness or distance from each other. They had to win their spurs in training of this mechanical sort before they were promoted to the reproduction of more "artistic" work. They worked at high tables so that stooping might be avoided, looking at the block through a magnifying-glass. At night the light was focussed upon the block through a globe of coloured water set up in front of the gas-lamp. Elaborate precautions of all sorts were taken to facilitate the arduous task. Papillon even tells you how to dispose of the belly while at work. In order to protect the original drawing from the moisture of the breath, engravers sometimes wore mouth-shades as well as the customary eye-shades. Or they covered up all but a small piece of the block with paper. In this way they must often have been uncertain what the exposed corner represented (whether sky, tree, rock or flesh) and their work consequently more than usually mechanical and deadening. They were for the most part men with little or no interest in art who probably never made drawings for pleasure. In the handbook on the practice of Engraving by Thomas Gilks (1866) you can read (under the heading "Importance of being able to Draw"): "The learner is now sitting at the table holding a block; which must have the required subject drawn upon it; *and here we must be permitted to say that the learner will find his advance in the Art much facilitated if he can draw.* Of course at the present day any kind of drawing may be made for the student better than he could do it for himself, but that is not the point; he that can draw"—and so on. The blandness and pathetic obsequiousness of the worthy Gilks and his sort are simply amazing. But they had a sort of pride, too, in their self-effacement. The Dalziels, who complain of the difficulties of the craft, of the ignorance shown by the artist of the capabilities of the material, and the lack of time in which to perform the task proudly, conclude that it was "a marvel that so much beautiful artistic work was done under such conditions."

One of the most distinguished wood-engravers of the latter part of the century was William James Linton, a man of considerable culture and great skill in his profession. Linton has left three books on the history and practice of Engraving in which the reader is brought into contact with a most independent and lofty mind gravely discoursing about what it thinks is Art and Beauty. Anybody who desires to re-create for himself the outlook of a representative Victorian upon a very important branch of Victorian Art can do no better than read Linton. One cannot help admiring the old man. He is so thorough, so sincere, so solemn, so monumental. But it is clear that this vast intelligence is exercising itself in the narrowest possible groove. Technique in general, and in particular a certain kind of white-line technique, seen at its highest in the pupils of Bewick, is Linton's cultus. Of the æsthetic of line, though he be eloquent for pages upon it, he seems to have had no clear grasp, and of the beauty of design *per se* he had no thought whatsoever. The elaborate reproduction of insipid and merely pretty pictures by inferior artists of Victoria's age, such was the vocation of this distinguished man—poet and historian, as well as engraver.

The later years of Linton were spent in America and he has left a book on the history of Engraving in that country where with the close of the century technique developed into an extraordinarily complicated system. Paintings and wash-drawings were photographed upon the sensitised surface of the wood-block, and engravers proceeded to turn them into the most unobtrusive linear arrangements conceivable. Self-abnegation was the main characteristic of the skilled engraver. The better the craftsman, the more subtle the arrangements whereby he concealed his personality and devoted himself to the most slavish reproductions of carelessly swept-in passages by young brushmen under the influence of Impressionistic painting. Their great dread was lest *their* art should not be concealed behind the painter's art, lest someone should see in a corner an evidence of the means employed. Even Linton is indignant at their servility and rightly claims that since Engraving is an independent art and withal an intellectual art aiming at the representation of forms by the means of line, then to neglect the forms at the expense of colour and moreover not to insist on the complete realisation of forms, because the painter has neglected them, is to be untrue to the Art of Engraving. Theoretically Linton was right. Engraving is primarily occupied with form, and colour is a secondary consideration. But if the editor of *Harper's* or some other magazine presented an engraver with a Corot landscape photographed on his block, what was the poor devil to do? To turn Corot's fleecy trees, his edges, with their lost-and-found quality, into hard matter-of-fact lines might have been true to his medium, but would certainly have been false to Corot. What the engravers actually *did* in such predicaments is made clear by looking at the pages of *Scribner's* or *Harper's* or other such magazines of the "'eighties" of the last century. With astonishing science they hit every tone in a painting, matched every gradation of colour with a system of lines or ticks. The result was something remarkably true to Corot or whoever they were reproducing, but so lacking in any real feeling for line that they simply cannot be seriously considered as engravings. They died, as it were, in their own too-much. But there was no end to this imbecile self-abnegation. They strained their medium to such an extent that you can find reproductions of the impasto of a fat oil-painting and even of the tiny shadows cast by prominent daubs of pigment.

But after them The Deluge. New photographic processes were introduced which made reproduction cheaper and absolutely faithful by infallible means. The brothers Dalziel, who for half a century were the most influential and prolific of English engravers, acknowledge this resignedly in the *Record* of their life-work. "When we look at the reproductions of tint drawings by the half-tone process, and when we think of the vast mass of wonderful illustration given to the public, week by week, of every conceivable class of subject, direct from the camera, in which the draughtsman has no part at all, and this work is generally of singular beauty and truth—we feel that our occupation is gone. In saying this" (continue the Dalziels) "we wish to add that we hail with satisfaction the marvellous results from these many ingenious adaptations of photography, and the consequent wide spread of the Art of Illustration, which has ever been our greatest delight."

BLAKE AND THE MODERN ENGLISH WOOD-ENGRAVERS

ALTHOUGH the isolation of William Blake from the main current of art in his day has been greatly exaggerated, there is no doubt that his appeal has been almost entirely posthumous. Of course the influence that he exerted upon a group of young men with whom he came in immediate contact was profound and educive of some remarkable work; but he made no broad impression upon the character of English art until our own time. It is therefore with the "moderns" that his work must be studied even in a history of Wood-Engraving, for it is by the artists of to-day that his appeal is felt at its fullest. The whole tendency of the art of the nineteenth century was towards fidelity to nature, at its extreme towards a scientific or photographic fidelity to nature, and to William Blake there was no real world but that apprehended by Vision.

Blake   From Thornton's "Eclogues of Virgil"

Born in 1757 and living until the age of seventy, the period of his life almost exactly coincides with that of Thomas Bewick, who is as eminently representative of the tendencies of his age as Blake is not. Surely a greater dissimilarity never existed between two artists than that between the sturdy countryman with his clear, robust, prosaic outlook upon Art and Life, and the neurotic inhabitant of the garret in Bolt Court with his Visions and his Prophecies and his belief in "Imagination the real and eternal world of which this Vegetable Universe is but a faint shadow." Bewick can only represent what his bodily eye has seen, Blake can only represent what has been revealed to him in vision. The one owes everything to his impassioned study of natural objects. The other complains that "Nature put him out." Bewick achieved fame at once and began a tradition which with modifications survived for a century. Blake, already very near his end, finds a little group of personal disciples, but has to wait until our own time before he becomes an inspiration and a model to artists.

So much has been written of late years about the wood-engravings of Blake to Dr. Thornton's edition of *Virgil's Eclogues* that only the exigencies of this history can compel us to add to the sum. The *Eclogues* appeared in 1821 with thirteen small oblong cuts by Blake, all of which illustrated Ambrose Philips' imitation of the First Eclogue of the Mantuan. These designs of extreme beauty and pastoral charm are engraved with great spirit but little attention to qualities of line or "finish." White line

Blake   *From Thornton's "Eclogues of Virgil"*

is used upon the black ground as though the artist had drawn the whole with his graver right off while the inspiration endured, without any preliminary pencilling, "lowering" and the like. Strong and ecstatic little figures, great suns and moons brooding over the low hills, and influencing the flow of broad streams that spread between fields, where sheep browse in regular rows, and great trees turn under their eave-like burdens of leaves—such are the features of these inspired cuts which made so immediate and lasting an appeal upon two young men. Contemporary engravers could not see beyond the crudity and child-like carelessness of the execution; but to Edward Calvert and Samuel Palmer the vision at the core was at once revealed. They met the old man in 1824, three years before his death, when he was living in a garret engraving the peerless set of plates for *The Book of Job* for the sum of one pound and fivepence a week. They had desired to meet the engraver of the cuts in Thornton's *Virgil* and they found him (as Mr. Binyon says) "at once a prophet and a creator—a kind of Michelangelo or Isaiah." To these fervent young men the tiny cuts were a revelation and a spiritual maieutic, and, in the few, too short years which they spent under his immediate inspiration both produced by far their best work.

The profound influence which Blake exerted upon Palmer, the younger of the two friends, was not, however, manifested to the same extent in

Wood-Engraving. We have seen only one design by Palmer which he engraved himself upon the block, and in this the model is manifest. It is a tiny thing but very lovely, and shows reapers at work upon a harvest, a deep clump of trees, a sickle moon and the "primitive cottage" which these brethren so loved and which appears first in Blake's designs for Thornton's *Eclogues*.

But contact with Blake and the inspiration of his designs caused Edward Calvert to turn at once to the wood-block to engrave prints of

Edward Calvert

The Cyder Feast

unparalleled beauty. Calvert had been a sailor until the age of twenty-five, but he had early felt a passion for the poetical and spiritual qualities inherent in nature which has something in common with the pantheism of Rousseau and of Wordsworth, but in Calvert is coloured by his love of the Idylls of Theocritus and Virgil, and a sentimental longing for bygone Arcadianism, hazy as were the golden washes of colour scrumbled over his later paintings. Blake's love of the pastoral, like that of Theocritus or Milton, the love of the townsman for the country, which he does not understand, was the side of his art which appealed profoundly to Calvert, and inspired the seven engravings upon wood and two upon copper which (with two tiny lithographs) were all that he made. From the very first he is master of his material, and, without the years of experience in the handling of the graver that Blake had, he easily excels his model in the technique of Wood-Engraving. Unless, of course, we take for granted many preliminary efforts upon the block, for which we have no evidence, the immediate maturity of Calvert will always remain a source of wonder. As in all fine Engraving, not only is the thing expressed beautiful but the means of expression are beautiful in their directness, clarity and eloquence. "With nothing am I more impressed" (writes the artist) "than with the necessity in all great work of suppressing the workman and all the mean dexterity of practice. The result in itself, in quiet dignity, is the only worthy attainment. Wood-Engraving of all things most ready for dexterity reads us a good lesson."

In the engraving of *The Ploughman*, the figure of the man at the hilts and of the angel descending to slay the serpent are quite definitely Blakean in type; but the forms of trees and vines, and corn, and furrows are sought out and realised with a completeness unparalleled in any of the other's designs. The great beauty of the forms, the swinging rhythm of the lines and the dark suggestiveness of the forest could not fail to appeal even to those who are indifferent to the symbolism with which it is charged.

The Cyder Feast is more straightforwardly pastoral, with no mystical significance, and unbounded gaiety and movement. The engraving is comparatively broad, but careful and undoubtedly worked out from drawings, for Calvert does not attack the block right off with the graver as Blake seems to have done. All his work is studiously wrought, and yet full of vigour, witness the leaping figures in the foreground of *The Cyder Feast* and those in the distance pirouetting against the enormous disk of the moon which might well have been the badge or emblem of these friends, and seems to have exerted such a fascination over them as it did over their contemporary, Keats.

In *The Chamber Idyll* Calvert might well seem to be competing with the professional wood-engravers of the day and to have carried off the prize, so sweetly and delicately is it wrought. Clennel and Nesbit might well have envied the obscure amateur his knowledge of all the possibilities of white line and his tact in the variety of textures. The tiny figures of the lovers have been engraved with spots rather than with lines. They are disrobing to climb into bed under the broad-beamed ceiling of a herdsman's cottage. It is night, and the stars illumine the fields without, revealing sheep-cote and flock, cattle and darkly-gleaming trees. It is the most exquisite wood-engraving that we have ever seen.

Even had Calvert done many more wood-engravings it is unlikely that he would have excelled these three. This note of the purest poetry latent within him was suddenly sounded by contact with the genius of Bolt Court. The rest of his career as an artist is a feeble anti-climax. He painted dozens of idyllic landscapes peopled with misty, golden Arcadians without ever again realising his conceptions as he had done with such startling completeness in these few engravings.

Burne-Jones   *From the Kelmscott "Chaucer" (Hammersmith, 1896. 6¼″ × 4¾″)*

Calvert's few prints were forgotten until in 1891 Sir Sidney Colvin exhibited them at the British Museum. Blake as a wood-engraver was remembered, but (if understood by men like Rossetti) was more an inspiration than a model until our own times. But the "Modern Woodcut," which owes so much of its qualities of freedom and directness to Blake, did not arrive at its present state until after a gradual development from the Reproductive Engraving which it has succeeded.

The Exhibition of Modern Wood-Engravings held in 1895 by the Vale Press Group marks the beginning of a new era. These artists, Charles

Ricketts, Charles Shannon, Sturge Moore, Reginald Savage and Lucien Pissarro, were alike in deploring the "artistic" engraving of the time and saw in all that elaboration and tonal work only suffocation and death. But their own work, "original" as it was and engraved by the designers themselves, was very unlike the prints of Blake and Calvert. In fact it was little more than facsimiles of pen-drawings with this

Burne-Jones   *From the Kelmscott "Chaucer" (Hammersmith, 1896. 6¼" × 4¾")*

novelty, that the designers did their own reproduction. Their engravings, in fact, form a transition between the reproductive work of the professionals and that of artists of this generation. In the same way Lepère in Paris may be considered as a Transitional engraver. He stood on Mount Pisgah and saw the promised land but he did not enter himself.

The greatest figure of this Transitional stage was undoubtedly William Morris. It is said of this man of tremendous energy that, even when he was a boy at Marlborough, his fingers were so restless that he had to make nets to employ them. To William Morris with his passionate love for mediaeval things the artistic crafts of his own time were rotten to the core with commercialism and required to be thrown away, and replaced with all that could be excited of that old-time joy and song and communal vigour which (he believed) had always accompanied the making of the artistic monuments of the Middle Age. It is therefore strange, considering the state of the Art of the Book at that time, that it was only at the end of his life that Morris turned his craftsman's instinct and his great knowledge of calligraphy and early printed books to bear upon the problem of Modern Book-Production. We are not here concerned with the history of the Kelmscott Press, nor of how Morris and his friends brought out in a few years books the most gorgeous seen since the decline of Venetian printing. But it concerns us to realise that his bias as a printer was all towards black letter, for upon this depended the nature of the woodcuts with which his books were adorned. He was obliged to design decorations suitable for the massive character of the two-columned page which he used in that incomparable gothic folio, the Kelmscott *Chaucer*, published at Hammersmith in 1896. In addition to deep borders of floral design and initials cut from the drawings of Morris, the *Chaucer* contains a wonderful series of illustrations by Burne-Jones. The treatment of these is derived to a great extent from the black-line cuts of Venetian *incunabula*. The lines are strong and open and the treatment frankly decorative. The figures are lank and anæmic as all Burne-Jones's figures are, but the rocks and seas, the gardens, interiors, etc., are designed in the most beautiful conventions. The gross tales of the Miller and other "churles" are wisely left unillustrated, and the artist concentrates on those sweetly-legendary or purely decorative passages in Chaucer which Morris and he were peculiarly fitted to portray. It is easy nowadays when it has served its purpose to put the *Chaucer* and other Kelmscott books aside as anachronisms; but modern fine printing and book-production begin with them. We must not forget to mention the wood-engraver, William Hooper, who deserves great praise, for he had to work from very slight pencil-drawings, so that it is good to think that Morris remembered him in the colophon of the *Chaucer*.

Morris was already what he thought "damned old" when he started to print. He was fifty-eight and had only a few years to live. But the same enthusiasm for *incunabula* that his circle shared was animating a group of much younger artists. These young men who still survive among us with unabating energy, although book-production has long since ceased to occupy their attention, have already been named as composing the Vale Press Group. In *The Dial*, "an occasional publication" edited by Ricketts and Shannon, original woodcuts by them all may be seen. There is a *fin-de-siècle* air about this magazine which was limited to 200 copies and had enormous margins. Contemporary activities

do not enter to disturb its claustral calm, wherein you may read solemn essays on Gustave Moreau and Maurice de Guérin, or adaptations from Rimbaud, and see "original lithographs drawn upon the stone" by Shannon, or "experiments in Line" by Ricketts; the whole production was "advanced," daring, and mysterious once; and a bit stuffy now, like an unaired room.

The Vale Press under the management of the same friends began to publish in 1897 and lasted until 1904, during which time

Charles Shannon   *From "Daphnis and Chloe" (The Vale Press)*

it published forty-five works, many of which were decorated with woodcuts by the co-partners. I believe that it was with these rebellious spirits (who have since become Members of the Royal Academy) that the phrase, of late so vulgarised, of "original woodcut" takes its origin. The edition of *Hero and Leander* which they published has "decorations designed and cut upon the wood" by Ricketts and Shannon and it is useful to know this, for you might take them for pen-drawings reproduced by some photographic process. It is difficult to see what they could have gained by making facsimiles of their own drawings, which the excellent Hooper or any other professional engraver could have done as well if not better.

Hero and Leander with *Daphnis and Chloe* are their most important books. The designers deliberately sought their models in the Italian cuts of the late fifteenth century, in particular in the *Hypnerotomachia Poliphili* of the Aldine Press. But even while basing their style on these early cuts they could not bar out contemporary influences. A whiff of the close air of the "'nineties" gets in, and the characters of Musæus and Longus hint to us of Wilde and Beardsley and even of "L'Art Nouveau." [1]

Sturge Moore   *The Little Mother*

Lucien Pissarro, son of Camille, the great Impressionist painter and one of a numerous family all of whom have at some time made wood-engravings, came over to England and joined *The Dial* group. Later he founded the Eragny Press and published exquisite octavos decorated with his own wood-engravings printed in several subdued colours. The effect of Eragny books is very sweet and decorative. Lucien Pissarro uses black line in his prints, and his very quiet and sincere designs have an engaging "gaucherie" which must have been very disconcerting to good people at the beginning of the century.

Another of *The Dial* coterie, the poet Sturge Moore, is the author of two or three small sets of wood-engravings full of strange feeling. Sturge Moore gets such a light and lyrical charm in these little illustrations to Wordsworth or *Le Centaure* of Maurice de Guérin that we are reminded of Calvert—but, at second thoughts, only of the Calvert of *The Cyder Feast*, for we are bound to confess that he is capable neither of the power

[1] So close was the collaboration that it is wellnigh impossible to tell which cut was designed by Ricketts and which by Shannon. In the example which we reproduce Shannon made the design but Ricketts transferred it to the block and *both* engraved it.

of construction shown in *The Ploughman*, nor of the exquisiteness of execution shown in *The Chamber Idyll*. Not being dependent upon his art for his daily bread, Sturge Moore can await the genuine promptings to expression, which, like the visitations of the poetic Muse to Gray, seem to be few but always leave treasures in their wake.

A more robust and popular spirit was William Nicholson who, as we have seen elsewhere, was much influenced by the elder Crawhall. This artistic ancestry is very significant. Nicholson holding Crawhall's hand (as it were) leaps right over the reproductive engravers into the period of the chapbooks. He is untouched by the methods of his time. The large simple designs which appeared in his picture-books (*London Types*, *An Alphabet*, etc.) were made with the graver on the end-grain, but they have all the breadth of knife-work. Nicholson, of course, is a painter and these cuts are a painter's conception. The figures are boldly modelled in light and shade in a manner resembling the old chiaroscuros, though something in the placing of the figures now and then reveals an acquaintance with Japanese design. But the application of the colours was not done as in colour-prints from wood-blocks proper, but by some lithographic process. The same process was used for the reproduction of the lettering in which the verses that generally accompany his cuts were written. Here again the influence of Crawhall is manifest, and, instead of employing metal types, the artist drew imitations of the fat, crazily-mustered types of the chapbooks as rendered by the whimsical Joseph Crawhall. Nicholson's picture-books appeared about the beginning of the present century and they have not "dated" yet. Nor is there any likelihood of their losing their appeal, for time will give a pleasant "patina" to these frank smiling books with their good-humoured rendering of the types of men and animals, their really admirable patterns of black and white and the delightful colours which enliven them.

In his book *Wood Cuts and Some Words* that genial egoist, Mr. Gordon Craig, tells us how he began to engrave under the instruction of Nicholson and the latter's brother-in-law, Pryde. In 1895 he began to cut little blocks to help him in his duties as a stage-designer, and he later used them to decorate theatrical programmes and for his magazine *The Mask*. Prior to the publication of *Wood Cuts and Some Words*, Craig had engraved as many as 517 blocks and in one year as many as 87. Such figures would be appalling in an artist who laudably refrains from over-production unless one reflected on the tiny scale and frequently nugatory character of the blocks. Craig has none of Nicholson's amplitude of design and power of draughtsmanship, but, to a rare talent for small rococo inventions, he adds great wit and ingenuity of engraving. His passion for stage-design is revealed in many little cuts wherein tiny figures are drawn as though moving upon a vast stage. The most commonplace subjects take on a charm under his handling. He can take a sphinx and a pyramid and can so place them and vary their contours, and subtly peck out spots, and gradate the distance between parallel lines as to produce a thing of rareness and charm. In Wood-Engraving, to apply a maxim of Joubert, it

Eric Gill   *From "The Song of Songs" (Golden Cockerel Press)*

is better to be exquisite than to be ample, and it is greatly to Mr. Craig's credit that he has seen this.

Most engravers cover the surface of the block with the thinnest film of white paint before making their drawing, but others, like Mr. Craig, enlist the aid of the wood with its curious grain to gather suggestions for the enrichment of their designs, just as Leonardo believed in seeking fanciful inventions from the markings on weather-stained walls. Nothing could be farther from such an attitude than the severe outlook of Mr. Eric Gill, who engraves upon wood, as he carves upon stone, designs of the most austere and intellectual character which would disdain such accidental aids. Whatever one may think of the cold, stark Neo-Byzantinism of his style, there can be no doubt about his sincerity as a man and his exceptional gifts as a craftsman. No living engraver can cut so steady and so eloquent a line, be it white line or black line, and no living engraver has done book-decorations more consonant with type. The criticism so justifiably levelled against woodcuts in modern books is that their technical crudity makes them fundamentally discordant when placed along with refined modern type-faces. To Mr. Gill's cuts this criticism is notably inapplicable. Beginning as a pupil and assistant to the calligrapher Edward Johnson, Gill has carved many noble inscriptions upon stone in Roman letters and the discipline of hand that he learned in such works has been invaluable to him as an engraver. In all his work there is the same striving for the abstract to the total elimination of what is called "character." All natural forms are stripped of extraneous adhesions and represented in the severest conventions or symbols. The result is often the creation of types of high and pure intensity, but sometimes the fire wanes and the result is merely dull and comic. His best engravings have such a white heat of intensity that we accept all the parts as moulded into one noble whole by the fire of his conception; but at other times only the droll mannerisms of his style are apparent, the breasts as round as sixpences, and eyes that occupy the whole width of a head. Mr. Gill shows no compromise and no sense of humour. The same searching intellectuality unsweetened by mere sensuousness, and sharpened almost to bitterness by a dæmonic urge, always in restraint, gets to the root of the matter in all his work.

So prominent an artist cannot fail to have followers. One of these, David Jones, like Mr. Gill a fervent Roman Catholic, has shared his voluntary exile from the world. Though Mr. Jones owes his style in the main to the influence of the older artist, he gives his figures more human interest, more "character" and shapes more contemporary. I do not mean to suggest that he draws figures like a "*Punch* artist"; but that occasionally he grafts on to his Byzantine types features that may be seen on men and women of to-day. In fact he is a less hieratic artist; and, indeed, something of a sense of humour (although never boisterous or warm-hearted) is discoverable in his designs. Mr. Jones in some of his most recent blocks for the limited editions of the Golden Cockerel Press shows a study of the white-line work of the fifteenth-century metal-cuts; but he is far from being an imitator, and is evolving a personal style that should win him a very high place in Wood-Engraving as in other forms of art.

Ethelbert White has made many delightful engravings of the country-side which he so loves. His life is spent moving in a caravan over the southern English counties. He had no art-school discipline but his work

David Jones

Oblation of Noah. From "The Deluge" (*Golden Cockerel Press*)

shows undoubted reminiscences of Spode willow-pattern plates and Old English sporting prints, as well as of the Douanier Rousseau and modern French painting. But he has made a delightful and really personal amalgam of such stylistic influences, and there is something redolent of the country-side in all he does. His wood-engravings, broad and frank and charmingly "swung-in," give us great pleasure; and his patterning of the shapes of trees and ricks and barns is as successful as it is bold. Particularly happy

Ethelbert White   *Paddington Barn* (8″ × 5½″)

is the way in which he combines the human figure with its setting, and shows us how

> Hob and Nob like blind men pass
> Down to the Bull for pipe and glass.

Indeed his engravings of great barns with rain-sunken roofs set against trees amid fat furrows of manured soil seem to afford a pictorial counter-part to Edmund Blunden's poetry. He has recently visited the Mediter-ranean sea-coast but has been inspired to nothing more than neat jobs by the sickly picturesqueness of the shore-towns and bays.

Gwendolen Raverat has devoted herself almost entirely to Wood-

Engraving which she has practised in most of its forms. Her work is always large in feeling, no matter what the scale of her blocks may be, and they vary greatly. At one time she made a series of symbolic designs in which the influence of Gill is clear, but they are rather strained productions. She has been praised for some of her illustrations, for example one of *The Ballad of Clerk Saunders*, and another of *David Old*, and a third of *Sir Thomas Browne and Death*; but all are lacking in real imaginative intensity. The *Clerk Saunders* does not convey the sense of "feyness," of the cocks crowing on merry middle-earth and the clinking bell

Gwendolen Raverat   *Sheep by the River*

going through the town. The David and Abishag is no more than a naked girl and an old man in a four-poster bed; while no vulgar skeleton of the Danse Macabre ever guided the pen of the author of *Urn Burial*. Some mighty form of sublime aspect such as Orcagna traced upon the walls of the Pisan Campo Santo was surely needed for that.

But the Gwendolen Raverat of the many calm and quiet landscapes is an engraver whose work will survive. On the charming *Duck Pond* and other pastoral subjects her reputation is firmly based. There is restraint and sweetness in her style and her cutting is broad and strong. In *The Duck Pond* the design is decorative in treatment but it is wonderful how simply the effect of strongly diffused sunlight is conveyed.

Eric Daglish has been dubbed "the Modern Bewick," but that is merely the journalistic way of saying that he also makes wood-engravings of birds and quadrupeds for books on Natural History. Both Daglish and

Bewick are naturalists who make their diagrams into things of beauty, and there the resemblance begins and ends. The work of Daglish reminds one of the animal-paintings of the Mughal School with their clearly out-

Eric Fitch Daglish   *The Philosopher (Barred Owl). From "Walden"*
                                      (Chapman and Hall)

lined markings and their lovely ambient shapes. He is a careful designer and the settings to his creatures are beautifully patterned and engraved with thin white lines. But in his preoccupation with pattern and colour he neglects form, and consequently, as diagrams, his engravings are not so valuable as those of Bewick. So that if one were searching for the most useful diagrams one would be wise to suspect an illustrator, who is so obviously an "artist," of suppressing useful information that did not

Paul Nash   *Winter Wood*

contribute to the effect of the design *per se*. Indeed, compared to him, Bewick is prosaic and intent only on telling us all he knows about animals and their dwelling-places. Mr. Daglish's are the most poetically conceived pictures of British birds and quadrupeds that we have seen.

He is very interested in the "colour" that the wood-block yields and loves to cut here and there passages of pure white, leaving them to sing out among the blacks and dark greys of his prints. He does this with rare imaginative effect at times as in his engraving of the nightingale, the dark-grey songster with its white throat amid small flowers of star-like purity against a black sky. Using a fine tool he cuts very nervous lines, every one of them with meaning. It is most refreshing to find a modern engraver who is so quiet in his methods. But these lines are often not more than scratches, and not deep enough to keep them from filling up if the block were to be heavily inked, so that Mr. Daglish's darkest passages are never a full black in intensity.

The most enterprising among English artists who have interested themselves in Wood-Engraving are the brothers Paul and John Nash. Their clarity and intensity of vision and their strong instinct for pattern are seen at their fullest in their prints. John Nash's work is gentler and more reticent than that of his brother, and not tortured with the same dæmonic urge. He is more sensitive and whimsical, more interested in natural objects for their own sakes. Podgy old men or languorous cats interest him as men and cats and not merely as shapes and forms. On the other hand, one feels that Paul Nash's conception of art is too austere to consider such things except (to adopt current critical jargon) for sake of their formal relations, their purely æsthetic aspect, to the elimination of all associated, implied ideas.

In his book called *Places* Paul Nash has seven landscapes in each of which he has caught the "genius loci" with remarkable intensity and expressed it with vehemence. His trees surge upwards and clash their branches together, or recede in arch after arch of cold, dark vaulting like the aisles of a mighty cathedral. Reeds shoot up like spears and the sun seems to boil in the sky. His landscapes are always sinister, tortured as though seen in a nightmare after driving through the dark in a car with strong head-lights. *Winter Wood*, which is reproduced here, is surely a great and most impressive design. The cold bare trees in their black aisles, the bitter white growth at the side, the figure that seems to haunt its paths, all these seem to me parts of an intense and personal reaction to nature. In his print of *The Breakwater* Paul Nash with fierce white lines has swept in a sense of the icy charging of the sea upon the impenetrable line of concrete, and yet has built up the design in the severest conventions with the waves turning over like rolls of paper. It is this

simple and bitterly keen vision of things that is the outstanding feature
in Paul Nash's art.

John Nash's artistic language is more easily intelligible, his conception

Paul Nash   *Design of Arches*

of nature nearer to the tradition of the great English water-colourists
which his work supplements. The nightmare element is quite absent from
his engravings and his use of line is less ruthless. The print called *The
Path through the Wood*, which is still his most interesting work, is full of
subtle counterchanges of white, grey and black, and is most beautifully

designed. He has done some interesting interiors and scenes of rural labour. His sense of humour which enables him to make the best comic

John Nash   *Black Bryony. From " Poisonous Plants" (Etchells and Macdonald)*

drawings of to-day (for he comes to it as a relaxation from more serious work and not as a means of earning a living) comes out delightfully in his engravings, notably in the edition of Swift's *Directions to Servants* which he illustrated for the Golden Cockerel Press.

Sydney Lee, the painter of huge decoratively treated landscapes, carries his preoccupation with textures into his wood-engravings. Large

John Nash

Autumn Crocus. From "Poisonous Plants"
(Etchells and Macdonald)

in scale and picturesque and sentimental in style, his engravings show great skill in the choice of systems of line and spot to represent the surface qualities of rocks and fields and water. He was early in the field and has had many followers. Brangwyn's engraving suffers, like all his work, from slipshod construction obscured but not concealed by the noisy rhetoric of his style. C. W. Taylor and John F. Greenwood are both engravers of architectural and rural scenes of considerable charm and their work deserves the popularity it has won. Noel Rooke as an instructor at the Central School of Arts and Crafts has earned the gratitude of many gifted students, among them Margaret Pilkington, Millicent Jackson, Lady Mabel Annesley and (best known of all) Vivien Gribble. The last-

Robert Gibbings   *From " Red Wise " (Golden Cockerel Press)*

named, like Mr. Rooke, has made book-decorations of "gentlemanly" restraint and severity. Both prefer to let the design come out in black line, which they use with simplicity and taste, and if their work had more verve and vitality they would be among the best book-decorators of our time. Eric Ravilious is a new-comer to Wood-Engraving who has already done some very personal and felicitous work. His designs are exceptionally graceful and his engraving very neat. His illustrations for Martin Armstrong's *Desert* were worthy of a better format. Most of these exquisitely designed little blocks were ruined by incompetent press-work. Bernard Rice, a young English engraver who elects to live in Yugo-Slavia, has recently made several very interesting large prints of a decorative nature. He goes out to the forest, selects his tree and makes his own blocks. Mr.

Rice employs a technique like that of Gauguin, and gets an effect like mezzotint by scraping out some passages very slightly and lowering others, as well as by engraving with the ordinary tools and with the multiple tool. Being his own block-maker, he is skilled at making the grain of the block contribute where desirable to the effect of the design. Until we saw his blocks we could not have believed that these prints were obtained by the ordinary method of printing. Although it is not part of our plan to discuss contemporary Wood-Engraving except in France and England, we must mention in this connection the prints of Josef Weiss of Munich, a young artist with a flaming and Grecoesque imagination, who has done some powerful wood-engravings of Apocalyptic scenes. Weiss like Gauguin scrapes and lowers his blocks but he does it with much more deliberation and craft. He does not, like Rice, use the cross-section of soft wood but the plank, and his mastery of tonal effect and all the qualities that the wood can be made to yield is extraordinary.

There are many other young English artists whose names might with equal justice be mentioned in this work did space permit. Indeed there is no doubt that the modern woodcut has come to stay and is certain to develop. The public have become aware, through illustrated books and the annual exhibitions of two recently formed societies, of the existence of what they consider a new form of art. In fact, there is danger of the woodcut becoming fashionable. This, however, would be a good thing if it brought with it any critical sense, but at present the modish people and the dealers who sell the prints are equally incapable of distinguishing between good and bad work, and equally avid of all and sundry, provided that it be liberally patterned with printer's ink. Before very long the novelty will cease and sound criticism develop. Indeed who knows but that some day original wood-engravers may be able to support themselves by the sale of their work.

GAUGUIN AND THE MODERN FRENCH WOOD-ENGRAVERS

In France the break from the old tradition of Reproductive Engraving was effected more gradually than in England, and not, as in England, by scholarly "amateurs," but by professional engravers. In 1897 a "Société des Graveurs sur bois" was founded by a few enthusiasts who felt that the art, although discredited by reproductive hack-work and threatened by the new photo-processes, was not only the best ally for typography but was on the eve of fresh developments. The organ of the Society, *L'Image,* under the artistic editorship of Tony Beltrand and Auguste Lepère, mirrors the state of Wood-Engraving at the close of the last century. All the pictures were engraved and what a hotch-potch of styles they form!—from elaborate tone-studies after the canvases of artists like Eugène Carrière, through the richly diapered black-line engravings by Lucien Pissarro to the freest of plank-cuts by Lepère himself. The work of the last-named epitomises the state of the art. Lepère was a professional engraver and could produce as brilliantly executed reproductions of his own and others' paintings as any American of the time; but he aimed at a more direct method of engraving, prompted partly by æsthetic disgust at the encroachments of Photography upon Art (and vice versa) and partly by his love of the cuts of the fifteenth and sixteenth centuries. In a letter to Roger Marx in 1900 Lepère complains that the robust art of xylography had been ruined by photo-processes. The best blocks were those most like photographs, and the taste for paintings was ruinous in book-illustration where the very definite and clear letters contrasted violently with the foggy spreading of the vignette over the page. What he most loved was "l'aspect franc, gras et vibrant d'un beau bois," and the earliest cuts were to his mind the most beautiful, the most true to the genius of the medium and to their function as book-decorations. Félix Bracquemond, the great etcher, had expressed similar opinions three years before, but Lepère made it his life-task to materialise them.

Edouard Pelletan was the publisher who set out to cleanse the Augean stables of the Book in France in the last years of the nineteenth century. Pelletan to great talent as a typographer added a rigorous insistence on order, but he was over-fastidious in trying to find the inevitable type and format to accompany each text. He had none of Morris's clarity of purpose and Morris's passion for *incunabula*, with the conviction it brought of the necessity for decoration rather than for illustration. Pelletan clung to the vignette and to the picturesque and anecdotal kind of book-illustration, which the reformers of the Book in England had entirely rejected. Anatole France's *La Terre et l'Homme*, and Renard's *Patrie* to which Paul-Emile Colin contributed strong and gloomy wood-engravings of the life of the peasant upon the soil, are Pelletan's last and only books which may be considered twentieth-century in spirit. Colin is an engraver of power and sincerity and practises not only in the ordinary way with knife and graver, but even with the knife upon the end-grain of boxwood, a method he claims to have originated. He was the only one of Pelletan's artists who engraved his own designs. All kinds of illustrators worked for these books, among them the facile Spaniard, Vierge, famous for his illustrations to Michelet's great *Histoire de France*. Pelletan never fully understood that, since white is the basic colour of the page, all designs should be kept to some extent open to expose that white, as a printed passage exposes it, if types and decoration are to be of one texture. Brushmen like Vierge took no thought of this, with the result that their vignettes are like grey stains on the page.

Far away from all such preoccupations, in Tahiti, in a native hut, attended by a native woman, Paul Gauguin died in 1903. This terrific, half-demented being had sought refuge from civilisation in the South Seas, but he carried his torment with him wherever he went. After his death several blocks were discovered which his native adherents were using to furnish a pigsty, and these have been carefully printed by the artist's son. In his Tahitian Eden, Gauguin had no access to proper implements, nor was his creative impatience at any time likely to have been governed much by the considerations of ordinary craftsmanship. Using the plank of soft wood of considerable scale he scored upon it with a knife and a gouge, scraping and lowering the wood at places, here softening an edge, and there leaving a hard outline, as he made his strange barbaric designs with their sexual and symbolic significance. There are only about a dozen of these prints of Gauguin, each of which

Félix Vallotton

Le Mauvais Pas

bears a title in the language of the islands, but they have exercised considerable influence upon the development of modern Wood-Engraving, both by their type of design and by their direct and not unsubtle method of cutting.

Until we recently examined some of the blocks of Bernard Rice, a young English engraver who obtains much the same tonal effects as Gauguin, we found it difficult to believe that direct printing in a press

Constant le Breton   *La Chute de la Maison Usher*

could have yielded such variety of colour, unless the thickness of the ink were varied at certain places or even wiping were employed. But we now know that parts of the surface of a block, if lowered ever so little with the ordinary scraper, such as etchers use for corrections, will print the delightful grey which one finds in Gauguin's prints. But, though some have been directly influenced by Gauguin's prints, most modern wood-engravers owe to him merely an incentive or inspiration towards the quest of new adventures in the art.

In the year before the Great War the veteran engraver and historian of his craft, Pierre Gusman, founded a Society of Original Wood-Engravers and combined with Lepère and others to publish the first part of an important venture in book-decoration. This experiment, called *Le Nouvel Imagier*, was in the form of three *fasciculi* in which short literary passages were chosen and (as the colophon says) "each artist charged to decorate a text has thereupon chosen a kind of type according to the style of his cuts, and has sought to resolve the problem of harmonising the two elements." For example, in the first number Pierre Gusman undertook to decorate a passage from Sophocles, but his engravings are not improved by the superimposition of a second block of yellow tint. Colin's decorations to Statius are admirably simple, but he is not at home in Arcadia, as he is upon the bleak furrows of his native soil. Laboureur (well known to-day as a line-engraver) uses massive outlines and no shading with excellent typographic effect, and Jacques Beltrand reproduces his own pen-drawings. In the second number Siméon shows two rollicking hearty cuts to an old drinking-poem, and Bonfils a crisp cut which is admirably consonant with the Cochin types which it decorates. The other contributions are not of much interest, but the experiment was a useful one and was crowned with some measure of success. All the artists chose sizes of types larger than those possible in books of ordinary length for common reading. This made their task easier, but rather evaded the real problem, which is not how to produce bibelots for the book-speculator, but how to produce cheap books beautifully adorned with woodcuts that are within the reach of the ordinary book-lover. The initials, *culs-de-lampe* and border strips are surprisingly bad, and none of the artists seemed to have any talent for designing pure typographic ornaments.

J. E. Laboureur   *Facteur rural*

French artists were already being attracted to Wood-Engraving before the war intervened, and since then their numbers have increased enormously. They employ all kinds of methods and all kinds of styles, but one common·spirit animates them—a joyous disregard for the difficulties of the medium. In this they follow Gauguin rather than the sober Lepère, for they improvise upon the block and trust to the shapes of the tools to suggest the character of the design. Fine gravers and the delicate tools for tone-work (called tint-tools and spit-stickers) are very seldom employed, though a multiple tool which makes a number of thin parallel lines at each stroke has of late become popular in use. This multiple tool or "vélo" (used by the commercial engravers to save labour in the lining of skies and smooth objects) is now made to serve all kinds of purposes, especially for the re-duction in tone of black passages.

P. Véra

P. VERA

Pomone

In the main the French are much less careful craftsmen than their English contemporaries. They make too light of the benefits of good workmanship. Most of the wood-engraving in modern French books is beneath contempt, technically inferior to the "imagerie" of the lower classes in the last two centuries and of course without the glamour that belongs to these simple and traditional designs. Wood-engravings are far more numerous in French books of to-day than in English, but on the whole the work is inferior in quality. Compared to English book-illustrations made by photo-processes the French woodcuts are obviously freer and more "advanced" in style. English publishers prefer to the starkness and intensity of a good original cut, an imitation made with

M. Vox   *Plaisir d'Amour*

white paint on black and in consequence sweeter and gentler in feeling. French engravers have more readily adopted the "advanced" conventions of modern painting, in which of course Paris sets the fashion to the world. The value of contemporary Wood-Engraving in France has been greatly over-estimated, largely in consequence of the exalted condition of French painting and sculpture and because artists of eminence such as Dufy, Derain, Vlaminck, and Marie Laurencin have made essays in the craft.

Three years ago M. Léon Pichon, of the publishing firm of that name, prepared for the *Studio* magazine a special number on "The New Book-Illustration in France," which has been of assistance to us in the course of this work, so that it seems ungenerous to criticise it here. Nevertheless, it must be stated that if the state of that illustration is to be judged by M. Pichon's plates and not by his word, then it is in a very poor way indeed. M. Pichon is the most generous and catholic of critics. As you read his pages you glow with enthusiasm and joy at the thought of so much impassioned effort brought to bear upon the book by artists so uniformly gifted with genius. But when you look at the plates, most of them from books decorated with woodcuts, disillusionment is complete.

F. Siméon

L'aimable Ingénue

These great decorators are very small fellows indeed, only M. Pichon has temporarily invested them in the purple which one and all must wear whose works are included in special numbers of the *Studio*.

Carlègle is one of the few illustrators whose work deserves the praise that it has received. His designs for *Daphnis et Chloé* (1919) and other classical texts of the idyllic type have strength and clarity of pattern, and are cleanly and sharply engraved. Fernand Siméon is a witty engraver who has done much work for the publishers. In his recent designs for Claude Tillier's *Mon Oncle Benjamin* he uses the multiple tool very cleverly with short jabs to convey effects of recession. A designer of great spirit, he loves all sensuous rounded forms, plump women, thatched cottages or great fruits. Galanis is perhaps the best-known exponent of the multiple tool.[1] It is the most misused of tools and can very easily produce monotonous and insipid effects; but Galanis manipulates it with great taste. His most interesting prints hitherto have been four still-life groups, one of them after a painting by Picasso. The arrangement of the fruits, jugs and serviettes which form these groups derives of course from Cézanne, but M. Galanis has obtained excellent effects of sheen and richness by crossing the multiple lines here and there, while wholly disregarding the real surface-texture of the objects represented.

Another French engraver who depends largely upon the "vélo" is Jacques Bouillaire. The streets and buildings which he loves to represent have a grim and brooding aspect and the way he uses white line to convey a sense of solidity is worthy of study; but his work cannot escape the charge of monotony. Constant le Breton has done capable architectural engravings, as well as several illustrated books. His illustrations to Poe's *Tales of Mystery and Imagination* are small but have considerable macabre power. Daragnès and Jou are other designers who delight in the representation of the grim and the weird. Daragnès uses white line with fierceness and certainty; but Jou is a tamer designer altogether, and prefers to reproduce his own black-line designs. Raoul Dufy uses the wood-block for the purposes of multiplying his admirable textile

[1] In 1912 M. Galanis first discovered and displayed the riches which the vélo offers when wielded in a freer manner—a manner the direct opposite of that with which it was used by its designers, the commercial engravers of last century. The result of his invention is seen in the beautiful *La Chasse* of that year, which we reproduce. M. Galanis calls this manner of engraving the "manière noire." Tint-tools and spit-stickers were the most common of all the weapons of the reproductive engraver. As many as twenty-five tint-tools would be found in most engravers' boxes. Spit-stickers cut a line of equal fineness and depth and can be used in making circular lines where gravers and tint-tools would be likely to bruise the edges of the block.

designs. Many of his independent prints are of a very trifling nature (I have seen one about the size of a postage stamp on which a sardine tin is crudely engraved); and all of them are slashed in with rather un-

Galanis   *La Chasse* (4⅝″ × 4⅛″)

necessary violence, though the animals in his cuts for Apollinaire's *Le Bestiaire* are delightfully designed. Had the order in which we treat of these artists been strictly chronological, Vallotton should have been mentioned before. Félix Vallotton, of Swiss extraction, belongs to the older tradition of which Nicholson is the outstanding exponent in England. He gets his effects of gloom and passion by large and careful patterns of black and white and quiet yet intense arrangement of contours. He has also cut several simple and expressive portraits. Gérard Cochet is only known to us by the edition of *Candide* which he copiously illustrated with little cuts. Cochet's technique is crude but his cuts have a spirit and gaiety that would have been lost in more careful work.

Out of the legion of engravers who are producing prints and book-decorations to-day, it is difficult to pick the most prominent, more difficult still to say anything just about them; moreover, there is danger of making this essay into a catalogue of names and works, and the time has not yet come for any estimate of the permanent value of their achievements.

Perhaps it would be better to conclude this account with a few general observations than to go over a lengthy list of names and strive to find the right adjective for each. Despite the valuable example offered by publications like *Le Nouvel Imagier*, the modern French engravers who work for publishers will not submit to the stylistic discipline necessary in fine book-production. They prefer to hack away with their knives as though the one thing that mattered was the communication of their own (often insignificant) natures. Most of them prefer cutting to the comparatively hard and mechanical practice of engraving. The distinguished painter, Derain, has made gouge-cuts in illustration of a poem of Apollinaire in which by the time he has laid down that formidable weapon there is so little surface left, and that little so difficult to understand, that criticism is almost silenced for want of grounds to build on. But not so praise—for Mr. Roger Fry, most sincere and learned of critics, discerns very remarkable qualities in the cuts of Derain. That he is a painter, and an exhibitor at the Salons, is not enough to excuse an engraver from completely disregarding the nature of the medium he employs. Engraving is a difficult craft and must be treated with respect. A good painter (Derain is a very good one) is by no means necessarily a good engraver. He is not an engraver at all unless he properly employs his medium. But most of the nonsense talked about "creative xylography" and "qualities of carved wood" comes from the professional critics who praise what it is fashionable to praise or what they fear (since they do not understand it), and who are ignorant of the practice of the craft. Unfortunately the jargon of the critics influences the weaker artists, and many of the woodcuts which are honoured to-day for their "strength" are merely violent.

Coming as the writer did a few years ago fresh from the old grey engravings after Tenniel and Millais to which he was accustomed, the discovery of the modern cuts with their juicy blackness and brilliant whiteness was for a while inspiring. These modern cuts looked so powerful, so expressive, so defiant of commercial laboriousness, so manifestly produced by the inexperienced hand propelled by uncompromising creative urge. But this was only the rapture of the young art-student. With the passing of a few months and the engraving of a few blocks it became apparent that the unbridled creative passion is more often than not a fashionable and simulated one, that the intensity is merely the result of so much printer's ink set abruptly beside so much white paper, that sincerity is not necessarily a synonym for bad workmanship, and daring cutting often merely the slipping of blunt tools.

MODERN WOOD-ENGRAVING: CONCLUSION

THE Wood-Engraving of the past was a reproductive medium involving a twofold division of labour. We have seen that this was the rule, and we have seen that there were notable exceptions to this rule. Giuseppe Scolari was probably one, Papillon and Bewick to a large extent, and Blake and Calvert entirely, were others, and we must not forget the horde of anonymous "imagiers" whose very lowliness doubtless obliged them to work in a dual capacity. When Linton says that "the white line alone is art" he means you to mistake him and his fraternity for "artists," because they did not always work line for line but often line for wash. But why are people always so covetous of the ambiguous title of "artist"? Craftsman, "Formschneider," surely these are honourable titles.

The old reproductive craftsmen loved their work. How they must have caressed the beautiful pieces of smooth box, and held no labour too much to bestow upon anything, were it a reproduction after Raphael or an advertisement of a bath-tub! Well, we have changed all that— "and a good thing too," we can hear some people say. But by removing the discipline of designing upon wood—lax as it had got to be before the end—we have let in the flux of "slick" illustration which makes abomination of so many magazines on every railway bookstall. To stem this tide of photographic garbage certain artists have revived Wood-Engraving; but in their horror of commercialism they have vetoed all reproductive engraving of any sort. Surely this is unwise. It is generally agreed that no photographic processes can give just that element of intensity and sharpness that is obtained by engraving upon wood. Would it not therefore be wise for designers to entrust their drawings once more to the hands of skilled engravers, as Tenniel did to Swain or Leighton to Dalziel?[1]

Theoretically, of course, a division of labour in art is a bad thing

[1] Since writing the above we have seen two recent books illustrated by Randolph Schwabe for C. W. Beaumont of the Charing Cross Road, viz. *Madrigals* of Clare and *The Café Royal and Other Essays* by Arthur Symons. In both of these Mr. Schwabe made careful pen-drawings upon the blocks which were then handed over to reproductive engravers. In the latter book there were portraits of Proust and Duse and other people which the engraver reproduced with extreme fidelity. The designs are very grey, and charming in their combinations of black-line and white-line work; Mr. Schwabe, smiling, suggested that the engraver had improved upon his originals.

and "original" engraving preferable to reproductive engraving: without doubt, if "original" engravers were less incompetent than they generally are; but since the craft is difficult to learn and few have time or patience to learn its grammar, it would be better for most designers to entrust their designs to others to engrave, or to have them reproduced by some photo-mechanical process—but to discuss the pros and cons of the latter alternative is not part of our business here.

After all is there anything wrong with the results of the old partnerships? What have we got against Burgkmair and de Negker or Holbein and Lützelburger or even Burne-Jones and Hooper, and who but the absurdest purist could frown at Utamaro or Hokusai, the Japanese designers of colour-prints, because they did not do their own cutting? If this writer has any quarrel at all, it is with the purists who drive so many fools to the wood-block. The only argument against reproductive engraving is that of expense, and on this point we must be silent, knowing nothing. But only a few years ago a charming edition of *The Decameron* was published, with illustrations in colour by Thomas Derrick (Chatto and Windus, 1920), in which the method of colour-printing from blocks (hatched here and there with the graver to reduce the strength of the tint) was employed with great success, as it had been by the same firm (Edmund Evans Ltd.) in the picture-books of Caldecott and Crane and Kate Greenaway, fifty years before; and, to this day, colour-printing from wood-blocks is used by French publishers for reproducing the water-colour drawings of artists like Maurice Denis and Marie Laurencin.

Good "original" wood-engravers have always been and always will be few. We do not mean by this to suggest that in our opinion a good original engraver should be thoroughly trained as Linton and his kind. Perish the thought! Blake, for example, did noble wood-engravings although his publisher felt it necessary to apologise for their lack of "art." No, good original engravers have a peculiar vision of things which differentiates them from other artists. We are not going to try to define this; it is unnecessary when we have eyes to see and can discern how Blake or Dürer, though themselves widely different as artists, have something in common which etchers like Rembrandt and Whistler do not have—an insistence on contour, a clear and intellectual vision which defines the shape and reveals the form of every object with equal completeness, which does not suggest but represents, and would see the glory behind a saintly head as a geometrically shaped nimbus and not as an irregular effulgence.

Eric W. Ravilious   *Church under a Hill*

All the old methods of making relief-prints are employed to-day and new variations devised. As far as we know, the manière criblée is alone in not being employed. Rice and Jakob Weiss, like Gauguin, get effects by scraping the surface of their blocks. Linoleum is often used, but seldom successfully, except in the wall-paper designs of Edward Bawden, and by the Viennese children, pupils of Professor Cizek, who do really lovely decorative designs upon linoleum, not with the knife, but with chisels with fine V-shaped cutting-edges (called "scrives"). The "scrive" enables them to get upon the soft ground something of the fluency of the graver-line. And now Eric Gill, in a recent publication of the Fleuron Press, tells us his method of intaglio printing from wood-blocks. But white line, used with freedom and spontaneity, as one might draw upon a black-board with chalk, is easily the favourite medium for creating prints. White line is hailed as the most "original" and the most "creative" of all these forms. Now, unless you make a great number of white lines your print will be very black. This blackness, however, is very much desired to-day. It is a sort of fetish. This is partly due to the violent re-action from the dull greyness of reproductive engraving, and it is no doubt good that the beautiful black which is one of the main charms of the medium should be exploited at last. But nothing is more depressing than a dead weight of printer's ink. Moreover you cannot get the full value of black unless you contrast it with greys and whites. Most exhibitions of modern woodcuts are gloomy as funerals.

Besides, what is wrong with grey as a colour? One suspects that not a little of the avoidance of greyness is due to the difficulty of obtaining it. A fine grey requires so much thoughtful hatching and so much skilful drawing that there is nothing which more exposes incompetence.

Another theory is that the material being wood the result should look "woody." The engravers of last century had taken pains lest their result should have anything of this quality, as far as anything done upon wood can avoid betraying its origin. So that to-day the engraver is urged to seek this very "woodiness," to make it obvious to the most ignorant that the result could not have been obtained in any other way than by chopping with a knife or gouge. As though one were to say, "Blake and Gauguin were great artists and so conscious of the wooden nature of wood that they aimed at conveying 'woodiness' in their prints. Go ye and do likewise, young blockheads."

Nothing could be more absurd. Blake is nothing if not a technician.

Did he not devise an original method of etching in relief for the printing of his books of poetry and prophecy? And was he not the author of the great set of line-engravings for *The Book of Job*? Indeed we may be sure that if Blake had done more wood-engraving he would have refined his technique without in any way checking the freedom of his utterance. And you will find no "woodiness" in the beautiful wood-engravings of his disciple Calvert. As for Gauguin, one must remember that he was in Tahiti and far distant from the makers of engraver's materials. Let us not blindly put down to inspiration that part of his work which is ascribable to lack of proper tools.

Even in Linton's time there was rumour of certain wild artists who "with block in one hand and graver in the other will walk into the full glare of sunlight and with abundant nerve-power and condensation of will, engrave directly what they see before them." Linton is vastly amused at the idea. "How can we dare to laugh!" says he (doubtless convulsed). "Yet I would not advise the expenditure of much time in this direction."

Recently we have heard of a certain painter of titanic mural decorations, who (worn out doubtless with the representation of colossal navvies standing among pumpkins to witness the Crucifixion or the departure of an adventurer for the Indies) sits up in bed and has a little light recreation by dashing off a block which would have taken Linton months to engrave.

It is time that we all got more reasonable. Wood-Engraving is a craft demanding at least as much concentration as any other. It must be learnt as laboriously as Painting or Tapestry-weaving, no matter how great an "artist" the engraver may be. Nothing is more ridiculous than to see beginners, wind-fed with current cant, violently stabbing the beautiful pieces of boxwood. What the art needs to-day is a number of designers of distinction willing to give at least as much pains to learning their craft as an etcher does, and capable of executing designs at least as skilfully as one whom the old commercials would have called "a capable lad."

A few words as to the use of woodcuts in modern books. There is a widespread belief that since woodcuts were the unique means of book-decoration in the Golden Age of Printing that they are the ideal accompaniment of types. And this is so. But there is a world of difference between the simple black-line cuts of the old books and the white-line cuts

Gertrude Hermes   *Fighting Dogs*

which pass as book-decorations to-day. In fact most contemporary woodcuts are not only too crude in quality but much too black in colour to act as book-decorations. Their origin is directly against them, for they are conceived of as white upon black and not, as in the case of the old cuts and of types, as black upon white.

There are only two ways of getting harmony out of this discordance: (1) to design types heavy enough to carry the weight in colour of the average modern woodcut; (2) to oblige the engraver to design specifically for the type.

The Germans love the juicy blackness of the modern woodcut which, as a matter of fact, is not so out of place in their books (where black-letter types have survived since Gutenberg's time) as it is in those of other countries. Moreover, Germany leads the world in typographical enter-prise, so that it is not surprising that they should endeavour to solve the problem by the first alternative. Rudolph Koch, the brilliant designer of the Klingspor type-foundry, has cut one face, the "Neuland," which was the outcome of his love of Wood-Engraving. "This type" (he tells us) "was made as in olden times by the punch-cutter being his own designer. The forms have been fashioned directly out of the metal with the tool, without being previously drawn on paper. Their shapes are the result of the tool." In one variation of "Neuland" little pieces of metal remain in relief just as in Wood-Engraving odd pieces of surface remain between the incisions of the graver. "Neuland" has no serifs and a massed page looks just like a page of a block-book. Notable example of Teutonic logic, to get a type fit to print with crude modern cuts we must go back to first sources—to the ancient block-books where the most perfect of all harmonies—technical harmony—was obtained by cutting both type and pictures with one and the same tool!

This Koch letter was used by the Nonesuch Press in their edition of the First Chapter of the Book of Genesis published not long since with engravings by Paul Nash. The arrangement was that of the block-books, on one side text, on the other picture; but of course it was much juicier in colour than any block-book, and (judged from a purely technical point of view) Nash's engravings were below the level of the best block-books. The first block was merely inked (to represent the void before God's fiat) and for each day of Creation more and more white was added, cul-minating in a cubist version of Adam and Eve. In this most amusing and artful book we see the logic of Koch's ideas carried to their farthest.

But what is successful in a pamphlet would be difficult and indeed maddening in a book made to be read.

Paul Nash also tried the block-book plan in his book of seven cuts called *Places.* Opposite each block he wrote in a heavy slanting hand a prose "illustration." It has also been suggested that the text might be

Blair Hughes-Stanton   *The Bull and the Beast*

engraved in white line upon black. We once saw a Shakespeare printed in white upon black paper.—But these are toys.

The second alternative, namely to oblige the engraver to design for the type, has been tried with great success by Mr. Robert Gibbings at the Golden Cockerel Press. Mr. Gibbings is himself a prominent wood-engraver and has done many decorations for his own publications. With one small hand-press, one pressman, two compositors and three sizes of Caslon Old Face, Mr. Gibbings by his intelligence and industry has won for himself a unique place in England as a printer of limited editions of books, nearly all of which contain wood-engravings. Mr. Gibbings has no patience for the æsthetic of Typography and no learned articles on the "Ideal Serif" flow from his pen. But he employs clever designers and makes them design for his types. Only at the Golden Cockerel Press are the ideal conditions for book-decoration to be found. The text is set up and printed pages are sent to the engraver, who designs his blocks to occupy the allotted spaces, and to take their places quietly in the page as a whole.

Trade conditions do not allow of this consideration for the artist. The larger presses call in the artist not by his decorations to make a book beautiful, but to make it saleable. He is given no specimen page of type for which to design and his advice is not wanted in the general "lay-out," which is planned by publishers who have no more aptitude for book-design than bankers or stockbrokers can be expected to have. The engraver sends his blocks to the printer who takes metal casts of them. They are then set up with types so light in colour that two printings are required to each page upon which text and block occur. Because, to get the full colour of a dark cut, so much ink is required that it would choke and blot the types, and therefore each has to be printed in turn. Double printing, moreover, is not only expensive but it nullifies the great advantage that Wood-Engraving has over Line-Engraving and other intaglio processes, namely that it can be printed at one impression with types.

One word more. Wood-Engraving is the true brother of Typography and the problem of keeping them together in peace and harmony in the House of the Book must be faced to-day. To us it seems that we must get back to greyness in our engravings, to greyness created by positive white lines made with gravers and other tools. This does not mean a return to the methods of Linton; rather than that we would advocate a return to the methods of the fifteenth-century metal-cuts. But other means of creating the greyness necessary not only to solve the typographic problem but for the sake of variety of colour in modern prints (and God knows we have need of it) will suggest themselves readily enough to the true original engraver. The future of Wood-Engraving lies in the development of the *métier*.

BOOKS CONSULTED

A Guide to the Processes and Schools of Engraving. British Museum, 1923.

ALLEMAGNE, H. d', *Les Cartes à Jouer du XIVe au XXe siècle.* Paris, 1906.

ARBER, A., *Herbals.* Cambridge Univ. Press, 1925.

ASHTON, *Chapbooks of the Eighteenth Century.* 1882.

BEEDHAM, R. J., *Wood-Engraving.* St. Dominic's Press, Ditchling, 1921.

BEWICK, T., *Works* (Memorial Edition). 1885–7.

—— *Vignettes.* Newcastle, 1827.

Bibliographica. 3 vols. See articles by Kristeller, Pollard, Rondot, etc. London, 1895–7.

BINYON, L., *The Followers of William Blake.* London, 1925 (Halton and Truscott Smith).

BLUM, A., *Les Origines de la Gravure en France.* Paris and Brussels, 1927.

BOUCHOT, H., *Un Ancêtre de la Gravure sur Bois . . . du Dép. d'estampes.* Paris, 1902.

—— *Les Deux Cents Incunables xylographiques . . . du Dép. d'estampes.* Paris, 1903.

BROWN, H., *The Venetian Printing Press.* London, 1891.

BUTSCH, A. F., *Die Bücherornamentik der Renaissance.* 4to. Leipzig, 1878–81.

CAMPBELL, *Annales de la Typographie néerlandaise au XVe siècle.* La Haye, 1874.

CHAMPFLEURY, *Histoire de l'Imagerie populaire.* 12mo. Paris, 1869.

CLAUDIN, *Histoire de l'Imprimerie en France au XVe et XVIe siècles.* 4 vols. Paris, 1900.

COCKERELL, S. C., *Some German Woodcuts of the Fifteenth Century.* 4to. Hammersmith, 1897.

COLVIN, S., *Early Engraving and Engravers in England.* London, 1905.

CONWAY, *The Literary Remains of Albrecht Dürer.* Cambridge, 1889.

—— *The Woodcutters of the Netherlands.* Cambridge, 1884.

COURBOIN, F., *La Gravure en France des origines à 1900.* Paris, 1923.

—— *Histoire illustrée de la Gravure en France.* 2 vols. Paris, 1923.

CUST, *The Master E. S. and the Ars Moriendi.* Oxford, 1898.

DAVIES, GERALD S., *Hans Holbein the Younger.* London, 1903.

DAVIS, H. W., *Catalogue of Early French Books in the Library of C. Fairfax-Murray.* 2 vols. London, 1910.

—— *Catalogue of Early German Books in the Library of C. Fairfax-Murray.* 2 vols. London, 1913.

DELABORDE, HENRI (VICOMTE), *La Gravure.* Paris, 1882.

DESNOYERS, "L'Imagerie populaire à Orléans" (*Mémoires de la Société Archéologique et Historique de l'Orléanais*, tome 17). Orléans, 1898.

DIEDERICHS, *Deutsches Leben der Vergangenheit in Bildern*. 2 vols. Jena, 1908.

DOBSON, AUSTIN, *Thomas Bewick and his Pupils*. London, 1889.

DODGSON, CAMPBELL, *Catalogue of Early German and Flemish Woodcuts in the British Museum*. London, 1903–11.

———— *Woodcuts of the Fifteenth Century in the John Rylands Library*. Manchester, 1915.

DUCHARTRE and SAULNIER, *L'Imagerie populaire*. Paris, 1925.

DUFF, E. G., *Early Printed Books* (Books about Books). 8vo. London, 1893.

DUFOUR, *Recherches sur la Danse Macabre*. Paris, 1873.

Einblattdrucke des fünfzehnten Jahrhunderts. 60 vols.

ESSLING, LE PRINCE D' (DUC DE RIVOLI), *Livres à Figures vénitiennes*. 3 vols. Paris, 1907.

FRY, ROGER, Essay on Dürer in *Vision and Design*. 1920.

FURST, HERBERT E. A., *The Modern Woodcut*. 1924.

GARNIER, J. M., *Histoire de l'Imagerie populaire à Chartres*. Chartres, 1869.

GILKS, *The Art of Wood-Engraving. A Practical Handbook*. 1866.

GUSMAN, PIERRE, *La Gravure sur Bois et d'épargne sur Metal*. Paris, 1916.

HAEBLER, *Early Printers of Spain and Portugal*. London, Bibliographical Society, 1897.

HATTON, R. G., *Craftsman's Herbal*. 1909.

HEITZ, *Büchermarken*. Strassburg, 1896.

HINDLEY, CHARLES, *Life and Times of James Catnach*. 1878.

HOLTROP, *Monuments typographiques des Pays Bas au XVᵉ siècle*. La Haye, 1868.

HUMPHREYS, H. N., *Masterpieces of the Early Printers and Engravers*. London, 1870.

JACKSON and CHATTO, *Treatise on Wood-Engraving*. London, 1839.

JENNINGS, O., *Early Woodcut Initials*. London, 1908.

KRISTELLER, P., *Early Florentine Woodcuts*. London, 1897.

———— *Jacopo de' Barbari*. Berlin, International Chalcographical Society, 1896.

———— *Kupferstich und Holzschnitt in vier Jahrhunderten*. Berlin, 1905.

LABORDE, LÉON DE, *Histoire de la Gravure en manière noire*. Paris, 1839.

LACOMBE, PAUL, *Les Livres d'Heures, etc*. Paris, 1907.

Le Triomphe de l'Empereur Maximilien I. Atlas. Vienna, 1796.

LINTON, W. J., *The Masters of Wood-Engraving*. London, 1889.

———— *Wood-Engraving. A Manual of Instruction*. London, 1884.

———— *History of Wood-Engraving in America*. London, 1882.

Lippmann, F., *Engravings and Woodcuts of the Old Masters*. 5 vols. London, 1889.

——— *The "Chevalier Délibéré" of Olivier de la Marche*. London, Bibliographical Society, 1898.

——— *The Master IB with the Bird*. Berlin, International Chalcographical Society, 1894.

——— *The Art of Wood-Engraving in Italy in the Fifteenth Century*. London, 1888.

Lyell, J. P. R., *Early Book-Illustration in Spain*. 1926.

Macfarlane, J., *Anthoine Vérard*. London, Bibliographical Society, 1900.

Mâle, "L'idée de la Mort et de la Danse Macabre" (*Revue des Deux Mondes*, 1906).

Moore, Sturge T., *Dürer*. London, 1905.

Morgan, J. P., *Catalogue of Early Printed Books from the Libraries of William Morris, etc., now forming portion of the Library of J. P. Morgan*. 3 vols. London, 1907.

Morris, William, "On the Woodcut Books of Ulm and Augsburg" (*Bibliographica*, 1895).

Muther, R., *Die deutsche Bücherillustration der Gothik und Frührenaissance*. München, 1884.

Muther and Hirth, *Meisterholzschnitte aus vier Jahrhunderten*. München, 1889–93.

Ongania, *L'Arte della Stampa nel Rinascimento Italiana*. Venice, 1894.

Palmer, A. H., *Catalogue of the Exhibition of the Works of Samuel Palmer*. 1926.

Papillon, J. M., *Traité historique et pratique de la Gravure en Bois*. 3 vols. Paris, 1776.

Pichon, L., "The New Book-Illustration in France" (*Studio*, Winter No., 1924).

Pollard, A. W., *Fine Books*. London, 1912.

——— *Early Illustrated Books*. London, 1893.

——— *Facsimiles of Early Printed Books in the Library of the British Museum*.

——— *Italian Book-Illustrations, chiefly of the Fifteenth Century* (Portfolio Monographs). London, 1894.

See also *Bibliographica* (*passim*).

Roberts, W., *Printers' Marks*. London, 1893.

Robertson, Robert, *Thomas Bewick and his Times*. Newcastle, 1886.

Rondot, Natalis., *Les Graveurs sur Bois à Lyon au XVe siècle*. Paris, 1896.

——— *Les Graveurs sur Bois à Lyon au XVIe siècle*. Lyon, 1897.

Rooses, Max, *Christopher Plantin, Imprimeur anversois. Biographie et Documents*. Fol. Anvers, 1896.

Salaman, "Modern Woodcuts and Lithographs in France and England" (*Studio*, 1919).

Schmidt, M., *Denkmäler des Holz- und Metallschnittes in München*. Nürnberg, 1884.

——— *Die frühesten und seltensten Denkmale des Holz- und Metallschnittes aus den XV und XVI^{en} Jahrhunderts*. München, 1883.

Schramm, *Der Bilderschmuck der Frühdrucke*. 8 vols. Leipzig, 1920.

Schreiber, *Manuel de l'amateur de la Gravure sur Bois et sur Metal au XVe siècle.*
  8 vols. Berlin, 1891.
Schretlen, M. J., *Dutch and Flemish Woodcuts of the Fifteenth Century.* London,
  1925 (Benn).
Segarizzi, *Bibliografia delle Stampe popolari della Biblioteca Marciana.* Bergamo,
  1913.
Silvestre, *Marques typographiques.* Paris, 1853–67.

Thierry-Poux, *Monuments de l'Imprimerie française.* Paris, 1890.
Thomas, *Spanish Fifteenth Century Printing.* 1926 (Benn).
Thomson, D. C., *Thomas Bewick.* London, 1903.

Updike, D. B., *Printing Types.* 2 vols. Cambridge, U.S.A., 1922.

Van Heurck, E. H., *Les Drapelets de Pèlerinage en Belgique et dans les Pays Voisins.*
  Anvers, 1922.
Van Heurck and Boknoogen, *Histoire de l'Imagerie populaire flamande.* Bruxelles,
  1910.
Vindel, *Bibliografia Gráfica.* Madrid, 1910.

White, Gleeson, *English Illustration; the Sixties.* 1906 (Constable).
Worringer, *Die altdeutsche Buchillustration.* München, 1912.

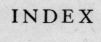

INDEX

INDEX